THE COMPLETE ENCYCLOPEDIA OF ANTIQUES

THE COMPLETE ENCYCLOPEDIA OF
ANTIQUES

Covers Antiques from the Middle Ages until the Early 20th Century

HIDDE HALBERTSMA

Grange BOOKS

This edition published in 2000 for Grange Books
an imprint of Grange Book PLC. The Grange
Kingsnorth Industrial Estate Hoo, Nr.
Rochester Kent ME39ND

Text and photographs: drs. Hidde Halbertsma
Photography: Ruurd Halbertsma and Marietje
Helbertsma
Translations: Stephen Challacombe
Coordination and guidance to author: Experttext,
Garderen
Editing, production, and coordination: TextCase,
Groningen, The Nedherlands
Design and layout: Signia Wischoten, The Netherlands
Cover design: Minkowsky Graphics, Enkhuizen,
The Nedherlands

B0442Rebo

ISBN 1 84013 400 3

Contents

This room is mainly furnished in 17th century style. The paintings, leather-gilt wall-hangings, and table are typical of this period. The chairs are from the early 18th century and the chandelier dates from the 19th century.

Foreword

It may seem a contradiction but in our rapidly-moving age antiques are becoming increasingly popular. It is as if in our throw-away consumer society we have suddenly recognized the value of old objects that were made by craftsmen. Granny's silver is polished and the chest-of-drawers from an ancient aunt is restored for use. Large numbers visit antique markets. Just the right time then for an 'everyday' encyclopaedia about antiques in which you can find much about the styles of the ages and also about collecting, restoring, and maintaining antiques. This is a book for the interested amateur collector.

This book would never have happened without the willing cooperation of my American sister Marietje Halbertsma, who was responsible for the chapter on American antiques. I would also like to thank all the many dealers and private collectors for letting us photograph their collections. Finally, special thanks are due to Katherine Gardner Cipolla, chairperson of the *Loring Greenough House* (Jamaica Plain, MA (USA), Patrick Byrne, owner of *Cobwebs* antique shop in Jamaica Plain, MA (USA), Venduhuis of Zwolle (NL), Meerwijk Antiquair en Restaurateur, Garderen (NL), Groot Antique, Grouw (NL), *De Trije Gritenijen* Museum, Assen (NL), and Mr J.J. Brakke of the Museum of Drenthe in Assen (NL) for making it possible to photograph the various interiors depicting the different eras.

Hidde Halbertsma
Zwolle, The Netherlands

Introduction

Antiques are all around us. We may pass them by or stumble across them in an old drawer where they have been forgotten. Mostly we do not give a thought to their age or origin but if we do ask then the reply is along the lines of 'Uncle John's watch' or 'grandma's chest-of-drawers'. Finding out about the history of the object gives it an extra dimension that might astonish its present day owner. Those who appreciate antiques are fascinated by objects from the past, some of which are quite remarkable but others were once quite commonplace. Antiques can be seen and touched and often also possess their own characteristic aroma. Antiques therefore provide a tangible and personal link with the past for many people. The idea of antiques only consisting of expensive works of art solely within the reach of rich collectors has been greatly modified in recent years. Interest in antiques is growing significantly.

Much has been written in magazines and newspapers by various experts and the popularity of antiques has been boosted by television programmes in which specialists value antiques. Once an interest in antiques is awakened many questions are then asked. For many this is a desire to find out more about the objects inherited from our parents and grandparents. This book is not just aimed at helping in this search for it can also be enjoyed by those who wish to browse and have memories evoked by the many illustrations of antique objects.

This book is ideal for the inexperienced person who owns or collects antiques. It deals with art history, furniture, ceramics, and glass etc. but also advises extensively on the subjects of collecting, restoring, and maintaining antiques.

The chapters about the different periods have been kept so far as possible in chronological order but a geographical division is also often made because these eras can differ from country to country. There is an extensive index at the back of the book to help you find specific information quickly.

Northern Borneo 'three dragon' gong, c 19th.

The main trends and styles

In each of the main trends and styles from the different eras a collection of influences were bought to bear on the arts and crafts of that age that lead to iden-tifiable styles that are associated with the period. The trends gave birth to styles and these were usually associated with a particular place or were determined by the preference of a particular ruler. Trends and styles influence one another of course but these influences do not always result in the adoption of every element from an earlier period. Trends and styles also occurred because people expressly decided to break with the current trend or with styles from an earlier era.

There are many objects that are true to the style of their period and purity of style is not an abstract concept. There are many objects though that are a mixture of styles in which the maker has been influenced by several different styles.

This might be the result of the preference or knowledge of the maker or the taste of the person who commissioned the object. It might also be a transitional piece during the change from one style to another. Some trends intentionally absorb styles from earlier ages to form a new unity (see Eclecticism). Folk art items are quite different from mainstream antiques and they often utilise a fusion of different major trends and styles.

Romanesque

The style of European art from the Middle Ages is generally known as Romanesque. This style developed more or less simultaneously in various places in Europe around 950 AD and lasted until about 1200 AD in most places or until about 1150 in northern France. Romanesque arts derived from the classical cultures of ancient Rome and the early Christians. The implementation of this classical style varies from place to place. The monasteries and priories of the cloistered orders were the buildings which preserved the classical style and these religious order such as the Benedictines, played an important role in the spread of the Romanesque style. Most artists were monks or friars and hence the principal manifestations of the classical Romanesque style is in religious buildings such as churches and monasteries.

The construction style of the classical Roman art was somewhat robust, fairly sober, and enclosed. This style of building developed into a more refined and slender form with rich decoration and greater openness. Sculpture was subordinate to architecture and restricted to the decoration of buildings. The art of the Romanesque image chiefly comprised frescoes on the walls of Romanesque churches but there were also illuminated miniatures painted in the prayer books and bibles. The gold-smith and silversmith's art reached great heights during this Romanesque period.

Gothic

One of the styles of European Medieval art is known as Gothic. This lasted from about 1150 to approximately 1420 in Italy but continued into the middle of the sixteenth century in northern Europe. The term 'Gothic' is derived from the Italian *gotico*. The term was used by the Italians from the sixteenth century for all art north of the Alps. The term was pejorative in tone – after all the Goths had put an end to Roman culture. The peoples to the north of the Alps were all simply dismissed as being descended from the Goths.

Gothic architecture

The form of Gothic architecture originated in the area of the Ile-de-France within the Paris basin. The difference in styles between Romanesque and Gothic is readily apparent.

Gothic architecture sought to achieve vertical lines or verticality in contrast with Romanesque. As much space as possible was reserved for high windows which were glazed with stained glass in patterns retained by lead.

Increasing use was made of sculpture to embellish the exteriors of the buildings. Although all Gothic originated from the French style, individual national styles of Gothic developed in each country.

Gothic art

Gothic sculpture developed beyond the ornamentation of the exteriors of buildings with statues of saints and the Madonna. The Gothic style is especially characterised by stylised folds in the figure's clothing, with flowing lines and these figures display emotions through their facial expressions and gestures. With less wall to decorate there was little need of fresco painters. Gothic is also reflected in paintings, miniatures, carpets, furniture, and jewellery with similar forms found in architecture with Gothic frontals, finials, pinnacles, ornamentation, rose windows and lancets particularly used in miniature paintings, furniture, and jewellery and as much use as possible of triangular and square forms in all manner of materials.

Gothic furniture

Furniture only became normal consumer objects in the late Middle Ages. Medieval noblemen travelled widely and so some

Spanish 16th century commode from Lugo on the border of Spain with Portugal. Such robust and down-to-earth Medieval pieces such as this with its functional design were kept long beyond their time in rural areas.

A 17th century Spanish cupboard in chestnut. It was originally built in to a house.

of their furniture needed to be portable. Most tables stood on trestles while others were firmly attached to wainscoting. Ordinary people sat on benches and stools. Chairs were for people of the higher echelons. Dressers were used to display valuables such as silverware. Decorated cupboards and chests were used for storing things. Strengthened chests without legs but with rounded lids and hand grips were used for travelling. Ordinary rectangular chests with straight legs were left at home.

English and transitional styles

The English Tudor style dates from around 1500, taking its name from the monarchs of the house of Tudor. The style epitomises the transition from late Gothic to early Renaissance.
The furniture makers art demonstrated a preference for oak. Elizabethan is the name given to furniture (mainly of oak) from the reign of Queen Elizabeth I (1558–1603) that has clear Renaissance influences.
Jacobean or early Stuart refers to the period of King James I (James VI of Scotland) and is derived from his Latin name of Jacobus. This period is characterised by sturdy dark oak furniture with turned legs, tables with hinged leaves on both sides, and carved backs to chairs, panels, chests-of-drawers, and cupboards.

Renaissance (to 1650)

Renaissance is French for 'reborn' and is the name given to a trend that transcended all European culture. The term is derived from the Italian *rinascita* which has the same meaning. The term was used initially in the fifteenth century to describe a re-emergence of classicism in pictorial art, literature, and science. The first traces of the Renaissance were found in Italy in the thirteenth century. The zenith of the Renaissance occurred

Bed from the transitional period between late Gothic and early Renaissance styles.

in the fifteenth and sixteenth centuries with some remaining influences into the seventeenth century. This cultural trend was at its strongest in Italy where it was fuelled by the city states in which merchants spent money on both art and science. The Renaissance did not find its way into the rest of Europe until after 1500. A characteristic of the Renaissance was the reduced role of the Church. In contrast with Romanesque and Gothic styles, the style of the Renaissance was felt throughout the elite of society. No longer was the Church the principal source of commissions for artists and craftsmen.
Instead the nobility became the patrons. External appearance and its effect were central to the Renaissance and the great advances in science were sources of inspiration for many artists. They studied both history and nature in great depth and acquainted themselves with anatomy

Large 16th century Dutch chandelier.

The lionís head was widely used as a motif on Renaissance style furniture.

Renaissance style pillow cabinet, 1684.

Friesian 17th century cabinet with Renaissance details. The columns on the door that are more than half-round are an interesting feature that shows this was an expensive piece of furniture. Instead of sawing a trunk in half for each column, the cabinetmaker has used the whole cross-section for each column.

Dutch 17th century Renaissance chair.

and perspective. They also happily made use of classical elements such mythological figures cherubs, urns, and laurel wreaths. The artist ceased to be an anonymous craftsman during the Renaissance, becoming respected members of society. The Renaissance took another form to the north of the Alps. Many Gothic elements were retained in the Low Countries and the style manifested itself in colour and excessive ornamentation. This became popular in Britain, Scandinavia, northern Germany, and France. The Italian influence was clearer in Bohemia, Austria, and southern parts of Germany.

Dutch 17th century Renaissance Zeeland-style bread cabinet.

Mannerism

The term 'Mannerism' is derived from the Italian word *maniera*, meaning 'manner'. Mannerism was a style that bridged the transition from the Renaissance to Baroque. It is most widely expressed in the visual art of paintings and sculpture. The artists expressly turn away from the idealism of the Renaissance. The emphasis was placed on form and led to elaborate and somewhat artificial results with people in unnatural stances and with ultra-slender faces. Mannerism was mainly a product of southern Europe.

Carolean and The Commonwealth

Carolean refers to the reigns of Kings Charles I and II of Great Britain but as a style period refers to the reign of Charles I (1625–1649) and was followed by The Commonwealth, describing the period of the republican government under Oliver Cromwell (The Protector of the Commonwealth), which was characteristically puritanical and hence austere.

Restoration

The Restoration is the period of English arts and crafts that started in 1660 with the restoration of the monarchy with the crowning of Charles II and continued to around 1714. The *joie de vivre* and ostentation of this era was a reaction to the austerity of The Commonwealth under Oliver Cromwell.

Baroque

Baroque initially referred to the architectural style that also influenced the visual arts of the seventeenth and early eighteenth centuries. The terms is often extended these days to describe literature and music of the period. The style is also confusingly sometimes termed as Late Renaissance. The word is French, meaning 'bizarre'. The word may also be derived from the Portuguese *barocco* meaning an 'imperfect pearl'. In any event the initial use of the term *baroque* was pejorative, referring to its pompous, exuberant, and grotesque character. The ornamentation was often so excessive that functionality was frequently threatened. Baroque was the last style to influence every aspect of European culture and in many respects it is a late and colourful remnant of the Renaissance. In common with the Renaissance, Baroque was born in Italy and spread itself throughout Roman Catholic countries where it became the established style of church and state. The Catholic Church manifested its power and glory once again which had been threatened by the Reformation.

Blue Bohemian neo-Baroque cabinet of 1835. Baroque continued alongside new trends in many places in Europe. See detail below.

For the Catholic states the ostentation of Baroque represented national pride and the absolute power of their rulers. Baroque was a reaction to the contorted forms of Mannerism. The artists of the Baroque style were inspired by their predecessors of the Renaissance who in their turn had found inspiration in classicism. Each element receives equal emphasis in Renaissance art but in Baroque every element is subordinate to the whole. Baroque's influence was much less outside Catholic counties. France accepted Baroque grudgingly and adapted it with introduction of classical influences.

William and Mary (1688–1702)

England adopted the main styles and ornamentation of Europe up to the eighteenth century. Generally these were simplified in style with English pieces generally being more modest.

After the Dutch stadtholder William III (of Orange) and his wife Mary Stuart won the throne of England from James II, Dutch style was introduced to form the first English style that was different from continental forms.

Louis' styles

The styles of the French kings Louis XII to XVI are known by the French numeration e.g. *Louis Treize.* The styles are generally sumptuous and exaggerated. During this era France gave the cultural lead. The styles and individual reigns of the kings do not precisely coincide though. Architecture and ornamentation of *Louis Treize* is somewhat disparate with manifest foreign influences in which both Italian and Flemish artists were of great significance. But there was already atension between Baroque and Classicism in these early stages. During the time of Louis XIV and XV Baroque held sway over French culture.
After 1750 – still in the reign of Louis XV – there was a classical revival against Baroque. French art during the reigns of the Kings Louis is characterised by the contrast between classical design of the outsides of buildings and the Baroque decoration of their interiors. This includes the fine curvilinear forms of the furniture, silver, porcelain, and furnishing fabrics.

Louis Treize (XIII)

Louis Treize is the first of the style periods of the reigns of the French kings Louis.
It is characterised by greater attention to decoration, turned wood, festoons, curlicues, chased pilasters, wide use of columns, and divided pediments.

Louis Quatorze (XIV)

Baroque was at the height of its sway in the world during the reign of Louis XIV (1643–1715). The Palace of Versailles, which is the Baroque masterpiece, had far greater influence on European culture than the religious Baroque emanating from Italy. The architecture was a fusion of classical forms with the Baroque originating from Italy.

A fine Louis XIII chair.

The style also greatly influenced furniture and ornamentation. These latter elements took on a strongly Baroque, heavy, and pompous style under Louis *Quatorze* with rich embellishment of swags, urns, cherubs, marble panels, ceiling painting, mirrors, festoons, and gilded plaster work.
The heavy symmetrical furniture was of monumental proportions with considerable use of luxury materials including marquetry inlays with veneers. Furniture is often embellished with columns, floral motifs, oak and laurel leaves, egg-and-tongue moulding, and edge mouldings. Greater use was made of exotic materials such as tortoiseshell and lacquer. Chairs had high backs and low seats and their trimmings showed a great preference for frills and fringes.

Dutch 18th century Louis XIV chair.

A Louis XIV style lavabo.

Louis XV

See Rococo

Louis XVI

See neo-classicism

French Regency

The period of the French Regency style relates to the regency of Phillipe of Orleans (1715–1723). This style preceded the Rococo of Louis XV and replaced the exuberant decoration of Louis XIV with its strongly Baroque curlicues and a symmetric wreaths and figures. The era following the death of Louis XIV was characterised by elegance and lightness. The luxurious life of city dwellers also reached the country through the aristocracy. The numbers of rooms in the châteaux and palaces increased so that some types of furniture became larger. French Regency can be regarded as a transition between Baroque and Rococo.

Rococo

The name Rococo is given to the style of the first half of the eighteenth century that marked the final phase of Baroque. The term is probably derived from the French *rocaille* used to describe rock grottoes or fountains and *coquille,* meaning shell or scallop. Rococo arose in France as a reaction against the gross-ornamentation, stateliness, and pomposity of 'high' Baroque. Rococo was more intimate, lighter in touch, and more elegant.

The *rocaille* or scallop is a characteristic feature of the Rococo style. Although elements of the Rococo style actually emerged during the French Regency, the Rococo era is largely contemporary in France with the style of Louis XV. The style first became apparent in the applied arts.

Chippendale bureau with leaf for writing while standing up.

A heavily ornamented Rococo sconce.

Porcelain – that was invented in Europe in 1709 – became heavily influenced by the Rococo style. French Rococo furniture is characterised by the fluidity of the various elements incorporated in lighter and more graceful pieces.
Chaises longues, wing chairs, and many other easy chairs were fashionable. Rococo spread to Italy where the style became somewhat exaggerated.

A rocaille decoration in a niche. The scallop form gave Rococo its name.

Italian Rococo furniture is heavier in design and ornamentation. Rococo manifested itself in England for a time through the asymmetrical carving of the Chippendale style. Sculpture of the Rococo style is busy and full of motion.
The style was generally more widely used for deco-ration in architecture than for the creation of works of art in their own right.

Louis Quinze (XV)

The lightness of touch of the French Regency changed somewhat with the extreme forms of Rococo during the era of Louis XV. The contrast between the classical exteriors of buildings and their Baroque interiors continued but was less pronounced. The style was characterised by light, elegant, and modest ornamentation with flowing lines, S-forms, and scrolls. Interiors were decorated with airy and asymmetric ornaments.

It became customary in the 18th century to decorate walls with painted tableaux with a dominate colour which then gave the room its name: hence in this case ëthe blue roomí. The Arcadian scenes are typical of the Louis XV and XVI styles of the later 18th century.

Dutch briar display cabinet in Louis XV style with raised top and crest in relief.

The curved line was often linked to that of the scallop or *rocaille* form. Pastel shades dominated during the Louis Quinze era. Furniture was intentionally more slender and graceful. Some craftsmen specialised in making certain pieces. Those making furniture with inlays of ebony veneer (ebony was the most widely used veneer for seventeenth century French furniture) were required to sign their work after 1743, except for those in the service of the King. Despite this it is difficult to establish the makers because these specialist also acted as dealers and

Louis XV tea caddy of about 1750.

tended to sign every good piece that passed through their hands. Individual elements of furniture such as legs and arm-rests began to lose their individuality. One part merged fluidly into the next. This was strengthened by the use of more refined and varied ornamentation than previously. Many new types of furniture appeared, such as commodes and book rests.

Eighteenth century English styles

Clawed feet are typical features of Queen Anne style furniture.

Queen Anne

This is the English style of the reign of Queen Anne (1702–1714). The broad curved cabriole leg was fashionable dur-

Inlaid Dutch Queen Anne style card table of about 1740. The table folds up.

Queen Anne chair.

Queen Anne table.

ing this period. The 'bull-and-claw' foot came in around 1710 with an animal's head or claw on a conical shaped foot. Windsor chairs did not have this feature. Queen Anne style cabinets were generally tall.

Georgian

The term Georgian is used for period of the reigns of Georges I (1714–1727), II (1727–1760), and III (1760–1820). The Georgian style is an English adaptation of the European styles of the eighteenth century with elements of Baroque, Classical revival, and later also Gothic revival.

Parallels can be found in Georgian styles between the furniture of Chippendale and that of French Louis XV. The refined neo-classical furniture and interiors of the Adam brothers echo that of French Louis XVI.

Sella curilis of late 19th C. The sella curilis chairs were originally the seat of Roman magistrates. This design was widely used during the revival of classicism.

George III style single door silver cabinet in mahogany with clawed feet.

Neo-classicism (1760–1830)

The term neo-classicism is given to a trend in art that arose in the late eighteenth century. It was a reaction against the rich embellishment of Baroque and playfulness of Rococo. The name points to the inspiration derived from classical art that resulted from archaeological excavations in Rome, Pompeii, Herculaneum, and Paestum. It meant a return to classical forms of straight lines and level planes.

Symmetry became important once more and classical ornaments and geometric shapes such as ram's heads, bull's and lion's faces, plaited braid, tendrils, rosettes, and urns replaced the overblown style of the preceding period. Neo-classicism became less important after 1800 with the arrival of the Romantic. Despite this the trend continued to be of considerable influence because it was taught at academies throughout the nineteenth century.

Louis XVI gentlemanís armchair.

Louis Seize (XVI)

The playfulness of Rococo became less fashionable during the reign of Louis XVI and the scallop motif disappeared. Symmetrical ornamentation was added to classical motifs such as corbels, olive wreaths, egg and tongue moulding, and sphinxes. Furniture parts such as arms and legs once more acquired their own identity. ook comfortabel. Furniture was rectangular and flat-fronted. Seats were both fine looking and comfortable. Chair legs that resembled fluted columns were very popular. Light colours were

Louis XVI chest of drawers.

Louis XVI half-moon table.

Louis XVI occasional table.

Louis XVI sconce.

Dutch Louis XVI era chest of drawers in rosewood.

popular during the time of Louis XVI. White lacquer and gilt were commonly used. There was considerable emphasis on elegance, smallness, and gracefulness. Sèvres porcelain, East Asian lacquer work, and miniatures were signs of a cultivated taste.

Directoire

Directoire is the name given to the style during the era of Napoleon's coup d'état (1795–1799). The style was in reaction to Rococo/Louis XVI and saw a return to more straightforward classical forms. At the heart of the Directoire style lay the classical style of ancient Greece. Symbols of the French Revolution such as the Cock and Virgin were associated with this, together with the Tricolour. The Directoire style mainly manifested itself in clothing and ornaments.

Empire

The Empire style relates to the fashion for furniture and interiors during Napoleon's rule (1799–1815). The style originated in France and was also popular in Europe and the USA. The classical inspiration was mainly derived from the time of the

Folding Consulate card table of the early 19th C. Consulate is the name given to the period of the French Republic before Napoleon became Emperor.

Consulate style secretaire.

Empire style chandelier converted first for gas and later for electric lighting.

Neo-Sheraton 19th century cabinet.

Empire style four-armed candelabra.

ancient Roman empire. Certain ancient Egyptian elements are also sometimes used, resulting from Napoleon's expedition to the Nile (1798). The Empire style was characterised in furniture by rigid symmetry, rectangularity, and solidity. Characteristic motifs that were used for decoration include the eagle, lion, sphinx, Neptune's chariot, urns, and quivers filled with arrows. The heavy and solid furniture can be recognised by its plain lines and flat planes.

Regency

The English Regency style arose during the rule by the Prince Regent (later George IV) during the illness of his father George III (1811–1820). In common with French Empire style, English Regency is inspired by classical culture and for this reason some call it English Empire.

Neo-Baroque 19th century candlestick.

Victorian mahogany ladiesí escritoire of about 1870.

Eclecticism and the neo-styles (1830–1880)

Eclecticism is a term used in visual arts when techniques, motifs, and elements from earlier styles are combined to form a new one. Eclecticism existed in the time of the ancient Greeks. Late in the Hellenic era Greek artists and craftsmen were already borrowing from the styles of older works. Elements for compositions were chosen from very different eras. Eclecticism became a strong movement in the nineteenth century with the re-emergence of older styles. Expression of these styles such as neo-Baroque, neo-Gothic, neo-classicism, and neo-Byzantinism were to be found into the twentieth century.

Victorian 19th century dressing table with tilting oval mirror.

Neo-Gothic armchair of about 1870.

Victorian

During Queen Victoria's long reign (1837–1901) the predominant influences in Britain on arts and crafts was the rise of the industrial middle class. House interiors were fussy and richly decorated with floral motifs and other adornments. The main intention was to display how well off the occupants were. Victorian furniture designs are typically comfortable. The excessive carving of the early Victorian era was later replaced by painted panels.

French Restoration

The style of the French Restoration originates from immediately after the fall of Emperor Napoleon I when the Bourbon monarchy was restored to the throne (1815–1830) in the form of King Louis XVII and Charles X. The style is characterised by rounded and curved forms. This was the era of Biedermeier in Austria and Germany.

Louis-Philippe

During the reign of King Louis-Philippe of Orleans (1830–1830) there was a revisiting of the style characteristics of Gothic and the Renaissance. A consequence of this is that furniture from this period is more massive and robust in style than during the Empire period. In common with German Biedermeier this period did not see a new style develop, rather adaptation of elements of the Empire style for the interiors and furniture of an increasingly bourgeois society.

Second Empire

The Second Empire was a poor reflection of the first. The classic beauty and grandeur of the clean lines of the period of Napoleon I were barely ever attained anywhere during the reign of Emperor Napoleon III (1852–1871).

Neo Louis-Philippe style table of about 1900.

Biedermeier

Biedermeier is a decorative style originating in Germany in the period 1815–1848. The name comes from Gottlieb Biedermeier, a nineteenth century fictional character of the poetry of Ludwig Eichrodt. Biedermeier was the typical sober but hypocritical bourgeois citizen.

German Biedermeier chair of about 1840.

German Biedermeier 19th century bureau. A nest of drawers is hidden behind the flap.

Biedermeier 19th century dining chair.

Dutch Biedermeier chiffoniËre of elm.

Walnut Biedermeier knitting chair with back of twisted pillars and fine fretwork.

The Biedermeier style was a reaction to the Romantic style of the Napoleonic era.
The bourgeois conservatism of Biedermeier was expressed in interior design, the visual arts, fashion, and literature. Interior style that was dominated by gentle curves and French polished wood was a bourgeois interpretation of the Empire style. Many decorative elements were borrowed from earlier styles.

Romanticism

Romanticism was a spiritual trend in the later eighteenth and early nineteenth centuries. It was a reaction against Rationalism and its logical expression in the form of neo-Classicism.
With Romanticism, arts and crafts became the expression of creativity and emotions of the artist and craftsman. Romanticism found little headway in France because of the strong influence

Screen with typical Romantic style of painting of the 18th century.

Painted leather 18th century screen. Compare the two screens: both are from the same era but are entirely different in style.

there of neo-Classicism. Romanticism had its greatest influence on music, painting, and literature.

Jugendstil and Art Nouveau

Around the turn of the century from the nineteenth into the twentieth a movement arose against the historical and bombastic attitudes of the 'neo-styles'. This trend was expressed through contemporary designs with flowing lines, new materials (iron and steel, glazed pottery, tiles, and concrete), and motifs taken from nature (flowers, animals, and other plants). Architectural and interior design was united into one cohesive style. These innovative movements appeared more or less simultaneously throughout Europe and quickly spread to USA and the colonial territories. The individual styles vary from country.

German Jugendstil decoration on this pewter item of about 1890.

Late Swiss Jugendstil electric lamp. Note the colour and design of the glass.

Arts and Crafts

The first manifestations of the movement appeared in England around 1860. The Arts and Crafts movement was a reaction against industrial mass production and sought to restore craftsmanship to the making of objects.

The Arts and Crafts movement made a logical link between the form and construction of a piece and introduced a new type of floral design.

Art Nouveau

IThe innovative and renewing movement in France and Belgium was known as Art Nouveau after the opening of the gallery of Siegfried Bing in Paris in 1895. Art Nouveau also placed an emphasis on hand-crafting of objects. The movement was characterised by extravagant and fashionable design with ornamentation to the fore. Wide use was made of organic elements such as flowers and other plants and animals.

Jugendstil

The name *Jugendstil* is dcrivcd from thc German periodical *Die Jugend* that was started by a group of leading creative people in Munich in 1896. Flowing lines and organic forms are characteristic of the style. Jugendstil also placed great emphasis on materials used and craftsmanship.

Sezession (Viennese Secession)

The new movement manifested itself within the Austro-Hungarian empire as the Wiener Sezession (Viennese Secession) which held its own exhibitions for more progressive artists. The Sezession is mainly characterised by decorative use of geometrical motifs.

Nieuwe kunst

The 'new art' of the movement sweeping Europe became known in the Low Countries as the 'Nieuwe kunst' – having precisely that meaning. It was also known as the 'salad dressing style' after a salad dressing manufacturer based in Delft used Jugendstil motives for his advertising and product labels. In Flemish speaking parts of Belgium the style was known as 'Palingstijl' (eel style).

Swiss Art Nouveau bedside cabinet of about 1920.

Jugendstil childrenís chair, early 20th century.

Art Deco

Art Deco was the principal style of applied art between about 1910 and 1940. The same term was used for this style in use in architecture, sculpture, and painting. There were two main movements within Art Deco. The first was centred on Paris and was richly decorative; objects were generally hand made from luxurious materials. The other movement saw links between Austrian and Scottish Art Nouveau, and German Bauhaus. This type of Art Nouveau sought to create undecorated objects of simple and functional form and was mainly aimed at mass production. New materials were put to use in Art Deco such as metal and glass for furniture. Plastic was used for smaller objects, including jewellery.

Collecting antiques

Collecting antiques is an art in itself and a great deal of knowledge can be gained by viewing them. This knowledge is not just about the antiques themselves but extends to their acquisition, maintenance, and restoration.

Old treadle sewing machines such as this early Pfaff are seen as on the border between antique and collectibles by most people.

What are antiques?

The word *antique* is of French origin and derived from the Latin *antiquus* or *anticus*. It means old, having existed since old times, aged, or venerable. The word gained meaning within art history in the seventeenth century and this meaning has been subsequently further widened. The use in this book is its general meaning of old objects made by artists and craftsmen and women.

Just how old does an object need to be to be described as antique? Some collectors will only consider an object as antique if it is 150 years old. Exceptions to this are jewellery, Chinese porcelain, and carpets. Jewellery according to these die-hards must date from before 1890 and they deem that Chinese porcelain should date from slightly earlier than 1800, while carpets are antique after fifty years. In the USA the term antique has long been reserved for objects dating from before 1830–1840 and some still stick to this. Most countries though term an object as antique when it is 100 years old and many dealers also observe this.

Louis XV pewter tray.

This age is enshrined in the law of some countries and can be of importance in respect of import and export of objects. It is probable that the 100 years 'rule' came about because early twentieth century antiquaries felt that the Empire style that was then about 100 years old was the 'last' of the great antique styles. This 100 year line is being increasingly eroded with the division between antiques and collectibles becoming increasingly diffuse.

This late 19th century cabinet once stood in a serving maidís room.

Antique dealers happily sell objects that are less than 100 years old and many collectors prefer to speak about objects 'of the period'. Use of such terms has led to a more flexible classification of antiques. This looser classification permits inclusion of late Jugendstil and even of Art Deco, which are not yet 100 years old, but extremely well represented in antique shops.

This book regards antiques as arts and crafts objects, including those made by craftsmen and objects of folk art. The makers must have some creative input into the process of making the object.
This draws the line at mass-produced articles and means that no two antique objects will be precisely the same, as is the case with mass-produced articles. A print from a seventeenth century etching in which a number of copies were produced is an antique. A Jugendstil picture of 1895 that has been created by a known artist but then produced by machine in a limited edition is a borderline case. Some deem this latter example not to be antique while others are more flexible.

Increasing importance is being currently attached to purity of style of an object in which an object should be representative of its period. On this basis, a Gothic style linen press of 1825 is not considered an antique. For some purists, this brings certain objects into contention as 'antique' that would otherwise have been dismissed by their 150 year 'rule', such as Biedermeier (1825–1860), Louis Philippe (1830–1850), and Victorian (1837–1901). Even the neo-styles (up to the twentieth century) and even Art Nouveau and Jugendstil (1890–1930) are thereby considered as antiques.

Anyone who starts to get interested in antiques will sooner or later come face to face with kitsch. This term came into being in Germany around 1900 where the craft-based industries were in decline as articles were increasingly mass-produced.

The term *kitsch* was used for objects of which their materials and method of production were not 'true'. An important characteristic of *kitsch* is the use of antique decorative elements.

Low Spanish bench of walnut, circa 1800.

A 19th century Spanish oak chest.

Country-style English commode of deal with replacement handles, circa 1910.

This generally implies the object is a copy but here too no hard and fast rules apply.

Not every *kitsch* object is lacking in artistry and the attitude of collectors varies in time so that certain objects that were previously dismissed as *kitsch* may later become highly regarded. This is all a matter of personal taste.

The Romans said long ago that there was no accounting for taste. It is also clear that the older an object is the less likely it is to be regarded as *kitsch*. Reproductions that would later be regarded as *kitsch* existed before the term was coined.

These were faithful copies of earlier objects that will never obtain the same value as the original object. Such reproductions can be highly sought after though today.

Czech larder cabinet of circa 1900, restored in late 1990s.

The round shape of this low salon table from Spain is unusual for this country. The legs of this Telavera de la Reine of circa 1900 have been cut short and the original painted finish has disappeared.

The collection

A collection cannot be assembled just by going out to buy antiques. The antique market is extremely complex. The value of a piece is in part determined by objective criteria such as its historical importance and originality but personal taste and preference can play an equally important role.

A newcomer to the world of antiques therefore needs to be able to learn to recognise the differences between different objects. Some imagine that all antique specialists are academically trained but if it was ever true, today there are countless well-informed self-taught persons among the devotees.

Furnishing or dressing a house with antiques or establishing a collection raises a great many questions. Someone without knowledge may have no notion as to whether a piece is worth £300, £3,000, or £30,000. How can the value be determined? Unfortunately there are no firm guidelines for assessing an antique's value but is something that is acquired through experience and knowledge.

Even experts cannot know everything and hence need to specialise in a particular area. Everyone starting out to collect antiques needs to have a clear idea of the aim of their collecting. This might be to collect a certain type of object ranging from a relatively accessible and affordable collection of thimbles to the more difficult and expensive matter of collecting works of art by Dutch masters. It might be Japanese carvings or seventeenth century nautical charts. Alternatively the direction might be to seek out a particular object or ones from a given region or style. Many, of course, merely seek attractive items with which to decorate their home. In every case it is essential for the newcomer to decide what he or she wishes to collect.

Four-door Basque chestnut cabinet of circa 1890 from northern Spain.

Describing this aim may be very difficult, especially for someone who does not yet know much about antiques. It is best for a newcomer to give themselves time to discover what they like and dislike, relying upon instinct.

A piece is not attractive because it is an antique or merely because it has managed to survive for a hundred years or more. What is it that attracts you to an object? Is it the colour or the material of which it is made? Or do you find a particular style attractive?
Soon you will discover a preference for a particular style and newcomers to collecting must trust their own taste. No-one else can tell you what is attractive for you.While you are acquiring the necessary knowledge about antiques, your eventual aims will probably become clearer.

One of the first steps in the learning process is to visit museums. They are a wealth of information on the descriptions of exhibits and in their booklets and catalogues. What is more 'just looking' in a museum does not attract questions from antique dealers who might regard you as a potential buyer. There are also courses on various aspects of antiques and lectures and books that tackle a specific area may be very useful too for a newcomer.

In addition there are specialist magazines that that contain a great deal of information.

The next step should be to attend viewing days prior to auction of the leading auction houses. This enables careful examination of items in which you are now interested. It is certainly worth getting the sale catalogues, which are also excellent books. Auctions give an idea of the kinds of prices that are paid. Following this, one might visit some antique shops. Most dealers will happily talk about antiques and they may be happy to give you pointers about what is best avoided, which are finer examples and even the best. They may also suggest books you can read on your chosen subject area. Of course they may also try to sell you something. It is best not to buy anything on the first visit and a good dealer will understand this and be aware that good advice can develop into a dealer–client relationship. Take ample time (at least a year) to get to understand the market and gain knowledge. This is mainly gained by looking, continually looking.

This Basque side-table was made in Spain around 1820.

Dealers and auctions

Once the fledgling antique collector has gained some insight into the market for his or her chosen area and – most importantly – has an understanding of the prices for relevant items, it is time to decide how much money he or she is prepared to spend on the first purchase. It is very important to set a limit for the first purchase and it is also sensible to start with modest amounts. The beginner still does not know enough about antiques or know their way around the antiques world and the risk of a bad purchase is quite high. It is therefore best to anticipate a potential loss and to take great care over the first purchase. Seeking out the right item to buy is in any event part of the pleasure of collecting antiques. For these same reasons it is best that the first purchase is of an object within the specialist area that has been chosen, which will become part of the permanent collection. If a poor buy is made it is difficult or impossible to get redress either in the case of private sales or auctions.

In the case of sale by private treaty neither the seller or buyer is probably able to make a proper valuation.

Where an auction house gives a guarantee regarding authenticity the purchaser will need to be able to prove that the item is not what is was described as in the sale catalogue but these often use vague terms to protect themselves, such as 'in the style of'. Often it is a question of your word against that of the auctioneer's staff and it is not worth going to law for a small amount.

Furthermore most auction houses have 'let-out' clauses in their terms of business. It may therefore be wiser to make the first purchase from a dealer.

Northern Spanish chestnut cabinet of circa 1800 in the process of restoration, without its handles and locks.

Since a dealer is deemed in law to be an expert, they are unable to use in defence that the buyer 'should have known better' but the standard advice for buying anything of 'let the buyer beware' still holds true. At one time auctions were mainly attended by antique dealers but nowadays many private buyers are also to be found. Auction houses vary widely. Those with the top *cachet* are international fine art and antique auction houses such as Christie's and Sotheby's. These establishments offer pieces of the highest quality and the same is true of the prices they achieve. Other auction houses reach a wider cross-section of the public.

An auction house acts as a broker between seller and buyer, rather like an estate agent but in addition to the seller paying a commission, insurance, and sometimes also for transport and catalogue photographs, the buyer also pays a 'buyer's premium' on the hammer price varying between 10 and 20 percent – with the leading houses currently pushing their premium towards 20 percent. Auctions are governed by law and by custom in most countries with the last bidder being obligated to buy once the hammer falls. It is important to understand some of the customs and practices at auctions and it is fear of these that often put people off from buying at auction. Dealers and other regulars often make their bids with almost invisible gestures and it may seem strange that the auctioneer rapidly raises prices without any apparent bidding being made. It is a good idea therefore for a newcomer to first visit an auction merely to absorb the atmosphere and customs.

Most items for sale at auctions come from either dealers and private collectors or from the estates of deceased persons. A price indication is usually given for each item or 'lot' by an expert based on the lowest and highest prices the expert anticipates. Sellers usually agree a reserve price beneath which the item may not be sold. This price is confidential between auctioneer and seller but is usually just below the guide price.

Catalogues for sales are issued several weeks before an auction. Those from the famous auctioneers are superb publications filled with interesting background information, descriptions of the lots with their numbers, and high quality photographs. The best auction houses indicate any damage or other negative matters regarding the item. Buyers need to realise that an auction house tries to get the highest price possible for the items which it sells and hence the descriptions emphasise the positive characteristics of a piece rather than the less favourable ones. Before buying expensive objects it is therefore sensible to discover as much as possible about the item in question.

A condition report can be requested which contains information additional to the catalogue.

This oak cabinet of circa 1885 is of Spanish origin with definite French influences.

Little escapes the experts of a good auction house and hence it is far less likely to find a true bargain in one. It can be well worthwhile though going to viewing for auctions of general effects with a keen eye. It is still possible to find a fine object that has escaped the attention of the experts and dealers and surprises can be found among hundreds of pieces of everyday 'junk'. These auctions are also interesting because their prices are usually much lower than the specialist auctions. There are three ways of bidding at auction: in person on the day, in writing, or by telephone. Telephone bids are usually only permitted above a certain indicated price. Written bids are safe for the buyer. After filling in a form, staff of the auctioneer then attempt to purchase the item for the lowest possible price (or so they claim) on the buyer's behalf.

For example, if a written bid of £900 has been made for a chest and the bidding in the room stops at £600, then the absent purchaser gets the chest for the lower price (plus the buyer's premium). There is always the chance of course that someone present on the day may exceed your bid. A further risk of written bids is that the auctioneer may start bidding high because he knows there is a high bid in writing. Strictly speaking the auctioneer should not be influenced by this but it happens of course.

Auctioneers usually start the bidding below the indicated price for the lot and then usually increases prices in steps of about 10 percent.

Auctioneers like to direct their attention towards two bidders and it may be of no point waving one's board around if not one of them.

It is then best to know who the bidders are. Dealers will generally not bid prices too high for they need to retain a profit margin. Some people get carried away at auctions and become determined to have a particular piece. In such circumstances it is almost inevitable that too much will be paid for the lot. Sensible people set themselves a limit for each item in which they are interested. And buying antiques should remain a hobby!

The success of auctions is the open nature of the selling process in comparison with the antique shop and dealer but despite this 'openness' customer's can be manipulated or duped.

If there are no bids forthcoming, an auctioneer can make out that he has received a bid – a practice with many epithets, some of which are not repeatable.

It is also not unknown for dealers to agree between themselves before the sale which items each will buy

This enables them to keep the prices down by not bidding against each other. It even occurs that they subsequently re-auction some pieces bought in this way between themselves and share the profits. Newcomers can best avoid such practices by only visiting an auction house with a solid reputation. Such establishments also protect their name by giving guarantees of authenticity in order to uphold their reputation and hence bad buys are far less likely.

It is a great shame if people pay too much for a piece which they then become tired with and store it away. The greatest pleasure from antiques is to be had if they are in the daily environment.

Display it, hang it on the wall, or put it in an appropriate spot. Although money cannot replace a cherished piece, it is sensible to insure it.

Norman French oak dresser of circa 1900.

Leather-clad Spanish stool originating from around Burgos circa 1900.

The purchase

It is not the intention to scare off potential new collectors. Most deals in the antique world occur without any problem but buyers can be less than satisfied with the piece they have bought and the price they have paid. It is for this reason that great care needs to be taken when buying antiques.
Considerable volumes of reproductions were once made of almost every type of antique and fakes are still made today. Sometimes these were and are made with the specific intention of selling them as genuine antiques.

The use of old timber in new furniture can have wonderful results but fraud is involved if a copy is knowingly sold as an antique in order to obtain a higher price.

This fine pewter tankard, beakers, and tray stem from before 1800.

The seller may not have been responsible for the copying or adaptation of a piece, which may even have occurred long ago. Back in 1900, English dealers happily sold antique chests from Germany, Belgium, and Holland but their plain panels were too austere for the English taste of the time and so they had carved decoration added. Some of these have found their way back into the antique market. The laws governing antiques differ throughout the countries of the world so that it is sensible if planning a major purchase to find out what the local laws are.
Prevention is better than cure and it is an essential character of English law that the buyer should take care when purchasing. For this reason it is advisable to thoroughly investigate a piece before buying and this is one of the reasons why a would-be collector needs to acquire so much knowledge. Knowledge and experience enable a careful study of a piece to reveal much.

A first indication of a piece of lower quality can be gained from its price. If a collector is offered a piece that would normally cost say £400 in a shop for a quarter of this price it should set off an alarm bell.
It is then sensible to study the item very closely and to get someone else with the necessary expertise to do so if not sufficiently experienced.

Checking out an item offered for sale is a matter of common sense. Keep an eye open for unusual marks of wear in places where a piece of furniture for instance would not be worn. If remnants of glue are visible then something must have happened with the piece. This need not be fraudulent reproduction but points at the very least to restoration. A check of the inside will help to show if the piece is genuine.

Lead shot has been known to be fired at furniture to give an impression of woodworm but shot holes always lead from outside inwards while woodworms always work outwards from the inside. Shot holes are always larger than those made by woodworms and shot will also press the grain of the wood inwards. Chemicals are also often used to distress wood so that it looks old and it can be blasted with sand or other matter to give a worn impression.

Mid 17th century pewter tray and spoons. Note the strange shape of the spoons for our time.

The person selling creates a particular impression about the piece in question and the buyers initially base themselves on this description. If there are things that reduce the value of the piece then they buyer certainly needs to find out. Only then can a true comparison be made between the piece and other objects of a similar nature and price.

It is extremely annoying to discover after the event that part of the piece is not original but restored. Buyers should therefore not only study the object very carefully but also protect themselves by asking questions. The laws of most countries require sellers to give truthful answers so do not be afraid to ask even what may seem the most silly of questions. It is better to be safe than sorry. Differences can occur over the characteristics of the pieces or over those that the seller indicated the piece possessed. Perhaps there is something wrong with the piece that the seller knew of or ought to have known about

Oak and chestnut cabinet from the Basque country of northern Spain, circa 1820.

A fine 18th century cabinet with pediment.

In all these cases it is difficult after the event to prove what was actually said. It is therefore a wise precaution to get the seller to give you a written description of the piece, if only for the insurance.

When a piece turns out not to be what the seller indicated, the purchaser needs to let the seller know this within 'reasonable time' after discovery of this fact. No action can be taken subsequently if this is not done. Where a dispute does end up in court, the judge will expect the seller to have given truthful information but also expects the purchaser to have taken 'due care' before buying.

Some countries place a higher duty on the seller where they are deemed to be a professional expert selling to someone who has no specialist knowledge.

Thefts of antiquities from both third world museums and archaeological sites has become more widespread in recent years. This worrying trade is thought to be driven by international dealers for whom items are stolen to order for onward sale to private collectors.

Aconvention regarding the rights of ownership was established in 1995 by which owners of antiquities and works of art must be able to prove their origin and demonstrate that they were lawfully acquired. Works are otherwise returned to their lawful owners with some compensation. This is not yet universally adopted in all Western countries.

French dresser, circa 1900.

Genuine, fake, and restored

The background to an antique may be uncertain. Sometimes written 'provenance' is provided which might include the opinion of a leading expert on fine arts or antiques.

This is intended to provide evidence of authenticity of the object or work in question. Without wishing to raise doubts about the majority of experts, their expert opinions can be a weak link in the chain for they provide no more than the expert's considered opinion. One's own research into the origins of a piece can offer a solution and sometimes may even find out the identity of the person who had the piece commissioned and of its maker.

When written provenance proves subsequently not to be valid this does not necessarily indicate that an object is an intentional fake. This can only be the case where the intention has been deception from the outset and many objects that are not genuine are not necessarily fakes.

Many objects were copied from earlier times during the nineteenth century because of the appreciation of their qualities which led to the rise of the style revivals, which are once more much in vogue. Early ceramics were also widely and successfully imitated in the past but the intention was always to produce reproductions and not fakes.

Something is only fake when it is intentionally represented as something it is not. Creation of fakes extends to 'over-restoration', creating of false provenance, the addition or removal of genuine indications such as maker's-marks, and forgery or removal of signatures. Professional fakers can produce deceptively good objects using modern technology.

The best weapon against fakes is knowledge. A well-informed collector can see that an object is a fake by means of historically incorrect details and by the traces of production of the piece.

Antiques are affected by their old age, through use, exposure to sunlight, and other factors. Previously the preferences of the restorer played a great role in the restoration.

They were generally less interested in retaining authenticity and repaired antiques according to their own ideas. They often 'improved' pieces. It was not until the nineteenth century that the notion of authenticity led to more careful restoration but this was not the restoration ethic of modern times and later additions were removed in efforts to restore to the original condition, with worn and missing parts being replaced.

Today two main rules of thumb are adhered to in restoring works. Firstly the restoration must be reversible, so that all traces of it can later be removed. There is a case in which an antique cloth was encased in glass. Although the cloth was well-preserved by this method it could never be removed from the glass and hence the restoration was irreversible. The second guideline for restoration lays down that the restoration can be clearly seen as such. With a restored chest for example this might be clear from the choice of a slightly different coloured wood. A plate that has been repaired with glue may look perfect from the front but it must be clear from the back that it has been restored.

A circa 1800 panelled Spanish cabinet in chestnut from Lugo on the Spanish-Portuguese border.

An 18th century oak linen chest. Like most such chests the original rounded lid on which nothing could be placed has been replaced.

These guidelines are not the laws of the Medes and Persians. Anyone wearing antique jewellery will not want any restoration to be visible. Restoration can create dilemmas that cannot be resolved with such guidelines. A studio in Cambridge was commissioned to restore an eighteenth century painting of a mounted horseman.

The restorer quickly discovered that the horse had been altered in the past and with the help of x-ray photographs it was seen that the horse had previously been much more sturdily built. Presumably several decades after the picture was originally painted more refined horses were preferred. What then was the restorer to do?
Should he remove the later layer of paint and return the picture to its original condition, or leave the later more slender horse?

Solid Spanish country-style of 1850ñ1870.

Restoring of antiques is a specialist profession. There are books about the restoration and maintenance of antiques but it is so easy to irreversibly damage a piece or to choose the wrong materials.

It is therefore far better to use a specialist who also has the knowledge to deal with unexpected problems and assess the best course of action. In any event find out from a museum or restorer what is the best manner of restoration. Owners of articles that require restoration are well advised to consider leaving the task to an expert.

There are differences of opinion over the different ways in which antique dealers and private owners have their pieces restored on the one hand and museums on the other. Museums place the emphasis on authenticity and restoration is clearly left in a state which shows its is not original.

An 18th century brass wine-cooler.
The legs are a later addition.

Private owners and dealers have a tendency to have their pieces invisibly restored. Private owners judge most on the outer appearance of a piece.

Whether or not a piece has been restored, and to what an extent, has a bearing on its value. Damage immediately lowers the value of a piece. It is not surprising that dealers can ask higher prices for pieces that look good which can then lead to over-restoration.

This can also lead for instance to the addition of bronzed handles and knobs being added that are not original to the piece. Since restoration affects the price, it should either be visible or notified in written provenance.

Portable bureau, circa 1900.

Two 18th century pewter beer tankards.

Two-door 18th century painted dresser.

Copper kettle inscribed ëweduwe (widow) Iwema 1850í.

There are no established rules about the extent to which a piece can be restored and still be called an 'antique'. It is a matter of course that old objects that were formerly in everyday use became damaged and have been repaired.

Small upright Spanish cabinet, circa 1800.

This Spanish cabinet of circa 1750 was originally built in to a house.

Miniature nineteenth century Spanish cashier's desk.

Some suggest that up to 30 percent of the object may be restored and still be described as antique while others set a lower level of 20 percent – with the additional proviso that none of the essential parts are affected.

A fine wooden clock case containing a modern quartz movement is quite ridiculous of course but even when objects have been restored with old and original parts they remain restored pieces. They are no longer in their original condition.

The simplicity of this nineteenth century French oak table is very attractive.

A past of its own

An antique or old building is much more than just something old: it has its own history. Often it is possible to uncover some of this past. A good example is an old family bible which has been handed down over the years. These often contain full details of births, marriages, and deaths, providing a fascinating family history.

An excellent example of the fascination on both a building and the objects associated with it is the former *Kurhaus* in Bergün in the Swiss canton of Graubünden (Grisons) which are now family apartments of the Swiss *Verein für Familienherbergen* (association for family inns).

The history begins with the raising of shares in 1903 to build a *kurhaus* in the

Escritoire, circa 1700.

This 18th century Dutch chest has been converted into a commode with bun feet.

Some original wicker chairs from the early 1920ís were discovered in the old Kurhaus some years ago.

village and this was soon followed by the other necessary facilities. The hotel was to be the village's showpiece and it was certainly one of the finest hotels in the canton for many years. Despite some difficult times the hotel did good business for many years but the lack of guests during World War II brought it to the verge

Wrought metal-work in fine Jugendstil above the main entrance.

of bankruptcy. The final blow was a fire in 1949 which totally destroyed the top floor. The local council bought the hotel in 1950 to save it from ruin.

A new roof was built without the original cupola and the building changed from hotel to family apartments. veranderd in familieapparteThese are highly sought after in summer and winter.

Jugendstil wrought metal-work on the front door.

The Kurhaus as depicted in a brochure from the 1920ís.

The Kurhaus today without cupola. Note the Jugendstil timber work on the fascia.

Art Nouveau detail in the lift screen at the rear of the lobby.

Jugendstil stained-glass in the main hall.

Today's interior is a mish-mash of older and more modern furniture with some of the original items still in use.

Original plans, and drawings of the *Kurhaus* though show how the architect envisaged the entire building with its interior fittings and furniture as an entity.

The chandelier as it now looks.

This fine Jugendstil desk is in one of the upstairs corridors.

Attention to detail: a brass hand-grip from a bedside cabinet.

Blueprint of the design for the main chandelier in the main hall of the Kurhaus.

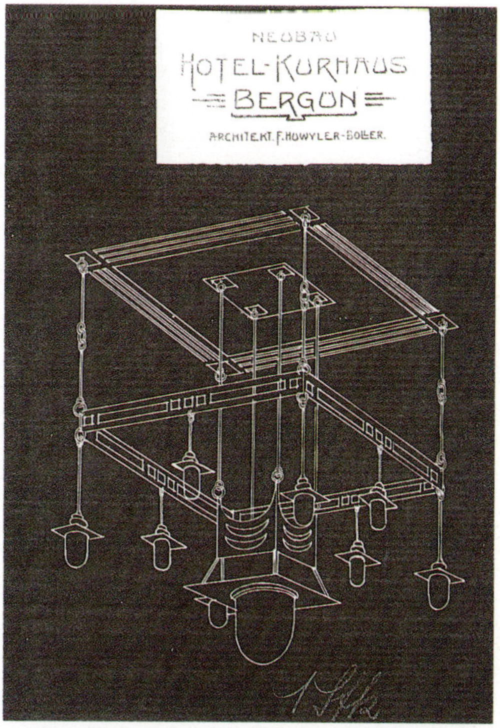

Fine detailing on the desk.

A rarity: an Art Nouveau chair with original fabric upholstery.

One of the original bar stools.

Fine ëwingedí door-handle.

Jugendstil architects not only designed the building, they also involved themselves in its interior style to form an entity of the whole. Special consideration was given in the design to both large and small lamps.

A small chandelier in the main hall.

A detail from the design for the buffet in the imposing main dining room.

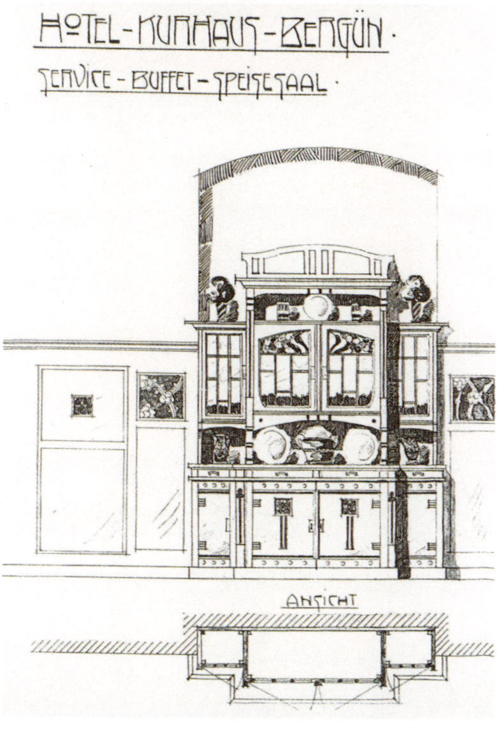

This illustration of the music room is from a 1920ís brochure.

Detail from a mirror.

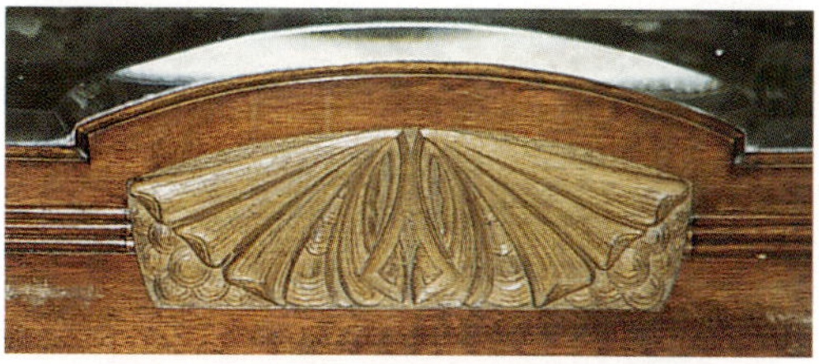

A fine lamp in the dining room.

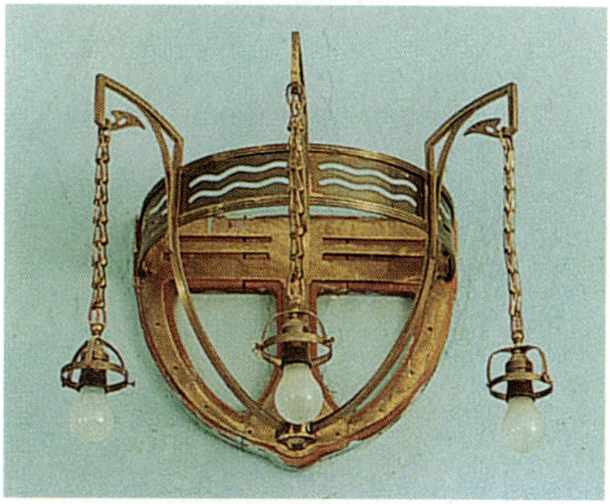

An illustration of the bar from a 1920ís brochure.

This stained-glass in the buffet doors is still in place.

This mirror formerly hung above a bench, which has gone, and now hangs above the staircase.

A fine dining-room chandelier.

A simple Jugendstil chair.

Another piece of furniture from the original interior: a Jugendstil wardrobe.

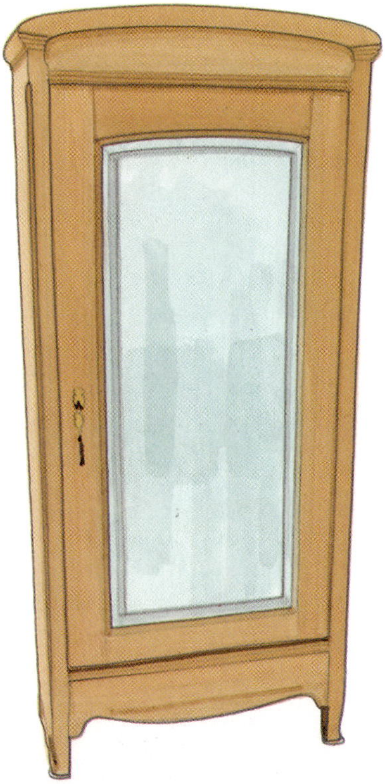

Furniture

The first humans were nomads who moved from place to place and found what they needed about them from what nature provided. When they learned to cultivate the soil humans generally ceased living as hunter-gatherers. They established homes beside their cultivated land and meadows. At first these were simple huts of wood and reed, perhaps daubed with clay or mud. Later some of them learned to make homes built of natural stone and baked clay but this was more the exception than the rule.

The walls of their houses were often weaker than the solid timber doors. It is not surprising then that the ancient Greek word for a 'housebreaker' has the literal meaning of 'he who breaks through a wall'.

Early furniture

Humans only began to make furniture when they started to settle in a fixed place.

Anntiques can sometimes contain surprises. The year 1703 is inscribed in the leaf of this table but when the table is turned around it becomes apparent the top was originally a door (the keyhole can still be seen). Does the date relate to the door or when the table was made?

The early furniture was understandably very primitive and entirely utilitarian but gradually the appearance of furniture also began to have more importance and it became decorated. The furnishings of wealthy households became more refined and unified in style.

Large-scale excavations and research have revealed a rich treasury of information about early cultures. These provide evidence of an abundant variety of design in crafts and architecture. A few surviving fragments of furniture and surviving illustrations show that the early Egyptians and people of Mesopotamia used tables, chairs, chests, and cabinets.
Furniture in antiquity was sometimes richly and extensively decorated. Inlay techniques with gemstones, wood, majolica, and metal were already known. They were not used again widely until the eighteenth century.
The ancient Greeks and Romans had stools, three-legged footstools, easy-chairs, and forms of *chaise longue*.

There were tables with one to four legs (card tables and folding tables) and also beds, plus large and small cabinets and chests. In Egypt these were made of different types of wood, leather, string, palm fronds, and reed. Luxury furniture was often decorated with glass and majolica with fittings of precious metal.

Greek furniture

Comfort and aesthetic appearance of furniture was intentionally combined in Ancient Greece. In addition to chairs, tables, and chests of widely differing forms they also made high-backed lounging chairs or *chaise longues* and lightweight portable beds. Typical decorations on such furniture included stylised acanthus leaf motifs, meanders, metopes, egg-and-tongue moulding, and parallel mouldings. Following the conquests of Alexander the Great, the Hellenic sphere of influence extended throughout the eastern end of the Mediterranean. This led to an interchange between the upper echelons of Hellenic society and the local populace which became apparent in arts and crafts.

This sewing or travel necessaire has had legs added and been re-arranged as a jewel chest. The legs are clearly a mis-marriage.

This chair of mixed styles is of no value to purists. The back is Louis XV, the legs are Queen Anne, and the sides are Louis XV.

THE CLASSICAL INFLUENCE

The Romans made contact with Greece and the Hellenic empire from the third century BC. In the centuries which followed, the Greeks became subject to the Romans but the Romans were in turn conquered by Hellenic culture.

The leading Roman scholars studied Greek and Greek literature and adopted Greek religions. Religious subjects were very important in Greek art and the Romans adopted this too.

Although there were differences between them it is possible to speak of a Greco-Roman classical culture.

The spread of this culture and its long-term influence was of great importance in the civilisation of western peoples and manifested itself in their arts. Think of the furniture makers of the Renaissance and Classicism who harked back to Greco-Roman forms of art. This classical influence has also been felt in later trends in which the specific intention has been to depart from the strictures of classical forms. Examples of this are Jugendstil and Art Nouveau around 1900 which determined to break free of both classical forms and their bombastic derived forms in the neo-styles.

Roman furniture

The Hellenic culture developed further during the rise of the Roman empire. Flexible furniture was made using metal and lathes were already in use. There were many forms of table but these were mostly round. Large pieces were decorated with plaster reliefs of chimeras, lions, and acanthus leaf motifs. Small numbers of folding chairs, tables, and bronze chairs have survived from this period. The Romans also had furniture with shelves.

Medieval furniture

Early Middle-age furniture

Knowledge of the majority of tools and techniques disappeared in Western Europe after the fall of the Roman Empire and were only rediscovered once more in the late Middle Ages. Certain techniques were retained though within the walls of monasteries.

An example is the lathe that once stood in the monastery of St Gallen in Switzerland. Knowledge of this technology and of other techniques spread once more through Europe from the ninth century.
A characteristic of the time was the lack of a fixed home. The rulers (kings and queens) travelled from castle to castle and took furniture with them that needed to be portable. bed-side cabinets, beds, dining tables, chests, lounging chairs, lecterns, foot stools, three-legged stools, and folding chairs. The many different styles and shapes from the early Middle Ages is the result of localised culture, and the tools and materials available.

The personal tastes of the persons ordering items also differed and hence so did the styles of their furniture. This ranged from outstanding to ordinary, from intricate to simple, from royal to bourgeois or even somewhat rustic.

CHESTS

Chests were very important during the Middle Ages. They were used to keep money in particular but also clothing and tableware in. Northern European chests were mainly of softwood such as deal and other pine. The main tool used to make these were an adze (specialist woodworker's axe), saw, and perhaps also a plane. These chests took various forms including those with saddle-form lids, elongated chests with decorative but straight moulding, and others that had the form of a coffin.

Middle-Age chests were also the first pieces of furniture to be artistically enhanced with very rich decoration. Northern European wood carving with arabesque motifs and twists was exceptionally imaginative.

New techniques for making furniture were first developed in southern and central Europe and the fronts of chests were embellished with copious curvilinear mouldings, irises, rows of stopped arc-forms, rosettes, and carved decorative mouldings. Iron fittings were not just used to join the wooden planks together but also formed part of the decoration. The few rare pieces from this period are mainly found in museums.

Gothic furniture

The feudal system began to change in western Europe in the twelfth century and standards of living gradually improved. The concept of chivalry, high moral principles, and courtly practices became increasingly more important. The nobility became increasingly more interested in pomp and splendour and much the same was true of the towns and cities, where the guilds in particular were of great influence in the development of the painting as an art form.

The guilds ensured the quality of goods and professionalism of craftsmen. The guilds also kept the various hand crafts entirely separate from each other. New guilds were even formed from within the timber workers' guilds for joiners, turners, and cabinetmakers who specialised in finer quality furniture. Furniture only became everyday items in the late Middle Ages. Pieces from this period only turn up for sale very exceptionally. The form, design, and standard of joinery often exhibit high standards of craftsmanship. The sawmill was invented in Germany in the early fourteenth century and this enabled cabinetmakers to make lighter and more elegant pieces.

It was now readily possible to saw pieces for the construction of a carcass and furthermore very thin pieces of timber could be cut to use as veneer.
These were used for inlay work of wood of contrasting colours. This development also led to a new style of art arising: Gothic. This first became apparent in the building of churches which we can still enjoy to this day, with great richness of sculpture, slender columns, and pointed arches.

GOTHIC CHESTS AND CABINETS

Chests were still the main form of show in his home for the increasingly better-off citizen. In the fourteenth century these were often decorated with reliefs of heraldic animals but this gradually gave way to a series of Gothic arches and by the late Middles Ages to finials. The type of ornamentation was determined by the wood used and varied from area to area. Timber from conifers decorated with leaf motifs was used in southern Germany, Austria, and Tyrol. Joiners in the Rhineland and North East France decorated pieces with garlands of fruit and flowers, and stylised vine stems. The hardwoods used in England, northern Italy, Scandinavia, and Spain was ideal for carving cruciform decorations and script panels.

Cabinets developed from chests and two chests stood one on another formed the first decorated cabinets, which became the second important item of furniture. A decorative moulding ran through the centre of the cabinet and they rested on a plinth. The first forerunners of dressers were made in Flanders. These were chests with a cupboard set on high legs.
The legs were joined together with cross-stretchers. Metal tableware was stored and displayed on these cabinets which had doors on them.

TABLES

Tables existed in a variety of forms. There were round and octagonal tops on a broad foot, long rectangular tables with broad cheeked supports on which the legs were joined by cross-stretchers. Chest tables and cashier's tables were made well into the eighteenth century.

SEATING

Little changed with seating. Folding chairs and those with three or four turned legs and also stools remained in use for some time. Throne like backed chairs were also used in France and the

Low Countries. These contained storage space, making them part chest/part chair. Benches were lighter and less robustly made. Some of these had folding back rests.

BEDS

The bed was a major eye catcher in the well-to-do home. In northern parts of Europe these had a full or semi canopy over them.

In France and the Low Countries, beds were often fixed to panelled walls.

Furniture and the Renaissance

There was a revolution in thinking in the fifteenth century which was much apparent in the visual arts but fed through more slowly to the design of furniture. Most of what was made was just a reworking of old themes and styles, even in Italy which was the forerunner of new forms of arts at this time. It was in Italy that late Gothic elements were first replaced by architectural forms such as pilasters, rounded arches, and columns. These designs were decorated with motifs borrowed from classical antiquity.

This included rosettes, toothed friezes, parallel, and egg and tongue mouldings. Where the structure of the furniture had previously been obvious it was now less obvious and greater emphasis was placed on the beauty of the shape of the piece itself.

Interior furnishing of the home was further extended during the Renaissance with hat stands, mirrors, busts, and bookcases. The choice of furnishings were largely dictated by the architectural character of Renaissance homes.

The functional form of the furniture was partly determined by aesthetic considerations.

CHESTS

This new style was found in chests of the time which became one of the main decorative pieces in the homes of the era. At first the chests were assembled from framing and panels which were initially solely decorated with simple geometric patterns. Subsequently the tops of these chests were embellished with human figures placed at the corners and the panels were often supplemented with mythological or historical scenes.

A 16th century carved cupboard attached to a wall.

A very English walnut secretaire of circa 1630.

Chests changed shape in the second half of the fifteenth century, becoming more cubic.
The geometric shapes of the surfaces were now enhanced with figurative decorations and also with plant forms. The feet of these chests were strikingly decorated.

CABINETS

Cabinets and cupboards became increasingly more important in the furnishing of homes. At first these had appeared in town halls and sacristies but they now started to turn up in private homes.
A credence table was used as a dresser. This is a two-door cupboard with sliding leaves beneath a folding leaf with quite limited decoration.

Two cupboards were placed one on top of another in less important rooms that were decorated even less. Cabinets sometimes also possessed a slide out or fold-down leaf which could be used as a surface to write on so that they could act as a bureau.
There were also bookcases, with and without doors and chests of drawers.

A 17th century oak pillow cabinet inlaid with walnut and palisander from the southern Netherlands.

Walnut Dutch cabinet, circa 1700, with cross-banding.

BEDS

A higher standard of living brought a further showpiece into homes – the bed. This formed part of the fitted furniture, attached to the walls. The principal end of the bed was raised and at first sat on a chest-like base but this disappeared around 1500.
During the high Renaissance the bed featured superb examples of sculpture. The richly embellished pillars bore a canopy.

TABLES

Ancient stone furniture inspired Italian craftsmen in their construction of tables leading to two or three highly decorative side-pieces, with caryatids, acanthus scrolls, and winged fantasy animals.

SEATING

Great value was placed upon elegance and comfort by people in this era and this is apparent from their stools, backed chairs, and other seats. Regional variations now arose in the different types of seating.

France

The French were the first to be influenced by Italian arts – because of their eager meddling in Italian politics. Hence

A 17th century armchair upholstered in golden leather.

The Gothic form of chair was retained but the armrests were raised and new 'architectural' details were added.
Despite the tremendous influence of the Italians, a new generation of French artists emerged who smothered furniture with a wealth of mouldings. These artists were mainly active in south-western France for in the north there was greater interest in functional design with both form and geometry arrived at logically. This found expression in an harmonic blend of neutral framework with modest decoration.
Cabinets were increasingly constructed with ever more slender legs. The body changed and was decorated with rich reliefs depicting the four seasons, the four elements, and ancient gods. Further south the form remained altogether more plump and cabinets still comprised two parts of equal size.

the first foreign country to adopt elements of the Italian Renaissance was France. The French were attracted by the reverence for classicism and the humanist attitude of the Italians. Italian artists were attracted to their court circles by the French aristocracy and yet the Gothic influences lived on long after this.
The early French Renaissance period saw development of the Frans I style, which saw late Gothic furniture acquire baluster legs, Corinthian capitals, friezes, pilasters, and decorative mouldings mixed with late Gothic characteristics. Chests, buffets, and benches retained an upright Gothic appearance.
Hence chests remained unchanged for a long time but dressers were used to store cutlery, tableware and other valuables.
The centre section was provided with a drawer for storage or was used to set out the cutlery and tableware. The top sat on Gothic pillars. Early dressers had the corners set back at an angle but later examples were more cubic in form as a result of the pilasters and pilaster legs.

France already led the way in terms of style for the building of palaces for Royalty and the aristocracy by the sixteenth century. These needed to meet the increasingly refined way of life of the nobility. France also led the way in the style of the interior decoration and furnishings of such aristocratic dwellings. High-backed chairs are very characteristic of this era.
By the late sixteenth century, the shape of people was once more a consideration in the design of chairs and chair backs were lightly curved in order to make them more comfortable. Armrests ending with ram's heads or scrolls rested on small turned column-like legs.

The high back of the Low Countries was exchanged for the low back of Italy. This development ended though when the Louis XIV style prescribed high chair backs. Very few chairs from this time have survived.
The bed with canopy established a firm place for itself in interior design in France in the sixteenth century. These

used upright posts in the form of pilasters or caryatids (female muse forming a pillar) in the Italian manner and for the design of their tables too the French looked to Italy. The leaf was carried by two moulded side-pieces in the form of chimeras or Hermes. There are often column supports between the side pieces and the table leaf. Column legged tables were very popular. These had horizontal stretchers linking them in the form of a double T.

The centre of large halls were often filled with tables with six, eight, or nine legs. It is difficult to differentiate between Louis XIII and Louis XIV tables. This often makes it difficult to date such a piece.

Germany

The Italian Renaissance style die not make headway in Germany before 1500. Its adoption is largely due to the German artists Holbein and Dürer. A great deal of work was done between 1525 and 1550 with drawings of ornamentation by the so-called 'minor masters'. Their influence only extended though to the decoration of the surfaces while form and function remained unchanged.

Only the aristocracy really adopted Italian examples. The citizenry continued to use furniture with Gothic style elements until the arrival of Baroque.
Furniture increasingly became more centrally made in France during the Renaissance but this did not happen in Germany, which was largely fragmented at the time. Furniture in Germany therefore differed from region to region.

NORTHERN GERMANY

The greatest response to the new style was in northern Germany, largely due to examples in the engravings of Heinrich Aldegrever. Yet here too the field was not wide open for greater ornamentation. There were two important types of cabinet: a large one with a Gothic style front with symmetrical mouldings, and a cabinet on tall legs that resembled a French dresser. The first of these types was decorated in a manner also found with chests from the Rhineland and Westphalia where the Gothic style endured. These chests were often decorated with long panels with lettering.
Most northern cabinets were made of oak while the preference in most other parts of Germany was for ash, larch, or deal (pine).

These timbers remained popular until well into the seventeenth century. High relief carving is particularly characteristic of northern German furniture of the time. The carcass was also decorated with allegorical or religious representations such as fertility rites and scrolls on the top moulding and also with sculptures of female muses as pilasters. This type of cabinet was made in Schleswig-Holstein until late in the Baroque era. Another type of piece that is typical of northern Germany is the small but tall 'farmer's' cabinet.

There were a number of variations in type of northern German chests of the sixteenth and seventeenth centuries. The variant originating from Lüneburg was the least changed of these from its predecessors. This type was made by joining planks together and it stood on tall legs.
Those from Holstein were supported on chest-like bases and were decorated in the same manner as cabinets from this region. Chests from Bremen had the form of cube that is slightly taller than it is wide.

SOUTHERN GERMANY

There was a marked preference for fine inlay in southern Germany. Italian architectural features were introduced via Augsburg where the local cabinet-makers were very active in the use of exotic woods such as palisander and ebony and also native timbers like maple, beech, cherry, and poplar for inlaying. A characteristic of late Renaissance furniture is the thoroughness of its making. Decorative designs were made by famous artists such as Burgkmair and Holbein. The plinths, centre parts, and cornices of these cabinets gave them a somewhat horizontal appearance. The main lines of southern German cabinets are largely lost beneath a welter of ornamental and architectural detail.

In reality they still consisted of two pieces. The decoration comprised Doric friezes, vines, symmetrical grotesque motifs, egg and tongue mouldings, and triglyphs. The sculptor and architect Peter Flötner exerted considerable influence on furniture of the time. He lived in Nuremberg during the first half of the sixteenth century. Chests were made as a result of his influence that were designed strictly according to architectural principles. Cabinets originating from Ulm are a variant of these, possessing niches between pilasters.

This early 18th century southern German or Czech trois corps or three part cabinet is of amboyna over deal. These cabinets incorporating a secretaire were made from Strasbourg to the Balkans.

A superbly finished 19th century German ladies writing desk.

The somewhat austere decoration on these cabinets is very superficial, being glued on to the chest and serving no structural purpose. In addition to chests with their surfaces harmoniously divided, more dynamic pieces emerged around 1600 with cornices and protruding feet. The vertical accent of these marked a transition towards the large two-door cabinet.

This type of cabinet developed into the typical southern German piece of furniture of the late Renaissance and seventeenth and eighteenth century Baroque. Sizeable chests were a Swiss speciality.

The preference for architectural detail was equally apparent with southern German washstands, and with large and broad buffet cabinets. Chests from the Tyrol often had fronts that were split into sections but subdivision into three to five sections was not uncommon. These areas were often decorated with marquetry.

The grain of the wood was also allowed its full expression. Southern German chests often had drawers in the bottom and the lids featured decoration divided into panels. The status of chests gradually reduced until eventually they were only found as furniture in farmhouses. Despite this chests were still made in southern Germany, with walnut being increasingly used.

Tables based on chests arrived in southern Germany from France and remained until late into the Baroque period. The influence of Gothic continued to be readily apparent.

Beds were free-standing with canopies mounted on posts with short valances or curtains. Very few chairs of this period from southern Germany have survived and those that have show clear signs of Italian Renaissance and German Gothic.

An exceptional 18th century German farmhouse cabinet. There are actually no drawers despite the handles. Its maker has attempted to imitate stylistic details from main trends in furniture.

Small 18th century oak document cabinet.

The 'farmer's chair' with square seat is the simplest form. Extensively carved chair backs and angled legs were adopted from Italy. This type of chair continued in existence until well into the eighteenth century in the Alps and southern Germany. In addition, there were many chairs with square rear legs that extended upwards to form the uprights of the back of the chair. Richly carved horizontal stringers were placed between the legs to make the chair more rigid.

Another widely found type of chair has arms, leather seat, and scissor-legs. A new type of 'Dutch' armchair appeared around 1600 with turned legs or moulded balusters that became very popular in the seventeenth century. Folding chairs also continued in use, especially in Switzerland.

18th century chair from Basle.

Late 18th century Friesian cloister table.

The Low Countries

The Catholic southern part of the Low Countries was mainly influenced by the French but the north went its own way. Furniture makers in the north were influential upon sculptors in Mecklenburg and Lübeck.

The preference in the Dutch Republic of the Seven United Provinces of the sixteenth and seventeenth centuries was for inlay with contrasting coloured woods, especially with ebony and rails, balusters, and carved pilasters were greatly favoured. Chests of this period exhibit the same features. Between 1725 and 1750 there was a marked preference for richly carved pieces.

By the late sixteenth into the seventeenth century many homes had a two-storey cabinet with protruding cornice. The upper part of the cabinet was slightly set back.

There were many regional variants on this theme with cabinetstypical of North and South Holland, Zeeland (with tall legged underframe), and Gelderland. This type of cabinet was also much desired in Cologne where they developed their own richly embellished style.

England

There was some small but increasing influence from the European mainland on England during this period. The dominant style was Elizabethan, after the name of Queen Elizabeth, characterised by simple interpretation of French but mainly Flemish Renaissance. Gradually the Gothic pointed arches and rosettes were replaced by heavy baluster legs, friezes, and other classical architectural elements.

The solid oak 'four-poster' canopy beds of this era are famous and many can still to be seen in castles and great stately homes.

Baroque

The principal characteristic of Baroque is its rejection of the rationalism of the Renaissance. Baroque is much more dynamic and lively, particularly with its use of light and shade in the manner of a painter. The design of a piece and its detail were subjugated to achievement of dynamism, which was at the core of Baroque. The eye for the main lines was expressed through the materials used. Wood was inlaid with gemstones or semi-precious stones, tortoiseshell, precious metal, and ivory. Light was reflected by polished wood. Supports were turned as scrolls and an overall impression of curved form was created by the use of projecting pediments, plinths, and cornices. Much use was made of acanthus stems with broad leaves and conch shell motifs.

It is difficult to determine with furniture when Baroque replaced the Renaissance because the two styles co-existed for a time. Furthermore the characteristic Baroque elements only became fully apparent during the late eighteenth century.

France

Most of Europe, with a few exceptions, fell sway to the dynamism of Baroque. France though preferred more rigid classical lines. This found its expression in an individual French style of furniture. It was precisely at this time that greater power came into the hands of the French king and with it a greater role in artistic commissions and hence of trends at the hands of the French court.

The best artists and craftsmen worked in the Royal studios – with the establishment in 1677 of the *Manufacture Royale des Meubles de la Couronne.* Cabinet making became regarded as an art in itself, with cabinet makers also working as *ébeniste* (specialist in inlay or marquetry – the name is derived from the French predilection for ebony inlay) and woodcarver.

In addition to the importance of construction and decoration in the making of furniture, consideration was also given to the location in which the furniture was to stand. The *ébeniste*, designer of the ornamentation, and the architect all made decisions about the final form of a piece. In the Middle Ages furniture had been largely portable or easily moved but during the Renaissance furniture was made for a more set place in the interior of homes. Now the far extreme was reached in which it was no longer intended that the piece should ever be moved.

A strange schism arose between furniture for the citizenry and very luxurious pieces. This also meant that different materials were used in the making of these different items. Instead of the customary walnut, more exotic types of wood were now used.

A good example of this is the use of ebony, which by the time of Louis XIII was already being decorated with coloured inlays.

The artist André Charles, who worked for the court of Louis XIV was exceptionally talented, and stood out from the other *ébenistes.* In his early period he also used Dutch motifs such as vases of jasmine, roses, and tulips in his mosaic woodwork. Later he was influenced by the designs of Bérain and Marot and replaced his motifs with banding linked together with acanthus stems. His designs were formed with both negative and positive inlays such as light pewter in tortoiseshell and vice versa. Later still he replaced the marquetry of the 1660's and 70's as it became less fashionable.

The bed was an important piece of furniture as the whole morning ceremony of rising or *lever* occurred around it. The enclosed square form of the bed remained with four posts and both outer and inner curtains. The bedroom had several ante-rooms attached in which there was much coming and going of court functionaries. The chest was banished from the furnishing of rooms and was replaced by the commode which became popular in France around 1700. The commode was a development of the chest with drawer which Boulle placed on legs. In the French *salons* table commodes also appeared, set on tall legs, encrusted with inlays of metal and tortoiseshell. These legs were furthermore decorated with bronze *mascarons* or grotesque masks. The drawers too were fitted with bronze handles which also held the encrusted decoration in the veneer.

The most important piece of *salon* furniture was a superbly made cabinet with drawes. At first the Boulle cabinets had separate plinths but later these were integral.

Tables were adapted to the considerable demands of the time and there were numerous variations. In common with other furniture, tables too were inlaid with metal and the same was equally true of cashier's tables, most of which had a small drawer. The older-style baluster legs were considered too plump and were replaced by cabriole legs.

Other rooms than the *salons* were often used for a number of purposes and as required night and toilet cabinets might be placed in them.

There were also heavy tables with marble tops plus smaller tables for lamps and suchlike. Console tables provided an architectural element.Seating in the form of *fauteuils*(armchairs), tabourets, sofas, and chairs formed part of the interiors of the homes of the wealthy and the aristocracy but cabinets did not. These were found in the homes of the citizenry but the new item of luxury furniture was the bookcase.

Many different types of armchair and chair were made. Armchairs with turned legs were widely used but later these legs were replaced with richly decorated baluster legs. These were joined together with diagonal carved stretchers or with H-form stretchers but these disappeared with the arrival of cabriole legs.

The backs of armchairs became more all encompassing and were upholstered and rounded off at the top in an arch. The curved arms of the chairs also became upholstered.

French furniture makers were also influenced by English furniture makers. This led to the introduction of the *commodité* – a kind of wide armchair – into France. The *canapé* was also partially developed from the English day bed or *lit de repos.*

German-speaking Europe and the Low Countries

Baroque expressed itself in Germany through very excessive and lively inlay and carving and was of considerable influence there. The elements of the Baroque style were incorporated with

Late Dutch Louis XVI mahogany cabinet.

Dutch Louis XVI tea pot stand with heating lamp.

both imagination and consistency. The output of German furniture makers was equally diverse as German politics.
Designs based on the Renaissance endured for a long time but alongside this a new style developed in the palaces, castles, and grand homes of the countless principalities, which adopted a great deal of the influences from elsewhere.
Furniture was imported into northern Germany for some considerable time from the northern Netherlands. After the death of Frederick I of Prussia in 1713 late Italian Baroque started to become more widespread and the artistic centre moved to Dresden, which became one of the most important artistic centres in Europe under Augustus the Strong, Elector of Saxony.

The Bavarian court in southern Germany was strongly influenced by French examples and items such as console tables with French baluster legs and lighter tables in the style of Boulle were made. The encrusted decoration of this maker and also of Marot found favour here too. Cabinets in ebony from Augsburg of this period are exceptionally fine. They have inlays of polychrome stones, ivory, wood, and *pietra dura* (mosaic of semi-precious stones).
Furniture was largely made from walnut with intarsia inlays of other wood. Great care was taken to ensure that the beauty of the grain of the walnut was revealed to its fullest potential.
The cabinetmakers achieved considerable results in such furniture. German Baroque ornamentation was dominated from the 1660's by heavy use of acanthus leaf motifs that had replaced conch shell forms, and by small arrow-like columns. Intarsia decorations became figurative from the start of the eighteenth century (bouquets of flowers were very popular) and no longer utilised vines, squares, or rectangular patterns. Baroque became increasingly more valid in Germany and this is clearly apparent with cabinets.
The older-style cabinet on bun feet was drastically altered. It changed into a four-door – later two-door – cabinet with heavy cornice, turned pilasters or columns, and angled fronts.
In terms of furniture, the northern parts of the Low Countries can be considered as an entity with northern Germany, although there were local style variations of course. Hamburg was an important furniture-making centre. The Hamburg four-door cabinet closely resembled Dutch Renaissance cabinets. In addition to these a fine two door cabinet appeared from Hamburg around 1700 with a straight cornice. The façade comprised large decorated areas with continuous pilasters. A similar cabinet from the Dutch Republic of this time is the linen cabinet for storing pillows.

The partial cornices of cabinets from Dantzig (Gdansk) gave them a less fussy appearance and their square panels were decorated with mythological scenes. By contrast, cabinets from Lübeck had arched cornices. The Baroque influence ensured that cabinets from Holstein and Westphalia were embellished with figurative decorations.
The influence of the naturalistic Dutch floral intarsia decoration remained apparent throughout the eighteenth century. In addition to the main show pieces many painted and non carved pieces were made in northern Germany.
In southern Germany, new life was given

to Renaissance cabinets at Ulm and cabinets from Augsburg were smaller and sometimes overwhelmingly decorated. The popularity of the *Wellenschrank* originating from Frankfurt was great from the beginning of the seventeenth century. This is a simply decorated cabinet in walnut veneer with an attractive curved front. Cabinets were also the most important item of furniture in northern Germany too.

There were various variants of these as elsewhere. Those from Hamburg were decorated with acanthus stems while Dantzig cabinets were smaller with one or two doors.

Commodes with pull-out leaf for writing and bureaux formed important pieces of furniture in the homes of the middle classes. Their chairs had spiral, turned, or cabriole legs and leather seats and these were also used to sit at table.

These chairs had high backs with heavy armrests and were decorated with carved banding and acanthus stems.

Many canopy beds with turned posts had large panels that were usually copiously decorated with intarsia inlay or carving. Gradually beds began to be made without valances.

Carving fell out of favour over the years so that cabinets had large plain surfaces on their fronts which gave them a monumental appearance.

The eighteenth century

The somewhat oppressive style of Louis XIV died with him. After his death life at court was characterised by elegance and a lighter touch. The effect was also felt in art with the salons of Paris being at the heart of the cultural life. The luxury of city life worked through to the country homes of the aristocracy which set an example to all Europe. The houses were extended with libraries, *boudoirs*, dining rooms, ballrooms, dressing rooms, bedrooms, workrooms and quarters for the servants being added. To give each room its distinctive function, the range of furniture also became extended.

France – Regency and Rococo

During the Duke of Orleans' regency rooms were still furnished with robust furniture but in the second half of the eighteenth century this altered radically. The fashion switched to lighter, more elegant designs that were also somewhat decadent in their decorative style. This made itself apparent in furniture with flowing lines, S-forms, and scrolls. Rococo was a fairly radical style period that endured for a shorter period in France than in other European countries. Customers made ever increasing demands on the furniture makers and furniture was required that was larger in size.

This caused a demarcation among the furniture makers with them specialising for instance in a particular type of expensive wood which they then made into furniture of the very highest standards. This was equally true of the bronze founders who engraved their adornments as if it were jewellery.

Increased demand brought about a certain amount of standardisation.

The *ébenistes* started to buy in timber, drawers, mouldings, marquetry, and handles and catches. All the *ébenistes* were required to sign their work from 1743, except for those working in the service of the King and yet it can be extremely difficult to identify a maker. This is because all the *ébenistes* also sold furniture made by others and it was their custom to sign all the furniture that they sold.

Daily life for the upper echelons of French society was extremely lively. Lots of callers were received and many visits also made, and in the evening they either attended or gave dinner parties. Lots of different types of seating were therefore needed which had to be comfortable.

Only curved forms would do for these. Among the new types of seating there was a short upholstered sofa of which one type was known as a *bergère*.

This had a closed back.

There was also the *bergère à joue,* which somewhat resembled a modern wing chair, and a number of versions of the *chaise longue* for lounging on. A *chaise longue* that was open at the front was known as a turquoise, while the variety with upholstered armrests was known as a *vieilleuse*.

A *canapé* has open armrests at the side, while a sofa has S-form closed side arms. The dressing table was accompanied by a *fauteuil de toilette* and a desk or bureau by a *fauteuil de bureau*. Rococo furniture was decorated with brocade, damask, velvet, or satin. Damask came from Genoa, Lyon, or Peking. Gobelin tapestry and cloth with petit-point embroidery from the state factory at Aubusson were used to upholster furniture. Woven reed was also used to make seats and chairs backs.

The gilt carved cartouches and shells of Italy disappeared from decorations to be replaced with unrestricted compositions with ribbons and flower stems.

The *rocaille* from which some say Rococo got its name came into vogue around 1750. There was a movement, up to the middle of the century, away from structure-led form towards ornamental design and was expressed also in the bronze embellishments. These were applied to table legs for example where stringers and legs met. A piece of furniture with a purely decorative function is the Rococo console which eventually replaced the console table.

Cabinets disappeared from interiors during the Rococo period except for in country homes and those of the citizenry, although there were half-height cabinets with two doors serving as wash-stand chiffoniers known as *meuble d'entre deux* and small bookcases with two doors. There would be a games table in the *salon,* sometimes with a chessboard inlaid into its top and the round *guéridon* or pedestal table was made for all manner of small items. There would be a large table in the dining room together with a whole series of smaller tables and for when they wished to talk without being overheard by the servants, there would be a 'dumb waiter' on which the staff would leave the food before retiring. In a ladies' room there would certainly be a dressing table or *table de toilette* which later became known as a *poudreuse*. The lady would also have a writing table or *bonheur du jour* in one of her rooms. Men's desks were much heavier in appearance, usually made from palisander but other words were also used for bureaux. Flat-fronted bureaux were popular until 1750 after which the cylindrical bureaux became more fashionable.

There would be several night tables in the sleeping quarters: the *tables de nuit* and *tables de lit*. During the Rococo period beds became more elegant and graceful but often with whimsical valances from which their names were derived of *lit à la Chinoise, l'Anglaise, l'Allemagne,* or *l'Italienne*. No chests or coffers were to be seen anywhere in the *salons,* these had been replaced by a commode with two attendant corner cabinets.

The form of the commode had also changed. The curves of the front had now disappeared and the bronze handles and catches were geometrically arranged. The bottom of the commode was bowed. As the years passed, Rococo became increasingly more complex. Bronze ornamentation and intarsia inlays now covered the entire fronts of pieces, without regard for the drawers.

Subsequently the decoration moved more to the sides of pieces. Bronze ornamentation became more simple with cleaner lines after 1740. Whatever their specialisation, virtually every furniture maker produced commodes during the Rococo era. Some of the famous names are J.P.

This room is furnished in Louis XVI style. The return of classical simplicity after the 'busy' Rococo is characteristic of the era. A central place is reserved for a display cabinet with Chinese porcelain.

Latz, J.F. Leleu, Nicolas Pineau, F. Oeben, J.H. Riesener, Bernard van Risenburgh, and Abraham Roentgen.

There was strongly exotic side to Rococo so that lacquered furniture was extremely popular at this time. Rococo flourished most during the first half of the eighteenth century and at this time French lacquer-work production overtook even that of the Dutch who had been the biggest producers of reproduction *chinoiserie* and the largest importers of Chinese and Japanese lacquer items. The Dutch Martin brothers were the major producers of reproduction *chinoiserie*.

Germany and Austria

The political situation had as great an influence on the furniture industry during the Rococo period as during the preceding era.

The artistic and cultural leanings of the individual courts depended both on their geographical position and political realities. Hence the main cities of Berlin, Dresden, Munich, and Vienna took their lead from the French court.
The German/Dutch Rhineland and the area between Liège and Achen differed markedly from the German/French Rhineland. There was a clear preference for Dutch and English style furniture in northern Germany.

The biggest variation in types of furniture and their styles resulted from the personalities of the persons commissioning them. When German makers did follow French inspiration they did not do so closely. This resulted in the *Bandestil* or 'banded style' which got its name from the banding motif popularly used until the mid eighteenth century on much furniture, but specially on bureaux.
A German Rococo secretaire had a style of its own, with a curved form which gave a far from restful appearance. The legs and corners were also slightly bowed and slanted. These secretaires were mainly made of ebony and fitted with drawers. Colourful marquetry was very popular for decoration. Frankfurt cabinets had a similar appearance and were therefore also extremely popular.

Northern makers who followed French ideas for commodes fitted them with three, four, or five drawers but they used no veneer. Further south, in contrast, a commode was deemed to be a tall cabinet finished in walnut veneer. This was finished unpretentiously with iron handles and fittings and had straight sides. The only decorated examples were those for aristocratic houses of the princes. The commode was a piece of furniture for the common folk. These were finished with refined carving in unvarnished oak and walnut in both Achen and Liège. These cities also made corner cabinets for tableware, wardrobes, small and tall dressers, and display cabinets.
The bureau was adopted from France too but German versions were both lower and less deep.The glazed fronted Dutch cabinet was further developed in north-west Germany and there was also clearly a Dutch influence in their lacquered furniture. Some chairs were both lacquered and decorated with inlays. The most common furniture though is made of stained walnut and oak.

The most precious pieces were gilded. Furniture made of beech or lime was usually painted yellow or white. Luxury items of furniture were also made in some places in Austria and Switzerland, often with the help of important artists. There are also delightful country pieces from this era. Rocaille motifs continued to be used in painted decoration until the middle of the nineteenth century.

This four-door mahogany Louis XVI cabinet on claw feet is very rare.

Louis XVI dining chair.

Louis XVI dining chair.

France – Louis XVI

A desire for the classical world returned in the middle of the eighteenth century resulted in a number of artists making journeys to Greece and Italy. Classicism became more widely known through their books, lectures, and works of art. Excavation of Herculaneum and Pompeii produced a great array of artistic treasures which inspired many contemporary artists.

This also coincided with a movement in art towards simplicity and naturalism. This trend manifested itself first in furniture, before the other arts. Furniture makers once more used motifs such as plaited garlands, egg and tongue mouldings, Hermes, nymphs, lion's heads, vines, rosettes, bull's heads, and Doric friezes. Rococo had shown a preference for gilding, white paint, and light colours. The mouldings and bronze ornamentation now faded into the background. Muted coloured veneers

Louis XVI dining chair.

Two Dutch dining chairs in the style of Louis XVI: right is the original, on the left a 19th century reproduction. +1

were now more popular. From the 1880's, at the end of Rococo, inlays of Sèvres porcelain had been used together with glass painting and lacquer from Asia. Floral motifs were popular for upholstery fabrics. Chairs were not just required to look fine but also to be comfortable. The backs of chairs became rounded or oval in the 1870's. These were crested with carved decoration. Legs resembling fluted columns were popular. The types of seating did not change though.

A newcomer was the three-seat sofa known as a *confidente*. The sides of both sofas and *bergères* were now generally straight. Console tables stood on a fluted column. Beds were no longer placed in an alcove and the side not against the wall was decorated.

The three-seat sofa was a newcomer under the Louis XVI style.

Louis XVI dumb waiter or étagère.

Louis XVI style small tables.

The common folk's furniture remained conservative. Items made for the citizenry included two-door cabinets, ladies' and medium height two-door dressers. Commodes were rectangular, smooth, and mainly set on conical legs.

A newcomer to less exalted homes was the cylinder bureau.One of the best furniture makers of the time was undoubtedly J.H. Riesener.

His pieces are decorated with marquetry flowers, urns, and fruits. Furniture was decorated with many allegorical figures and bronze embellishments. Riesener partially changed his approach towards the end of the eighteenth century with the introduction of straight legs and more geometrical marquetry. He undoubtedly gave his closest attention to his rectangular secretaires and commodes

Louis XVI table with drop leaves.

Louis XVI screen.

Louis XVI display cabinet of which the glazing bars have been removed during restoration.

Louis XVI dining room lavabo for washing hands.

with rounded corners Most of the *ébenistes* working for the French court were actually German.

Great names among suppliers to the court include J.F. Schwerdtfeger and Adam Weisweller. The greatest of all were Abraham and David Roentgen, who also sold to the courts of other European rulers.

David Roentgen's speciality was furniture with secret mechanisms. His marquetry decorations were based on designs by the fresco artist Januarius Zick.

David Roentgen lived in Paris between 1775 and 1780 and it was at this time that his finest pieces were made. Most of them were light in colour with bronze decoration.

A provincial Louis XVI cabinet with basin for rinsing glasses.

Small Louis XVI table.

The first to incorporate English ideas in furniture in France was G. Jacob, a woodcarver, who made armchairs of mahogany. The backs of his chairs were in the form of an oval medallion and they had console legs.
The fan-like fretwork form of his chair backs was very fine. The German maker J.G. Bennemann specialised after 1779 in large horizontally arranged dressers that were decorated with bronze adornments specially made by P.P. Thomire.

Classicism, Empire, and Biedermeier

England

English furniture makers between the sixteenth and eighteenth century adopted both the ornamentation and forms of continental furniture, although with a British tendency towards modesty and simplicity. There are three main periods of English furniture. The first is the Elizabethan era in which solid oak dominates. This lasted into the reign of the Stuarts. At this time Dutch furniture, which had much in common with the character of the English pieces, was imported together with luxury Flemish and French furniture.

The first new era of a distinctive English style was that of William and Mary when walnut was widely used.
The form of chairs brought over from the Dutch republic were adapted. The fretwork backs were raised in height and given scrolls. Fabric upholstery was replaced with harder woven seats and chair backs. Other types of chairs also evolved from this original type. A bench with a back was also created (a settee), a two-seated bench (double stool), and small sofa, known as a lover's seat. These types were made well into the eighteenth century.
Oak furniture was often covered with walnut or other veneers and decorated with inlays. The Dutch example of tulips, other flowers, and birds was also adopted.
Both the cabinet and secretaire on turned legs were important pieces of furniture, which were fitted with drawers. Both marquetry and lacquer along the Dutch lines were popular between 1680 and 1720. Things continued in this vein until 1750.
The most important piece of furniture though was the chest of drawers, made in the form of a low or taller commode.
The wide and curved cabriole leg was very popular during the reign of Queen Anne (1702–1714) but was being replaced by 1710 with the bull and claw foot. The ubiquitous English Windsor chairs has neither of these characteristics.

THOMAS CHIPPENDALE

English furniture making was significantly altered in 1754 by Thomas Chippendale. He preferred to work in mahogany and had taste preferences drawn from French and Asian examples. But he was also inspired by native English Gothic. He brought together Rococo shells for instance with late Gothic elements.

Chippendale produced a number of types of table including reading tables, bookcases closed at the bottom and enclosed with glazed doors above, card tables, glazed dressers with a taller central section, three-part cabinets, a small table on bowed legs, a round folding table, and bureaux or writing commodes.
His commodes shared a curved front with those of France. But his greatest love was probably for chairs. Following on from his Chinese and Gothic influences he produced chairs with square legs and the merest hint of decoration. All his creativity went into the decoration of the backs of his chairs.

The curved central 'splat' of the back was fretcut and carved in the form of woven leaves and flowers, with curls, scrolls, 'ribbons', and loops.

ROBERT ADAM

Robert Adam gained great fame in the subsequent stage of English furniture design. Adam used Classicism in a very decorative way.

His semi-oval commodes have their front decorated with painting and extremely fine marquetry. The painting took the form of banding, garlands and laurel wreaths, mounted trophies, oval forms, urns, and columns.

Robert Adam's storage furniture with its geometrical lines was made solely using light-coloured timber. This was mainly sandalwood. The top leaf and stringers of tables were decorated with either carved or burnt in patterns. These too utilised simple geometric motifs.

SHERATON AND HEPPLEWHITE

Thomas Sheraton and George Hepplewhite differed from Adam. Both made different types of cabinets but instead of using carving they preferred to see the natural figure of the grain of the wood.

Both Sheraton and Hepplewhite had a hand in the development of several types of table and they also made bureaux with cylinder locks, dressing tables, tables for placing against a wall, and bedside tables.

In common with Robert Adam they gave considerable attention to the backs of the chairs they made. Sheraton made the simpler type of chair, using sober, fitted for the purpose, and geometric designs. After 30 years as a furniture maker he reintroduced the use of rush seats for his chairs.

Hepplewhite in turn introduced the Prince of Wales feathers or ears of corn designs into the oval framing of his chair backs. More pointed oval forms and heart shape panels were also used by Hepplewhite.

ENGLISH REGENCY

The great flourishing of English furniture making drew to a close at the end of the eighteenth century. The English Regency period is considered by some as a mere variant of the French Empire style. It was not again until the 1860's that English furniture once more emerged with fresh ideas.

France – Louis XVI and Empire

A new style arose in France out of the Louis XVI style known as Empire. It was directly derived from the Napoleonic ideal of a Roman Empire.

French *ébenistes* were not greatly inspired by theexamples from classical antiquity given by wealth of treasures uncovered by excavations.

A child's bureau from the late 19th century made as an apprentice's piece.

A 19th century linen press.

Fortunately it was an era of artists with vivid imaginations and this included the architects P. Fontaines and Christian Percier who drew on the classical past for their designs for interiors, covering walls with carpet or colourful silk. Classical

Early 19th century mahogany half-moon table.

Elm ladies' bureau with certain Empire characteristics, circa 1800.

antiquity was glorified at this time so that artistic concepts of these idealistic days gained a romantic heroic overtones. This expressed itself through an almost pathetic level of ostentation, which was revealed in interior furnishings.

It is striking how similarly Empire furnishings are worked, making them readily distinguishable and rather uniform in appearance.

The furnishings were uncluttered and derived their form from architecture. The solid looking furnishings are strongly symmetrical with straight lines.

The Empire style also expressed itself in the design of furniture for the rooms. Important elements for Empire furniture are the cornices, pilasters, and columns

The decorative mouldings of acanthus stems, dolphins, egg and tongue mouldings, nymphs, laurel wreaths, lions, palmettes, sphinxes (which referred

Dutch East Indies teak dining table with classical legs, post 1800.

A very fine Empire bed with its matching night cupboard (below). The form is derived from early Egyptian ships.

Empire night (or pot) cupboard.

to Napoleon's Nile expedition), urns, and swans created their own identity.

The finest ornaments came from the workshop of Thomire.
The names that stand out during the first twenty years of the eighteenth century among the *ébenistes* are G. Jacob and his son Jacob Desmalter.

Empire dressing table with fine curved legs.

Empire style tables were fairly lavishly made for a range of purposes. Many four-legged tables served as writing desks but there were also bureaux with shutters and desks with pedestals.

Ordinary tables were round as was the case in ancient Greece and Rome. But tables were also made in various polygonal forms. Initially the table top was borne by a carved figure but this was

Late Empire childís chair with brass inlay on the chair back.

Chiffonier circa 1820. This was a forerunner of the documents cabinet. Cardboard boxes were stored in the lower cupboard.

later replaced by a plain columns with inlay and bronze capitals The wash stand also evolved.

A separate leaf was added for a water jug and the wash basin was often supported by a swan. The sliding drawer of the dressing table was often fitted with a mirror for hair styling.

Serving tray with silver of 1837. This tray had legs added in the 20th century and is now used as a table.

Secretaires were an enclosed but compact piece of furniture. Commodes were simples and without curves, with two drawers or two doors. A new item in the bedroom was a large swivel cheval glass mirror or *psyché* set in a frame on a stand. Considerable attention was given during the Empire period to the design of beds. Although these no longer had canopies they still remained pretentious. Furniture makers happily used a boat form for beds, known as *lit de bateau.* Matching style bedside cabinets and night cabinets with decorated fronts were also made for such beds.

Chairs and other seating from the Empire period is characterised by an emphasis on woodworking skills and heavy construction.

At first these had round turned legs but later these stood on arched sabre legs. Interiors were also furnished with dumb waiters, plus flower and sewing tables and a bird cage. The strong love of music also meant that pianos were increasingly found that were mainly imported from London and Vienna.

Germany

German furniture making reached a crescendo in style shortly after the French Revolution. It is entirely unfair to compare the German style of this period with the style of Louis XVI.

New directions in art in Germany generally arose from philosophers rather than practitioners. The Louis XVI style had reached Germany by 1760 by way of the Rhineland. German copies lack the same finesse of the French originals and did not fully implement the style.

Furthermore Baroque influences still endured in Germany and affected this new style import.

Free-standing German cupboard, circa 1870.

Furniture from the area around Liège and Achen was much closer to the French examples. Further north in Germany, along the North Sea coast and around Lübeck, the Louis XVI style was diluted by traditional Scandinavian styles.

The heavy in scale white furniture from this region was influenced by the simple beauty of furniture from Sweden and Denmark. German furniture makers were increasingly influenced as the years passed by their English compatriots. Wide use was made in Berlin and Hamburg and other major cities of veneer.

In addition to the use of native wood from cherry, conifers, walnut, and pear, mahogany was imported on a greater scale. Eventually the native timbers were forced to yield to the imports. Types of furniture dating back to the time of Queen Anne were copied from Britain, such as double commodes, sawing and dressing tables, and bureaux.
These were later followed by bookcases and glazed-fronted cabinets. English style tended to rule until the emergence of Biedermeier.

Display cabinets though were mainly inspired along French lines, largely due to David Roentgen. These pieces were largely made of course for the palaces and castles of the ruling German princes. These were decorated with inlays of animals, birds, and floral still life designs at Roentgen's instigation.

After some time these designs were supplemented with allegorical scenes and chinoiserie along Dutch lines. The sober way in which ordinary German folk furnished their homes stood in stark contrast with the overwhelmingly ornate interiors of the palaces.

It is impossible to over-emphasize the longevity of the influence of Baroque throughout the whole of Germany. We have seen how English style influenced the north. In Prussian Berlin Karl Friedrich Schinkel was open to both high classical and emancipated popular classical examples. In the south, in Munich, Leo von Klenze was rather more inspired by French style. Vienna in Austria was another matter though. Furniture makers there combined decorative tastes with comfort.

GERMAN BIEDERMEIER

The first tendency towards more approachable furniture for the 'ordinary' home could be seen in the work of
Klenze of Munich and these were popular with the generations leading up to the revolutionary year of 1848.

Biedermeier style became popular in the German-speaking countries of Germany,

Biedermeier dining chair with well-upholstered seat and back. Comfort was extremely important during the Biedermeier period.

Biedermeier occasional table. Biedermeier interiors were busy places because they were filled with many small tables.

Austria, and Switzerland but also in The Netherlands.

Biedermeier style was a counter to the rigid and pathetic Empire. It was inspired by furniture design that was popular with ordinary people around 1800.

The ordinary citizen preferred more approachable furniture with rounded corners and lightly curved surfaces, circles, ovals, and curved broad lines. The popular notion of comfort meant for instance wide sofas and divans. Sets of tables and chairs were given pride of place in the 'ordinary' home. Little use was made of bronze encrusted decoration or fittings in Biedermeier furniture. This was restricted to small turnkeys, horns of plenty, and key escutcheons.

In Germany, as in England, bookcases consisted of three parts. The three-piece display cabinet in the style of Sheraton

Single door Dutch oak wall cabinet, circa 1860.

Two door Dutch Biedermeier cabinet with internal shelves in mahogany, circa 1870.

Single door 19th century Biedermeier china cabinet.

A 19th century Dutch Biedermeier mahogany bonheur.

German Biedermeier bureau in mahogany, 19th century.

A comfortable Dutch Biedermeier three-seat settee in mahogany, circa 1860.

was also adopted from England. Wardrobes, linen cupboards, and china cabinets had pilasters at their corners and otherwise were entirely glazed. Secretaires managed to stay in existence during the Biedermeier period but their style varied from area to area.

The tops of these secretaires were sometimes reminiscent of a cathedral. The inside of a secretaire was subdivided along architectural lines with small drawers, mirrors, and small columns. It is fun to find all the secret cavities.
The most widely used woods were native beech, ash, cherry, and pear plus 'exotic' mahogany. Most secretaires were decorated with paintings or veneer.
Furniture was often covered in floral cretonne with intensely coloured roses or with cotton rep. The walls were hung with plain wallpaper or with paper with floral or vine patterns. This made the rooms look busy even before the many items of furniture were added. These included sewing tables, dumb waiters for books and china, and wastepaper baskets.

The period of Eclecticism

The Biedermeier style is regarded as the last creative style of the nineteenth century. Furniture makers had started casting their eyes back to examples in classical antiquity during the period of

The 19th century saw style eclectic revivals. This German neo-Gothic cabinet is a such an example.

Secretaire, circa 1870, with certain neo-Gothic elements.

Late 19th century English Windsor chair with finely constructed chair back.

This late 19th century English dining table can be cranked out with a handle to seat up to 12 people.

Reproduction Robert Adam style display cabinet of the second époque.

An exceptionally fine 19th century English rosewood bureau.

Victorian mahogany ladies' bureau, circa 1870.

This pink neo-Louis XV chair was made circa 1850–1860 and was originally part of a chaise longue.

French oak cabinet circa 1860–1870.

French Louis-Philippe style cherry table with drop leaves, circa 1900.

Normandy table with drop leaves and Louis-Philippe style legs, made just before 1900.

A 19th century walnut dressing table.

A 19th century lawyerís oak writing case with fold out writing leaf.

Elm study chair, circa 1850.

A Swiss bureau of the 19th century.

Finely detailed 19th century corner chair.

Classicism. This trend continued as the Romantic style during the first half of the nineteenth century, which led in turn to the neo styles or Eclecticism.

The first was neo-Gothic in Austria and Germany between 1840 and 1860, which was overtaken by a Rococo revival. In the 1890's there was a revival of Renaissance style elements with characteristically heavy forms of credence tables and dressers.

Tea dumb waiter, circa 1900.

A 19th century Colonial style writing case with double doors, counter top, and brass handles.

Round Colonial style salon table, circa 1900. The foot is made from one piece of timber.

Commode or chaise percée, circa 1900.

It became fashionable to decorate and furnish in oriental style at the end of the nineteenth century. Furnishings such as carpets and rugs, vases, mother-of-pearl decorated furniture, and divans were widely found at this time.

The heroic style of the first Napoleon was overwhelmed beneath a welter of large upholstered pieces and drapes in the France of Napoleon III.

This excess and ostentation covered up a lack of creativity on the part of the *citoyens* who now held the leading positions in industry and commerce. This also brought about an increase in mass production. The flood of cheap and indiscriminate furniture led to a marked reduction in fine hand-made furniture by craftsmen. This process was also hastened by the attitude of the schools for the applies arts.
Eclecticism manifested itself in virtually every branch of the arts. Only Michael Thonnet contributed new creativity at this time. He discovered in about 1830 that it was possible to make thin lightweight sheets of oak veneer which could be bent and laminated in order to make furniture. He bent laminated sheets of oak veneer with the help of steam.
Another raw material which was also popular in the past for making lightweight chairs is rattan.

German Perzina made Jugendstil piano from Schwerin, circa 1910. +1 teveel

Typical Jugendstil ornamentation on the piano.

Jugendstil, Art Nouveau, and Art Deco

Opposition to Eclecticism arose in the late nineteenth century. The imitations of old styles and tasteless mass produced items were detested. Artists formed themselves into groups in many countries and strove for pure craftmanship and simple art. Above all objects were to be functional, original, and logically constructed.

Munich became an important centre in this movement. A publication entitled *Die Jugend* was established there and this gave its name to style which arose: Jugendstil.
This was more of a movement and trend than a style in itself with many different approaches in different countries.
An important group formed around John Ruskin in England for which the social aspect was also important. The emphasis was placed on craft traditions that still existed and had done so since the Middle Ages. The Arts and Crafts movement, as it was known, placed its main emphasis on craftmanship in the making of pieces. Another group of artists in Scotland, led by the architect Charles Rennie Macintosh, went its own way. Another important centre was Vienna where Sezession was formed, under leadership of the artists J.M. Olbricht and Gustav Klimt.

France had been pushed into the background during the previous period of furniture making and Art Nouveau arose as an innovative movement which tied in with activities elsewhere at that time. The main centres of French Art Nouveau were Paris and Nancy.
The British Arts and Crafts movement had hardly any effect on France and certainly none on its furniture designs. Hence the French developed a style of their own. French artists produced many delightful decorations with elegant

and original designs, using expensive materials. Generally these new styles started from a standpoint that the eclectic character of nineteenth century furniture was pompous. The new designs were therefore lighter, more transparent in their construction, more fluid, and more 'honest'. The silhouettes used were still of classical origin. Decorative elements were drawn from nature and the extent to which these were then stylised depend on the individual movement. This can be seen in the difference between Jugendstil and French Art Nouveau. Jugendstil's decorations are more naturalistic than the stylised forms of Art Nouveau.

Major names of furniture designers of the time are Van der Velde and Horta in Belgium, Bugatti in Italy, and Louis Majorelle and Emile Gallé in France. The German makers included names such as tioners in Britain. In addition to Macintosh, another great name from around the turn of the century is C.F.A. Voysey.

A further detail tends more towards Art Nouveau.

The matching Jugendstil piano stool.

The Viennese *Werkstätte* was led by Josef Hoffmann who found himself drawn to the work of the Scot Macintosh. In common with other centres, the artists of the *Werkstätte* did not fully subscribe to the ruling ideas of either Jugendstil or Art Nouveau. They did not consider that only traditional hand-crafting was valid and they also used machinery. Reproductions of the popular main great styles continued to be made up to the outbreak of World War I.

The styles of the French Kings Louis, Sheraton, and Chippendale continued to be very popular and not everyone admired the modern art approach of Jugendstil and Art Nouveau. After World War I a new style was discerned – Art Deco. Art Deco absorbed much of Art Nouveau but rejected its adherence to hand craftmanship and expressly chose to machine make objects. It was not furniture of the mid eighteenth century that inspired Art Deco designers, rather than that of Louis XVI and the Directoire at the end of the century.

The influence of Cubism can be readily seen in the modern designs of this time.

Ceramics

Ceramic is the term given to all earthenware, china, and porcelain and it applies to all objects fashioned from clay and then hardened by drying or firing in a kiln. The history of ceramics is closely related to the history of humankind. People discovered various materials and techniques, learned them from each other, and further developed them.

Over the ages a wide range of ceramic forms have been created, reflecting the diversity of human activities. These uses range from religious and mystical or magical objects through objects on which to serve and eat food and works of art, to present day material for turbochargers for motors. Ceramic materials also form part of the heat-shield of space craft.

This chapter is an overview of the most important forms of European pottery. Chinese and Japanese ceramics are handled in the chapter on Oriental objects.

The first pottery

The basis of all ceramic material is pottery clay. This clay has been deposited as a sediment from rivers which have eroded rocks and carried the material downstream. The constituents of clay therefore depend on the geology of the rocks upstream. If a river flows through granite for example, the clay can contain kaolin. Clay containing kaolin that has been baked is so dense in structure that it is no longer porous and is known as china or porcelain. Such clay is also known as china clay.

Clay with too little kaolin is more porous and can therefore only hold liquids for a limited time. Ceramics developed across many centuries. The clay was at first shaped by hand so that the end product was always irregular. The potter's wheel was invented around 4,000 BC – probably in Egypt. This enabled the clay to be shaped more consistently into round forms. Besides forming clay by hand on the wheel, the technique of shaping clay by pressing it in double moulds to make parts was also developed. The individual parts were then later joined together and the seam was smoothed over to hide it.

While mankind roamed the earth as hunters, the struggle for daily existence prevented the creation of objects of art. Those objects that they did make were mainly practical in nature: tools with which to create shelter, for hunting, and to make clothing. Water was not carried in fragile earthenware containers but in hollow organic objects such as gourds. The easily kneaded sediment from the rivers was only used to make idols and other ritual images of animals and other figures. These hunters did discover that the clay hardened if left in the sun to dry and perhaps it was a chance discovery that drying with fire gave even better results.

Early developments

Greater use of clay only started once people started to settle and turn to agriculture.

Food from one harvest could be stored until the next in jars or pitchers and this was one of the essential requirements for settled agriculture.

The first agricultural communities formed the basis for the later larger towns, nations, and cultures. Clay also served another very important function in Sumeria. Tablets of fired clay were used to preserve texts. It was also discovered

that when firing certain types of clay metal ores were released.
Hence earthenware also formed the basis for the winning of metals such as copper, silver, gold, and iron. Ceramic techniques were greatly stimulated by the essential role of clay in the founding of metal objects. Jugs of earthenware and bronze were made in the same way in China for centuries, from the Shang to the Qing dynasty, as a result of this development.
\
The desire for and extent of decoration of objects is not just a reflection of the way in which the people lived but also of their standards of living and pottery techniques and the type of ceramic objects made.

Glazes and porcelain

It was discovered that pottery could be given a different colour and also be made impervious by the addition of glazes.
This made it possible to keep and transport liquids in an hygienic manner. Furthermore, pottery changed from being purely practical objects into ones of artistic expression through the addition of pigments. Ceramic objects therefore became subject to trade with peoples who had not yet developed the techniques able to buy them from others who had.

The Chinese earned a great deal of money for a thousand years by exporting their porcelain. Their markets reached as far as Persia and Europe. Porcelain objects were highly desirable and considerable efforts were made in Europe to discover the process by which they were made.

It took until the start of the eighteenth century before people in Meissen in Germany managed to produce a similar type of ceramic.

Two Friesian earthenware brandy goblets of 1864, made for the marriage of Henrietta Catharina Meeren and Tjalling Justus Halbertsma.

TILES IN ANTIQUITY

The techniques used to produce tiles down the ages did not differ from those used to make other earthenware.
The difference was in their use as floor-covering and – perhaps the most interesting form – as wall decoration. The oldest tiles with a coloured glaze are Egyptian, dating from 4,000 BC.
Most ancient Egyptian tiles are blue in colour. Because glaze is not particularly opaque, different effects can be achieved by using thin or thicker coatings.

Ancient Mesopotamia – the country of the two rivers that incorporates present-day Syria and Iraq – also had tiles 3,000 years before Christ.
These tiles were quite different to those of the early Egyptians. Use was often made of imposing effects with sparkling colours. The large group of glazed tiles of the Ishtar gate of Babylon are such an example.

Grecian-Roman antiquity

Countless Grecian and Roman trading vessels have been discovered in the Mediterranean with many earthenware amphora still intact. These were used to ship wine and olive oil. Ceramic items were highly desirable trading goods in the past and they played an important role for the ancient Greeks from early times.

The Greeks combined functional design with a good feeling for decoration. The high quality of their pottery was due both to their extensive experience and the well-developed practice of specialisatio. The Greeks used ceramics for a wide range of purposes from household objects to dedication to their gods. The end use of the item played a part of course in determining its quality. Renowned Greek pottery originates from Corinth and Athens.

The production of Greek pottery was carried on until into the era of the Roman Empire.
The Romans enriched ceramics with their *terra sigillata*. This term is derived from the potters stamp often used to mark their work.

An 18th century blue and white coffee pot from Islamic Persia. The Chinese influences are easily recognisable.

European pottery from the Middle Ages

Cultural development stagnated after the fall of the Roman Empire. It took well into the Middles Ages before there could be talk of creative revival in the crafts. Ceramics only truly re-emerged in the Romanesque era. Pottery of this time is fairly mediocre from an artistic standpoint.

Islamic influences

Southern European culture was influenced during the later thirteenth century by the fine ceramics from the Muhammadan Middle-East. The Arabic world had maintained the rich classical traditions and absorbed them into its own style. Their ceramics were very advanced, both aesthetically and technically. In the simplest technique, porous earthenware was covered with a thin layer of slip clay to make slip earthenware. This provided a base for *sgraffito* or engraving of a simple painted decoration. The object was covered before firing with an often colourless, easily melted and lustrous lead glaze. This technique was known as *mezzamajolica*.

Majolica arrived in southern Europe in the fourteenth century from the Islamic world of Turkey and Persia. By the fifteenth and early sixteenth centuries it was being widely produced by Italian potteries.

POROUS AND IMPERVIOUS CERAMICS

Ceramics can be divided into impervious stoneware and porous earthenware. Porous earthenware is generally fired at temperatures of 500 to 800°C (932–1,472°F) at which the individual grains of clay remain intact. With stoneware, the pottery is fired at about 1,300°C (2,372°) at which temperature the grains fuse together to form an impervious ceramic.

Majolica

THE ARRIVAL OF MAJOLICA IN ITALY

Majolica meant a tremendous step-forward in pottery. Such pottery was exported to Europe by Arab merchants. Some English-speaking experts call early majolica *maiolica* and reserve the name *majolica* for the nineteenth century copies of this ware. The name was once used for the island now known in Spanish as Mallorca or in English as Majorca which was once an important trading centre for Moorish pottery that found its way to Italy.

The production of majolica ware expanded significantly in Italy in the mid 1500's and a style of their own had emerged by the end of that century. Majolica formed part of the Renaissance in the early sixteenth century which saw a change in both function and form of majolica ware. In the fifteenth century majolica ware was still predominantly consisted of everyday items such as jugs and pitchers or jars.

During the sixteenth century though this ceramic ware decorated the homes of the rich patricians and embellished the festive table. Majolica was also an expensive present that people were pleased to receive. These items were mainly flat tableware because the decorative effects worked best on plates and dishes. Dinner services acquired more subtle and elegant proportions through greater thought in their design and throwing of the clay and the quality of the glazes improved continuously. This was especially true of the opaque in glaze forming the ground for the decoration which was now covered with a transparent lead glaze that made the majolica sparkle after firing. At the same time the painted decoration took a new direction. As a result of the great admiration for Chinese porcelain being imported through Venice, majolica also quickly started to be widely produced with a white ground. The town of Faenza took the lead in this and it is from here that the term faience is derived. The characteristic dominant colours of faience are blue, purple, orange, yellow, and green.

FRENCH MAJOLICA

Tin glazed pottery in France for some time was only imported from Italy with French potteries mainly producing lead glazed wares. Some sporadic use was made in the sixteenth century of tin glaze – mainly in the making of tiles.

Production of majolica type wares only got under way in France during the Baroque period. The first impetus for adoption of this technique was probably the emigration of Italian potters to France during the sixteenth century. Their products were decorated in the Italian manner but started to exhibit different detail and colour characteristics. The technique was not yet adopted by French potters.

SHIFTING THE CENTRE OF GRAVITY

Majolica-type wares north of the Alps were mainly restricted in terms of local production to southern parts of Germany. The technique had not yet been adopted throughout the German territories. During the seventeenth century, the centre of gravity of development of earthenware and production of majolica-type wares shifted north of the Alps. The production of majolica related ware became important in Germany, France, and the Low Countries. England was the leading centre for the production of stoneware.

This development eventually led to the discovery of how to fire porcelain, the production of which began in Meissen near Dresden in the eighteenth century.

DELFT

The production of majolica wares started in the Dutch Republic of the United Provinces in the second half of the sixteenth century. Countless Protestants who were driven out of the Catholic south moved into the northern provinces and these included potters from Antwerp where majolica ware started in the sixteenth century. Their knowledge had probably been gained from Italian potters. The production of majolica type wares was concentrated mainly in Delft from the start of the seventeenth century.

This was due to its proximity to the necessary clay and its position on navigable waterways over which the Delft pottery could be transported. Dutch merchants took over the trade in oriental porcelain from the Portuguese at the start of the seventeenth century and the newly formed Dutch East India Company starting to import porcelain. The trade flourished enormously and oriental porcelain became highly fashionable. This naturally had its effect on the style of Delft. Chinese porcelain of the Ming dynasty was even reproduced in the early seventeenth century.

This applied both to the blue decoration on a white ground and the patterns and motifs used. The production of tiles was on an even larger scale but this was mainly concentrated in Amsterdam, Haarlem, and Rotterdam.

A wealth of rural Dutch antiques can be seen in this room: brass, Delft, tiles, and oak furniture are all characteristic of the farmhouse style that existed for several centuries.

FOREIGN INFLUENCES ON DELFT

The import of Chinese porcelain dropped off and even stopped entirely in the second half of the seventeenth century. Although Dutch merchants succeeded in gaining a monopoly on the exporting of Japanese porcelain, the volumes were far too small to meet demands. For this reason potters in Delft began to improve their imitations of oriental porcelain. There were a number of potteries in Delft between 1640 and 1706 that were making Delft's majolica-type ware. The quality of their output was such that it was able to compete successfully with imports from Japan. The Delft potters ascribed their success to their enterprise, craftmanship, ability to adapt to the wishes of their customers, and the high standard of the Japanese and Chinese examples on which they based their work.

Their relationship with Dutch artists also played a great role. Delft is mainly marked with the individual pottery's mark. Delft was of such quality at this time that at first glance the earthenware could be confused with porcelain.

Red was added to the colours to be fired and the painting techniques were also enhanced. The only area in which they lagged was in design with the majority of their work being based on oriental products.

There was a tremendous range of both domestic as well as foreign decorative motives available to them from which they developed separate domestic and oriental lines.

Delft blue scene of 1747 when Willem IV was appointed stadtholder with 'Vivat Oranje'.

DOMESTIC AND ORIENTAL LINES

Domestic styles still dominated during the third quarter of the seventeenth century. This showed predominantly figurative compositions such as town scenes and seascapes.

There were interiors and landscapes, biblical scenes from the Old and New Testament, and sea battles. Mythological motifs were rarely used. The style of painting is related to the art of Dutch painters of the time. Oriental styles existed alongside the domestic scenes but started to take over around 1760 and became the most important direction for Delft.

The determination to imitate Chinese porcelain was aesthetically very successful. In addition to blue there was also polychrome decoration which was initially just with the use of enamels but enriched by red at the end of the seventeenth century. Delft started to reproduce Japanese Imari and Chinese *Famille Verte* at the beginning of the seventeenth century. They created new compositions based on examples, with a colourful mixture of widely varying motifs brought together. The effect of light was sometimes strengthened by creating a ripple effect.

Pottery that imitated Chinese *Famille Rose* saw the greater use of more muted colours. It was with these that Delft achieved its greatest heights between 1725–1735.

NEW FORMS OF ENTERPRISE

The nature of the Delft enterprises were already changing by the late seventeenth century. Management of the potteries shifted from artists and craftsmen to commercial individuals. If the master potters of great character had not resisted them the artistic level of output would certainly have fallen. Delft responded to

Two unique Delft blue strainers, circa 1600.

market demand in the eighteenth century based on several traditions. Influenced by Baroque, tableware was produced in new and bizarre forms such as the finger bowls and several piece pyramid-form hyacinth vases.

At the same time the northern parts of The Netherlands were sending wooden models for porcelain to the Orient, resulting in *chine de commande* (see also Oriental objects). The artistic quality

A fine Delft blue pot with brass lid.

A Delft blue cabinet set.

of Delft came under pressure from two directions in the second half of the eighteenth century. More intensive trade meant that the prices of the now readily available Chinese porcelain dropped and in addition Delft found stiffer competition from potteries in Meissen and elsewhere in Germany and also from the new type of English stoneware. The red stoneware that was mainly used for teapots is closely related to Delft.
This copied the Chinese who did not make their tea in porcelain teapots but stoneware ones. These teapots arrived in Europe with porcelain.

A unique Delft blue tulip vase.

Dutch potters in the north of the country started to copy this type of ware around 1670.

FRENCH FAIENCE

The Dutch example was quickly followed in both France and Germany. The impulse came from mercantilism: an economic policy intended to improve welfare by increasing the export of goods while limiting imports.

This economic system gave a stimulus to the switch from making things by hand to mass production with efficient distribution of work. This is not yet a question of mechanisation, just of better distribution of manual work. There were numerous companies in the later seventeenth century which manufactured textiles, earthenware, and porcelain. Because the products were still hand made they still had individual character. Production of faience was given an impetus at the end of the seventeenth and start of the eighteenth centuries by edicts in France that the population was to hand in their silverware in order to help a government in financial difficulties as a result of expensive wars. Much of the silverware that was melted down was replaced by faience ware.

French Baroque faience can be split into two categories. The first of these dominated until the mid 1700's and used the well-proven Dutch and Italian technique of painting enamel over unfired glaze.
The other, new method decorated the fired pottery with muted colours. This method enabled greater choice of shades of colour.

Independent of adoption of artistic and technical influences from abroad French faience showed a character of its own.

FRENCH POTTERY

Nevers can look back over a long tradition but never developed a style of its own. They copied the styles of their competitors such as the Urbane style, Delft, Rouen, and Mouters. The best known Nevers product is *Bleu Persan*.
Majolica style ware was already made in Rouen in the sixteenth century where the first good European results with porcelain were achieved.
Rouen potters recognised the need to choose a different direction than Delft and Italian majolica, and hoped to win customers by innovation. A new form of decoration with blue drapery and vines was developed in the late seventeenth century.

The main motifs were uniformly arranged around the piece in the *style rayonnant,* repeated in countless variations. This type of decoration greatly influenced other faience produced elsewhere in France in the late seventeenth century. Rouen developed colourful *décor à la corne* ware in about 1750, decorated with deeply coloured glazes, in reaction to the monochrome symmetry of faience at the time.

Two manufacturers led the way at that time in Moustiers: these were Clerésy and Olery. Moustiers was also important in creative terms. Moustiers introduced blue painted decoration at the end of the seventeenth century and the Italian influence on the painted decoration of plates and dishes is clearly apparent. The fine ornamentation on the rims though are inspired by Rouen.

An original form of decoration originating from Moustiers is *Béraindecor,* which became established in 1720 after a period of development. Twenty years later this gave way to a new polychrome form of painting by the artist Joseph Olery (1697–1749), following his visit to Alcora in Spain.
Moustiers then started to produce brown, green, yellow, mauve, and sometimes blue coloured decorations using Spanish-

style patterns. More or less at the same time Moustiers also developed *décor à la guirlande.* These same motifs were being used at this time in Alcora in Spain. This makes it difficult to tell the products of these two centres apart. Both the Olery and *Bérain* styles were widely adopted by other business in central and southern France.

Strasbourg played an important role in later French faience of the Rococo period. Just as in Germany, faience was produced in Strasbourg with the same muted colours used in porcelain production. These methods were also subsequently used on minor products from Rouen and Moustiers. Other companies managed to achieve high quality artistic results with these new methods.

Marseilles, for instance, produced the best French faience decorated with muted colours and a school was established in Marseilles in 1756 for faience painting, which also pursued new directions. Inspiration was constantly drawn from nature, which provides an inexhaustible source.
This resulted in exceptionally fresh painting. The palette of colours used was dominated by carmine and pink.

DEVELOPMENTS IN GERMANY

Mercantilism was also a spur to the development of their own production of faience in Germany. The potteries were protected against imports with special concessions. The great admiration for Chinese porcelain created demand for ever increasing quality and thereby greatly stimulated development.

Porcelain remained outside the pockets of most Germans long after the first porcelain works was established in Meissen. This also created demand for the cheaper faience as in France.
In Germany too the new ware also replaced silver as tableware. The number of businesses expanded rapidly with the strong demand, so that there were 80 producers in Germany in the eighteenth century. Although these producers were widely scattered and at some distance from each other from the Rhine to the Oder and the Alps to the Baltic, their products were broadly similar.

The reason for this is that the painters moved frequently from one establishment to another and therefore introduced their style into various localities.
German faience from the second half of the seventeenth century attained similar standards as majolica-type ware of the northern Low Countries and set out expressly to copy them. With the passage of time though changes of decoration and shape were introduced. These were influenced by Baroque, Rococo, and later by Classicism.

After 1720 the monochrome blue Oriental style was relinquished with a change to European motifs and polychromatic colour glazes. In common with other countries, Germany also switched to muted colours and European styles of painting during the eighteenth century.

GERMAN PRODUCTION

Two Dutch men founded an extremely productive pottery in Hanau in Germany in 1661 to produce majolica-type ware. The *chinoiserie* designs, landscapes, and oriental flowers from this source were mistaken for a long time for Delft and much the same applies to the production that started in Frankfurt am Main in 1666. The artistic and technical quality of the Frankfurt faience meant that it was even a competitor for Delft for a while.

In addition to the blue decoration, the Frankfurt output used strongly Baroque motifs, flowers, and mythological scenes at the end of the seventeenth century. The Delft influence is clearly apparent in early Berlin rippled vases decorated

in the Chinese manner with both blue and coloured enamel. Berlin was the other place in addition to Delft that also used yellow.
Similar methods of decoration were also used in some smaller production centres. The third important German production centre was Ansbach where a refined Baroque style with arabesque banding was developed.

After 1720, decoration similar to that of Rouen was also used, and there was contemporaneously a resurgence of Chinese *famille* verte. This led to a remarkably delightful form of painted faience from Ansbach.
The influence of porcelain – especially that of Meissen – was plain for all to see in German faience after 1740.

STRASBOURG'S INFLUENCE

Strasbourg played a key role of artistic influence on German ceramics in the second half of the eighteenth century. Although the works were established in 1721, it did not blossom artistically until the middle of the eighteenth century.

This was when Strasbourg switched to the use of muted colours and new decorative motifs. These lively designs were extremely popular. The changes in the designs of the pieces were also very important.

A romantic 18th century Louis XV terracotta garden statue.

The handles of tableware acquired the form of figures or fruit and was decorated with leaves, vegetables, and fruit in relief. The coarse faience figures of Strasbourg were not of the same quality as the porcelain with which they must compete.
The Strasbourg style of decorated faience figurine extended during the early eighteenth century to France and Germany but the influence was not widespread. Strasbourg's influence though was much greater in northern Germany and along the North Sea and Baltic coasts.
Production of faience only started here after 1750, during the Rococo period. Because the area was not established and hence was open to outside influences, the Strasbourg manner found ready acceptance here. These producers have their own characteristic forms in which richly embellished reliefs are given full expression.
The faience was decorated in a porcelain manner but usually of a lesser quality.

Terracotta statues of the 18th century are typically romantic in style.

Elsewhere, Strasbourg extended its influence throughout central Europe through works established at Holitsch in 1743.

These were the first industrial concern to be established in the Austro-Hungarian empire. Holitsch was expected to compete in the production of both porcelain and faience for the export market while dominating the home market. It was also expected to keep abreast of the fashions of the day.

Hence Holitsch adopted a number of decorative styles from elsewhere.

PAINTING OF MAJOLICA/FAIENCE

The best works of ceramic art in the second half of the seventeenth century were made by home workers who painted majolica type wares and glass. The influence of oriental porcelain and Delft lessened gradually in the 1820's as the Baroque style gained its hold. The best of the majolica-type wares between 1715 and 1740 were the faience from Bayreuth and Nuremberg in southern Germany.

Nuremberg mainly engaged itself with the blue decor style and the style of work of the home artists had less influence on these. Generally the entire surface was painted. Like Bayreuth there were landscapes and still life paintings, Rouen wallpaper patterns, and biblical scenes. Bayreuth also used pale blue but the influence of the home artists can certainly be seen in their polychrome decors.

MAJOLICA VERSUS STONEWARE

The production of stoneware in central Europe began from 1786 onwards to oust majolica type wares as elsewhere in Europe. In its heyday Holitsch had influenced other works at Proskau in Silesia (later Moravia) and Tata in Hungary. A number of smaller scale faience works were active in Thuringia.

Red Böttger stoneware was very popular and hence was widely copied. A pottery in Ansbach made 'brown porcelain'. The Böttger stoneware was imitated in Bayreuth by the so-called 'brown ware'.

RECOGNISING THE ORIGINS OF MAJOLICA

The origins of majolica and related wares can be established by means of marks. There are excellent books in which these marks are illustrated. Not every mark is a factory mark: some are the mark of the individual potter or painter, and other marks refer to measurements.

The origins of unmarked pieces need to be established by means of the material used, decoration style, and shape of the piece. This if often extremely difficult. Sometimes one has to be satisfied with establishing a certain area where the piece was made.
Many originally everyday pieces have no strong identifying characteristics.

An 18th century Wedgwood fruit dish.

Stoneware

ENGLISH CERAMICS

Ceramics in Great Britain developed more or less independently of continental Europe.
The most important development in Britain was that of stoneware.The basis for this had been established by previous continuous developments in the making of ceramics.
The high point was achieved by the master potter Josiah Wedgwood during the later eighteenth century. The majority of England's ceramics industry was concentrated in Staffordshire.
In the seventeenth century, British potteries developed slipware, a popular product made with red clay that was decorated with slip or diluted clay and then coated with a lead glaze. The finest of these products were made by Thomas Toft and family.

Wedgwood jasper ware pot. Josiah Wedgwood was a neo-classicist and knowledgeable about classical antiquity. His factory was named Wedgwood of Etruria. The Etrurians lived to the north of Rome and play an important part in Roman history. They ruled Rome for some considerable time. Josiah Wedgwood's legacy still produce products in a classical style.

Both Dutch and German potters sourced their clay for Rhineland stoneware and *faience* Delft from Britain. The British too began to make a form of majolica known as Delftware during the later seventeenth century but this never equalled the quality of Delft itself.

WEDGWOOD AND THE DEVELOPMENT OF STONEWARE

The early development of stoneware began in 1671 when the Englishman John Dwight was granted a patent for the production of ceramics.

There were many busts in his works made of stoneware with a salt glaze. This stoneware was a pale grey-white colour, sometimes with a transparent body. A further important contribution in the development was made by Astbury in 1720. By adding quartz to the clay

A 19th century Wedgwood stoneware cream jug.

A 19th century Wedgwood stoneware sugar bowl.

he succeeded in creating a hard white body. Because he used a yellowish lead glaze instead of saltglaze, his products can be regarded as stoneware.
The Astbury's white stoneware was made in Staffordshire until 1780. Its place was taken by the more highly regarded Cream Ware, from the works of Josiah Wedgwood. Josiah Wedgwood was a good organiser as well as possessing great technical knowledge and artistic ambitions.

He gained knowledge of every type of ceramic being produced in Staffordshire in his father's works and from the other great potteries of the area.
By the time he joined the business of Thomas Whieldon in 1754 he was an experienced craftsman. With Whieldon he mainly dedicated himself to experimenting with coloured glazes. He set up his own works in Burslam in 1759 where all manner of Staffordshire pottery was made. He was joined in partnership by his friend Thomas Bentley in 1768. Together they established the new Etruria works in 1780. Both men favoured classical art. In addition to classical forms, Wedgwood pottery uses classical styles of decoration. Several new types of ceramic were introduced in the new works.
The discovery by the Astburys was of great significance for Wedgwood. He perfected the technique and then mass produced such wares, making them available for a wider public.
With Astbury's stoneware as his basis, Wedgwood introduced Cream Ware in 1759. After appointment as potter to Queen Charlotte, its name was changed to Queen's Ware. By adding additional quartz and kaolin he was able to create a pale body. Because stoneware had great benefits in everyday use it quickly also became popular in Europe.
With porcelain, it became the most widely used material in the nineteenth century

A 19th century Wedgwood vase.

OTHER DISCOVERIES BY JOSIAH WEDGWOOD

Wedgwood not only made stoneware, he also continuously worked to improve it. In addition to cream coloured wares he also started to make 'black basaltes'. This ceramic was used for busts, medallions, plaques, and cameos. The material was ideal for luxury objects. There was also a similar 'redware' known as *Rosso antico*. This was used for tea and coffee services, and tea and coffee pots.

The most famous of the other Wedgwood ceramics is jasper ware. At first this was just the famous 'Wedgwood blue' plus sage green, and plain white.

After 1775 the colours were light and dark blue, sage green, olive green, black, and occasionally yellow. These single colours were decorated with moulded reliefs – usually in white.

In addition to tableware, jasper ware was also used to make all manner of small items such as chains, knots, ear-rings, and shoe buckles. Jasper ware plaques areform of decoration for walls.

Wedgwood Jasper ware cream jug.

Wedgwood Jasper ware vase.

Jasper ware is so popular that it is still in production today.

STONEWARE WORLDWIDE

In the last quarter of the eighteenth century majolica-type wares were replaced by stoneware. Stoneware dominated in the nineteenth century and replaced porcelain in the ordinary home. Efforts were made in continental Europe – often without much success – to imitate the English ceramics. Success lay in the right choice of materials, which were

Wedgwood mark circa 1900.

readily available in Staffordshire. Some factories though managed to imitate both the style and material of English wares.

During the time that stoneware was being developed the public turned against excessive ornamentation. The material itself therefore became of greater importance.

Since the mass-produced stoneware suited the taste for modesty at the end of the eighteenth and early nineteenth centuries, it was able to be sold in considerable volume. Porcelain was no competition for stoneware because this continued with its artistic approach and could only be afforded by the really well-to-do.

Porcelain only succeeded in winning a larger share of the world market when its prices dropped.

An 18th century glazed earthenware Portuguese vase.

CONTINENTAL EUROPEAN STONEWARE

The first examples of stoneware on the continent of Europe were based on other ceramic products. The earliest French stoneware was influenced by silver tableware that from 1760 was decorated with Baroque, Rococo, and Classical styles. It was quickly realised that these forms and styles were not appropriate for stoneware and instead simpler, more sober, and fluid lines of English pewter were used.

Rococo motifs were hardly every used in Britain except for the rims of plates. The British developed the feather edge which was then copied by continental factories. The feather edge held sway throughout the whole of the first half of the nineteenth century. The true stoneware style was created along classical lines by Josiah Wedgwood. During the main period for stoneware Wedgwood's laid down that the form and material should set the tone. The sober relief decoration merely served to emphasise the form. Open 'fretwork' that was cut with a metal die was very fine. The artistic play of light and shade is created by the nature of the material itself. This type of decoration was adopted by all the stoneware factories in Bohemia, Moravia (former Czechoslovakia), Germany, France, and Britain.

Through general adoption of relief moulding and open 'fretwork', painted decoration was pushed into the background. The best painted wares were made in Prague and Reinitz but this merely copied Viennese porcelain of the Sorgenthal era.

Apart from these individual examples of painted decoration there was also some good simple painted decoration with the character of folk art. From the time of Queen's Ware, expensive hand-painting was replaced by cheaper printing which was easier for mass production.

Developments in the nineteenth century

Coloured glazes were popular in Great Britain in the eighteenth century. By the end of that century and beginning of the nineteenth the technique was also adopted by continental factories. At the same time the French began to apply lustre to their pottery. This was regarded as extremely modern in the second half of the nineteenth century. This saw a movement away though from the original principles of stoneware.

This return to an earlier look caused some to look for alternative types of ceramics around the mid-nineteenth century such as *hydrolith*, *siderolith*, and *terralith*. Porcelain had won its battle with stoneware by becoming less expensive. The levelling out effect of industrial production in the first half of the nineteenth century led to a style vacuum which led producers to revive Classicism in an attempt to also bring back former ceramic techniques. This set up the creative conditions for the following generation which took the techniques of their predecessors and improved them. When people were confronted with oriental art at the World Exhibition in Paris in 1878 this found its way into ceramics. The search for new concepts was coupled with general movements in the arts and the efforts to break free from historical style influences.

Jugendstil and Art Nouveau led the way in this. France now became the leading creative producer of ceramics.
Because of the Art Nouveau creed a new appreciation was created for hand-made articles and this in turn led to ceramics adapting to the times and becoming more closely associated with the other forms of art.
Ceramics from other European countries became more important around 1900.

GLAZES

Most ceramics, with the exception of porcelain, had been porous down the ages. It was quite late on that a means was found to overcome this disadvantage. Different types of combustible materials created a layer of a different composition on the porous earthenware. This was how it was discovered by chance that this glazed layer made the pottery waterproof. A further advantage is that pigments can be added to glazes so that the practical ceramic items can also become an expression of art.

There are three main types of glaze: salt glaze, lead glaze, and tin glaze. Salt glaze is created by throwing salt into the kiln. A colourless glaze is formed on the product as the salt mixes with the silicic acid in the clay. This glazed layer can be turned brown by adding birch bark to the kiln. Salt glaze was not used for long in Europe.
It is found mainly in English white saltglaze pottery (1725–1775) and hard stoneware like pottery known as grès produced along the Rhine. Lead glaze brought about a significant improvement in ceramic production.
This transparent glaze was created by means of a moulded product being dipped in a lead solution before firing. Even items that have not been fired lose their porosity by this means. It was later discovered that the addition of copper oxide to the lead solution resulted in a green colour. The potter can also choose between yellow-white or red clay.

Figures can be applied to dry objects by means of a 'bull-ring' or grooves created which are then sprayed with yellow-white slip. Glaze is then applied over the top of this decoration. Another technique is *sgraffitto* whereby a thin layer of yellow clay is applied to the object into which decoration is then scratched or engraved to reveal the red clay beneath. Everyday items of pottery were produced

for many centuries using these techniques. With tin glaze a dried ceramic object is dipped in a tin-based solution. During firing the ware acquires an opaque and lustrous white layer. It is possible to add further colours to this layer and therefore to make polychrome products.
Sometimes a further transparent lead glaze is applied over the top for a really sparkling lustre as happens with the best quality Delft. Tin glaze, like salt glaze, is an extremely ancient process, probably discovered earlier than six centuries before the birth of Christ in Persia.
This discovery appears to have become forgotten though and was rediscovered in the Arab world in the eighth century. Tin glaze found its way from Moorish Spain and Majorca (Mallorca=majolica) to Faenza in Italy (hence *faience*).

European porcelain

THE ORIGINS OF PORCELAIN

The Chinese were the first to discover the composition for hard paste porcelain. They kept the production method strictly secret. Chinese porcelain reached Europe in small quantities in the Middle Ages through Asian trade routes and as a result of trade with the Islamic world. The Chinese porcelain of the fifteenth and sixteenth centuries in particular achieved high standards of perfection. Portuguese merchant venturers brought large quantities of Chinese porcelain to Europe at this time.

Japan also started to produce hard paste porcelain around 1500 and in the seventeenth and eighteenth century Dutch merchants shipped large volumes of Japanese porcelain to Europe. Porcelain was so highly regarded in Europe that people went to great lengths in their efforts to discover the secrets of the process. The Tuscan ruler Francesco di Medici established a works to produce soft paste porcelain in 1575. This works produced Medici porcelain which lay somewhere between hard paste and soft paste. No more than 60 pieces of this ware have survived.

DISCOVERY OF THE PORCELAIN PROCESS IN EUROPE

Medici porcelain was merely a stage in the development of European porcelain. The problem of how to make white and translucent porcelain had still not been overcome around 1700. Geological research was carried out in Saxony at the end of the seventeenth century to find raw materials that could be of economic benefit to the country. Count von Tschirnhaus, who led this study, was also responsible for constructing a glass-blowing works and sought suitable fire-resistant materials to coat the furnace. Firing experiments used loam from Colditz which was later to become a major constituent of hard paste porcelain. In 1704 he was given supervision of the young Johann Friedrich Böttcher (or Böttiger) who was being held prisoner by Augustus the Strong of Saxony in Meissen. Böttcher had studied alchemy in Berlin but he fled when the Prussian king Frederick I decided to use Böttcher for his own ends.

While furthering his studies in Wittenberg he came within the territory ruled by Augustus the Strong of Saxony who denied him access to Dresden and put him into 'protective custody'.
Böttcher was required to make gold for Augustus the Strong but when this failed he succeeded in convincing the ruler that he should establish a works to make hard stoneware.

The necessary means were made available to him in 1707 and the co-operation between Böttcher and Tschirnhaus finally led in 1709 to solving the question of the right composition of materials to

A 19th century Dutch oak porcelain cabinet.

make hard paste porcelain. Tschirnhaus had died in 1708 and therefore did not join in the success.

The discovery first had to be assessed and approved by a commission. When this happened, the first European porcelain factory was established in 1710 in Meissen. Böttcher managed the works until his death in 1719.

Meissen

MEISSEN: THE BÖTTCHER PERIOD

During the Böttcher period, the Meissen factory produced both red stoneware and hard paste porcelain. Copies of Chinese porcelain forms were mainly produced with both bodies with only the bell-shaped beakers being a new design. Both the white porcelain and stoneware were ornamented with naturalistic plant relief mouldings and with printed decoration. The mouldings were hand-formed and individually applied. Painted pieces from this period are extremely rare. It is also claimed that Böttcher invented the pink violet mother-of-pearl glaze.

MEISSEN: THE HÖROLDT PERIOD

The period of painted decoration began with Böttcher's successor, Johann Gregor Höroldt. The famous sculptor Johann Gottlieb Kirchner worked for the factory under Höroldt as the master model maker. He was succeeded in 1733 by Johann Joachim Kändler, who completed the development of an entirely European style of porcelain. The Meissen factory was managed by Camillo Marcolini from 1744, under whose leadership it went steadily downhill. The Meissen products of this period have little artistic merit.

During the Höroldt and Kändler eras, Höroldt introduced the more muted colours which had a lower melting point and a broader ranger of colours. The factory began to produce brown, yellow, yellow-green, grey-green, pale green, red, and violet in 1722. This was followed by fire-hardened gilding in 1725. Oriental styles were copied for tableware until 1735 for both the shape and painted style of the porcelain.

This included the well-known *indiansche Blumen* (Indian flowers), with motifs such as bamboo, chrysanthemums, dragons, fantastic birds, beetles, and peonies included. Pseudo Chinese drawings were used between 1725–1735, based on Dutch and German *chinoiserie* engravings.

Höroldt also succeeded in his efforts to create different porcelain bodies. These blue, yellow, or turquoise bodies gave a different ground for painted decoration. Miniatures followed the oriental manner from 1735, mainly featuring landscapes. Chivalrous groups became popular after 1740. Both of these forms were inspired by the Dutch school of landscape artists. No underglaze decoration was applied prior to 1740 for technical reasons. The famous strawflower (everlasting flowers) and onion patterns arose around 1740. These were still in use on porcelain of much later dates. In terms of the design of the form of pieces, Meissen was happy to adopt oriental patterns.

MEISSEN: THE KÄNDLER PERIOD

The designs changed under Kändler, especially after Kirchner came to Meissen. Kirchner gave Meissen what it had been missing until then: a Baroque style of its own.

The impulse for a more expansive and creative style for the porcelain came from Elector Augustus the Strong himself. He wanted to decorate his 'Japanese palace' with life-size white porcelain figures. Kirchner was commissioned to create these statues but he was sacked in 1733 so that the commission had to be completed by Kändler, who created a large number of mouldings but the plan for the Japanese palace did not go ahead because of the death of Augustus.

Kändler introduced the decoration of plates with bas-relief plaiting. Various versions of this type of decoration were made. These sometimes carried the name of the persons who originally ordered them or descriptive names such as : 'New Willow, 'Old Willow', 'Old Brandenstein', 'New Brandenstein', 'Gotzkowsky's raised flowers', and 'Dulong relief decoration'.

Although these came into being in the 1730's, they were still being made in the second half of the eighteenth century. During the Rococo period (circa 1745–1775), changes were introduced to the motifs after 1740. The decoration was limited to German flowers together with insects, twigs, birds, and fruit.

Small specialised porcelain works were set up in Meissen in the second half of the eighteenth century. Kändler assumed the management of the modelling studio around 1740. All fifty of the employees were artistically above average which was a great support for him.

The factory produced mouldings with various themes at this time, ranging from

A 19th century Meissen Pièce de milieu.

mythological and allegorical scenes to soldiers, hunters, cavaliers, ladies in wide skirts, farmers, merchants, and scenes from the Italian Commedia dell' Arte to craftsmen and native figures. The designs were adapted to the renewed fashion for Classicism in the 1860's

MEISSEN'S GLORY DAYS COME TO AN END

Inspired by classical art, the tableware changed during the 1780's under Marcolini (1774–1814) to more rigid and simple designs. The style of decoration also changed significantly. In common with Sèvres, Meissen decorated the entire outer surface with *bleu de roi,* except for the medallions that were to be painted. The miniatures, town views, and symbolic objects were executed in either polychrome or *grisaille*.

Meissen lost its way under Marcolini and the works no longer held the leading position in its competition with other European porcelain factories. Meissen even began to copy examples from

A 19th century Meissen candelabra.

Dresden porcelain figurine, circa 1880.

A 19th century Meissen vase.

Vienna and Sèvres and to produce biscuit. The grainy Meissen biscuit has a cool blue colour and is not of the quality of Sèvres biscuit. This brought the great period of Meissen porcelain production to a close. The nineteenth century production cannot be compared to that of Höroldt and Kändler.
Commercial considerations and a lack of creativity led Meissen in the nineteenth century to produce new production from old moulds of the previous century.

MEISSEN PORCELAIN MARKS

Meissner porcelain of the Böttcher era is unmarked. Between 1720 and 1725 many items were marked with imitations of Chinese inscriptions. From 1723 the KPM or MPM mark was made in blue underglaze. This is an abbreviation of Köningliche Porzellmanufaktur or Meisner Porzellmanufaktur.
Alternatively, pieces were marked with a simplified drawing of Mercury's staff. Large pieces in Chinese of Japanese style

of 1725–1730 are marked AR (Augustus Rex), as are those later pieces produced for the Saxon court.

The first appearance of what was to become Meissen's traditional mark (two crossed swords), borrowed from the Saxon coat of arms, was in 1720. There is a dot between the hilts of the two swords on porcelain of 1763–1774. In the Marcolini era (1774–1814) this dot became a star. Between 1814 and 1820 a Roman numeral appears beneath the swords as a date mark. Classical style biscuit figurines have the mark painted or printed in blue with the swords forming a triangle. When the mark is scratched through with one or more oblique strokes it denotes a piece of lesser quality.

The scratches were applied when the pieces left the factory. It is uncertain when Meissen started to place the mark on the cutting edge of the two swords but this probably meant that the piece left the factory undecorated and was painted elsewhere. It is not used on pieces with relief moulding.

VIENNESE PORCELAIN

Following Meissen's success, a porcelain works was set up in Vienna in 1718. This remained a private enterprise until 1755 when it was purchased by the state. The factory then had a number of very artistic employees.

A 19th century Meissen cup and saucer with lid, decorated with the letter 'G'.

HOUSE-PAINTERS (HAUSMALER)

Porcelain was painted at home by artists in the eighteenth century, just like glass. The hausmalers (literally 'house-painters') mainly worked to order. Although most of them were insignificant artists, a few were exceptionally talented. It was extremely difficult for them to obtain porcelain, especially in the early days of European production when the factories took great care that no unfinished pieces left the works.

Hence they used the more readily obtainable oriental porcelain that had already been treated with cobalt beneath the glaze.

The sound financial basis of the company enabled the company to make great advances but these developments were abruptly brought to a halt by the Seven Years War (1756–1763) between Prussia and Great Britain on the one side and a coalition of France, Austria, and Russia on the other.

The factory had a number of difficult years too following the war. After the management was taken over by Konrad Sorgenthal Vienna overtook Meissen. The importance of the Viennese works quickly reduced though in the nineteenth century and the government closed them in 1864.

THE EARLY VIENNESE YEARS

At first – during the era of the Dutch man Claudius Innocentius du Paquier – output of the Viennese factory was restricted to making and painting tableware. Vienna developed an individual style of both decoration and form and achieved remarkable results during the first decades. The pieces were quite different from those of Meissen. Between 1720 and 1730 the factory almost exclusively

Mug and bowl of Ludwigsburg porcelain.

produced polychrome chinoiserie. The designs were often inspired by Japanese Imari ware.

The first painted European flowers appeared as early as 1725. Between 1730–1740 chinoiserie was increasingly replaced by designs that suited the Baroque of the time, with ribbons, foliage, flowers, fruit, baskets, shells, plaiting, and also landscape miniatures. In contrast there was also monochrome decoration painted in dark magenta, sepia, or silver in the style of an engraving. Viennese porcelain of this time was unsigned which makes it difficult to separate originals from reproductions.

In the pre-Sorgenthal era, new colours, patterns, and forms were developed in Vienna. The products were adapted to suit the Rococo style. From 1750 Viennese porcelain was no longer different from the products of the German porcelain factories. In the decade before 1750 Vienna had produced porcelain models with a character of their own: scenes from life and also mythological and allegorical scenes.

The Viennese figurines were characterised by their gracefulness, animated movements, and quite unusual heads with laughing mouths. The colour palette of brown and red in combination with a broad range yellow, gold, and lilac tints with black was a characteristic of Viennese porcelain. Vienna gained its leading position in the European porcelain industry through the master modeller Johann Joseph Niedermeyer.

SORGENTHAL AND GRASSI

The production of coffee, tea, and dinner services was extended during the Sorgenthal era (1784–1805). Sorgenthal brought a period of both artistic and commercial success to Vienna. Vienna regarded the production of painted decor highly and hence also worked to improve the colours.

The blue known as *Leithnerblau* was discovered by the chemist J. Leithner. The ground was kept vermilion or pale lilac and the painting was often executed *en grisaille*. Vienna increasingly covered the entire surface of tableware with painted decoration, a layer of coloured glaze, or ornamentation. These were often copies of famous masterpieces from the galleries of Vienna.

After the death of the trend-setting Niedermeyer in 1784, his position was assumed by Anton Grassi who introduced Classicism and relief moulding. His pastoral and metropolitan subjects radiate the freshness of everyday life. After 1790, Grassi also created portrait busts and groups in biscuit in the manner of Sèvres. He was succeeded after his death by his pupil Elias Hütter, who worked in his style. He tended strongly towards the prescribed academicism represented by the Empire style.

VIENNESE PORCELAIN MARKS

The Viennese porcelain mark of the period 1744–1749 is derived from the state arms. It was impressed in pieces. The mark is a shield with two diagonal stripes. The same mark was used between 1749–1770, often asymmetrically applied in blue underglaze.

From 1770 the shield was smaller and symmetrical. Impressed marks are often found on Viennese porcelain from 1827

and this has also been the case for the year marking after 1783. Until 1800 only the last two numbers of the year were used (e.g. 1792 as 92) but from 1800 three numbers were used (1814 became 814). The numbers relate to the year of manufacture and not the time when the piece was decorated.
There are sometimes also painted marks alongside the impressed ones. These indicate the painter who carried out the decoration.

HOECHST PORCELAIN

Two financiers established a new porcelain factory in Hoechst with a porcelain painter from Meissen in 1746. The business did not flourish. Although the works was taken over by the Elector of Hesse in 1778, its finances remained troubled. The factory was closed in 1796 after the French occupation. Tableware from Hesse was strongly influenced by Meissen, especially in the beginning. Hoechst ware during the Rococo period is characteristically painted in shades of purple. The relief moulding done by a succession of modellers is extremely interesting and quite original.

HOECHST MARKS

Hoechst was marked until 1763 with a wheel with six spokes, based on the Elector's arms. Marks were painted or printed in golden or red overglaze.
Between 1765 and 1775 the Elector's crown is also often pictured above the wheel.

BERLIN PORCELAIN

In common with the other German rulers, the King of Prussia wanted porcelain to be produced within his domain. It was not necessary however for him to establish his own works for two were established in the capital Berlin by private initiatives, although the second of these was set-up at the King's wish. Two years later this second works was taken over by the Prussian Kingdom.

WEGELY

The first porcelain factory in Berlin was set-up in 1751 by Wilhelm Kasper Wegely. The artistic management of his business was in the hands of I.J. Claure from Meissen and E.H. Reichard as modeller. He also succeeded in attracting several employees from Hoechst. The painting was dominated by magenta or blue. German style flowers were painted in pale multi-colours. The relief decoration of Wegely's tableware was too crude and their designs too heavy for the elegance of Rococo.

The initial output by Wegely's works had an incorrect mixture for the porcelain body. Because kaolin from Saxony was added, the body was white but the surface became cracked. The material was actually too hard to be painted well. Production ceased in 1757, a year after the outbreak of the Seven Years War.

GOTZKOWSKY

The merchant Johann Ernst Gotzkowsky made renewed efforts in 1761 at the request of King Frederick the Great. His new factory employed some of Wegely's work-force. The manager was J.G. Grieninger. Gotzkowsky attracted a modeller from Meissen to work for him named F.E. Meyer. The modeller was supported by the painters K.J.C. Klipfel, K.W. Böhme, and J.B. Borrmann.
The state took the business over after two years. It was not yet possible to acquire kaolin from Saxony and as replacement the works used a mixture of Silesian kaolin and loam from Passau. This produced a fine porcelain with a cream-white body. In its first ten years the factory concentrated on production of tableware with painted decoration and raised ornamentation. The creativity was such that there were virtually no instances of borrowing ideas from elsewhere. One innovation was the creation of relief ornamentation. The entire surface was covered with relief Rococo

Pottery is sometimes used to mark special occasions and as instruments of propaganda. The Dutch House of Orange was a frequent subject of decoration in the northern Low Countries. Cup and saucer to mark the marriage of Wilhelmina of Prussia with stadtholder Willem V in 1767

ornamentation. The rims of pieces were often open as if plaited. The painting is characteristically monochrome, supported by painted gilt. Except for the floral decorations in brown, crimson, or orange, tableware was often decorated with Boucher engravings. The edges were finished in a mosaic style of decoration. The Prussian king ordered a dinner service in this style between 1765 and 1767 for his palace at Potsdam, likewise the services ordered for his castle at Breslau – today's Wroclaw, Poland – (1767–1768) and his palace at Sansouci (1769). In 1780 the Berlin factory followed the Meissen relief mouldings known as 'New Osier' and 'New Brandenstein'.
Gotzkowsky first used bleu mourant in 1784. It was the favourite colour of the Prussian king.

The Berlin factory was less important than the output of Meissen. The standard of its output though was raised by the Meissen modeller, F.E. Meyer who worked in the spirit of Rococo. Meyer was the spiritual father of the tableware for the new Potsdam palace and figurines representing the four seasons that accompanied the dinner services.
Wilhelm Christian Meyer followed his brother to Berlin in 1766. Rococo had more or less ebbed away at this time and his style showed a strong tendency towards an academic Classicism. The Meyer brothers worked together on the factory's most important order: the table centrepiece that formed part of a dessert service for the Tsarina Catharina II of Russia. The brothers succeeded in creating a composition in which a large group of figures were kept manageable. When W.C. Meyer left Berlin his brother was unable to maintain the standard of modelling in Berlin. In common with other porcelain factories, the designs became simpler in the 1780's. The dominant colour of painted decoration remained though. The cool harmony of pink with grey and iron oxide red with gold was typical of products from the Berlin works.

BERLIN PORCELAIN MARKS

The Wegely works marked its pieces with a blue underglaze 'W'. From 1757–1763, Gotzkowsky marked his porcelain with enamel or with a blue underglaze 'G'. After the works came under state control, the Royal Prussian Porcelain Works used a variety of forms of the royal sceptre as mark between 1763–1837.

These were made in blue underglaze. From 1837–1844 the letters 'KPM' were added in blue beneath the sceptre. Between 1844–1870 there was an impressed Prussian eagle above the letters 'KPM'. The mark reverted to the sceptre from 1870 but with a diagonal stripe in the centre.

FÜRSTENBERG PORCELAIN

As elsewhere, the Fürstenberg porcelain works were established by the local ruler. In this case it was Charles I of Braunschweig. After several false starts, the works finally got into production in 1753 following the arrival of the Hoechst porcelain chemist Benckgraff.
The modeller S. Feilner and painter Zechinger were added to the staff. Tableware from Fürstenberg was influenced by

Meissen yet it is possible to discern original ideas of their own in the pieces. In order to cover up for an inadequate mix of raw materials, the extravagant relief mouldings were excessively decorated during the 1850's and 60's. The strongest aspect of Fürstenberg porcelain was its painted decoration with exquisite colouring. The works produced large dishes between 1765–1770 with paintings resembling framed works of arts.

[The relief mouldings of Feilner, who worked at Fürstenberg until 1770, were rural peasants and craftsmen, mythological representations, and a series of figurines based on the Italian Commedia dell' Arte. Under the leadership of master modeller J.C. Rombrich, Meissen examples were followed after 1770 or engravings were used.
Fürstenberg biscuit by the Frenchman Desoches is very graceful but these too are merely reproductions. In 1795 management passed to Frenchman L.V. Gervelot, who introduced the Empire style. This resulted in the gilt decoration on a CCbleu de roi or black ground for tableware. The relief mouldings such as biscuit cameos, were also based on the Empire style.

FÜRSTENBERG MARKS

Fürstenberg marked its pieces with a blue underglaze 'F'. Busts were marked with an impressed outline of a horse until the start of the nineteenth century.

Five piece pottery cabinet set with decoration in honour of stadtholder Willem V (1748–1806).

FRANKENTHAL PORCELAIN

The Palatinate elector Carl Theodor extended a privilege to Paul Hannong for the establishment of a porcelain works. Hannong established his own factory in Frankenthal in 1775. His son Charles François was put in charge. After his death he was succeeded by the younger brother Joseph Adam. The business was taken over by the Elector for the Palatinate in 1762 but sold after just over thirty years to the Van Recum brothers. The Frankenthal porcelain works closed in 1800.

The model master at Frankenthal from 1755–1761 was J.W. Lanz. Under his leadership the products were markedly artistic in nature. The decorations were predominantly realistic representations of groups along the lines of French engravings of country tableaux. Lanz's successor, Konrad Link, produced almost perfect busts, dancers, and cameos. The famous J.P. Melchoir (who later went to work at Nymphenburg) worked for Frankenthal between 1779–1793. It was through him that Classicism became dominant at Frankenthal. One of the later modellers was a pupil of Melchoir, Adam Clair, who followed him to Nymphenburg in 1799.

FRANKENTHAL MARKS

Frankenthal porcelain was marked between 1756–1762 by printing the letters 'PHF' (Paul Hannong Frankenthal) or 'PH' (Paul Hannong). Between 1756–1759 pieces were marked with a blue underglaze with a lion rampant. From 1762 Frankenthal porcelain was marked in blue underglaze with 'CT' and a crown, representing the initials of Carl Theodor, the elector.
From 1759–1763 the initials 'JAH' for J.A. Hannong were applied and from 1770–1780 an abbreviated form of the year date was also indicated. The 'VR' initials of Van Recum first appeared in 1795.

Nymphenburg pièce de milieu.

NYMPHENBURG

A porcelain works was established in 1747 by F.I. Niedermeyer in Neudeck, a suburb of Munich. The business was not successful but this changed when Jakob Ringler was attracted there from the Viennese porcelain factory in 1753. At this time production was taken over by the Bavarian state but it returned to private ownership in 1762.

The company moved to a new factory at Nymphenburg in 1761 from which both the company and its products then derived its name.

During the Neudeck phase, relief modelling had been more important than painted tableware. The master modeller from 1754 until his death at Nymphenburg was Franz Anton Bustelli who was one of the best Rococo style modellers in Europe. His pieces all have great movement and meaningful expressions. Nymphenburg became famous through his delicate, animated groups and figurines from the Italian Commedia dell' Arte and he also created the famous musical Chinese figures and child figurines.

After Bustelli's death in 1763 he was replaced by the Czech sculptor Aulicek whose most important work was done between 1763–17772. Aulicek's work once more radiated the truth and simplicity of Classicism. He produced 25 hunting tableaux, classical gods, and a number of mythological groups. The successor to Aulicek was J.P. Melchior who had worked at both Hoechst and Frankenthal. Until he ceased work in 1822, Melchior was the master modeller of the Nymphenburg works. His work includes a number of allegorical groups and busts in biscuit.

NYMPHENBURG MARKS

The first Neudeck pieces were marked with a hexagon in blue underglaze. This was accompanied by various letters. The famous square shield bearing the Bavarian coat of arms was already applied in Neudeck. Nymphenburg used this shield in a variety of sizes. Bustelli's own work is signed with his initials 'FB'.

LUDWIGSBURG PORCELAIN

Carl Eugen, Duke of Würtemberg, took over control in 1758 of a porcelain works that had been set-up in Ludwigsburg in 1756.
The duke appointed Josef Jakob Ringler as manager in 1759 who had previously worked for Hoechst, Strasbourg, Nymphenburg (Neudeck), and Vienna. When Duke Carl Eugen held court in Ludwigsburg from 1760–1767, this provided great stimulus for the company. After this the artistic flair withered and production was stopped in 1824.

Ludwigsburg is famous for its models by Jean Louis, Beyer, and Lejeune. Beyer worked for the state company from 1759–1767. He was a proponent of Classicism and created allegorical figures, folklore characters, and contemporary figurines.

LUDWIGSBURG MARKS

Ludwigsburg is marked from 1758–1793 in blue underglaze with several interwoven letter 'C's', sometimes surmounted with a crown. This was followed by a period in which the current ruler's initials were used. From 1793–1805 an 'L' beneath a crown represented Duke Ludwig, 'FR' from 1806–1810 for Fredericus Rex, and 'WR' from 1816–1824 for Wilhelminus Rex.

These initials are mainly applied in a gilt. From the end of the eighteenth into the early nineteenth century the deer antlers of the Würtemburg coat of arms are also used.
This sometimes even appears in triplicate or more with interwoven 'C'.

OTHER GERMAN PORCELAIN MAKERS AND THEIR MARKS

There were also German porcelain works at Ansbach, Fulda, and Kloster Veilsdorf. Ansbach was established in 1759 and still exists. Ansbach pieces are marked with a handwritten 'A' in blue under glaze. Figurines sometimes bear a roof with three fishes, which is the Ansbach arms. Other models are not marked.

The Fulda works existed between 1763–1790. Fulda porcelain between 1763–1788 is marked with two 'F's' in blue under glaze.
Pieces from the 1765–1780 period sometimes bear the cross from the Fulda town coat of arms.

There were numerous small porcelain works in Thuringia at Gera (1779), Gotha (1757), Ilmenau (1777), Limbach (1772), Volkstedt (1760), and Wallendorf (1763). The Kloster Veisldorf works was the only Thuringian makers of any significance. Kloster Veisldorf was set-up in 1760. In the period after 1797 it belonged to Greiner. The mark consists of interwoven letters 'C' and 'V' in blue under glaze.

FRENCH HARD AND SOFT PASTE

France became entirely taken with porcelain in the eighteenth century. At first soft paste porcelain was made in large volume and with support from the king. After discovery of kaolin in Limoges, Sèvres also began to make hard paste from 1769.

SOFT PASTE, HARD PASTE, AND BONE CHINA

Soft paste porcelain resulted from European attempts to make true porcelain. The clay from which it is fired is a mixture of white clay and frit (raw material of glass) or soapstone, or bone-ash.
Soft paste is known as pâte tendre in French.Hard paste is true porcelain of a similar character to the original Chinese wares later also made in Europe. The major constituents are kaolin (China clay) and petuntse (China stone) or later feldspar. The French call this pâte dure. Hard-paste porcelain is slightly translucent and not porous.

An important improvement of hard paste was the development of bone china by Spode in England in 1794. This porcelain adds a high proportion of bone ash to hard paste ingredients, making it better able to withstand high temperatures.

EARLY FRENCH PORCELAIN

The first commercial porcelain in France was made at St-Cloud in 1702. Pierre Chicaneau was granted the rights that year to make soft paste porcelain. His business quickly went into very considerable production. The tableware from St-Cloud was a very clever reproduction – in both form and decoration – of Chinese porcelain. Even after Böttcher's discovery in Meissen in 1708, St-Cloud was imitated in France by Chantilly (1725) and Mennecy (1734) where mainly enamelled soft-paste porcelain was made.

Chantilly operated until 1789, initially following Meissen but later Sèvres (see later). Mennecy-Villeroy initially started in Paris in 1734 but moved to Mennecy in 1748. The business ended up in Bourg-la-Reine. Mennecy-Villeroy followed the fashion of the time.
Initially for floral decor on tableware the Meissen examples were used but later this changed to reproduction of the Chinese style, with some pieces being reminiscent of St-Cloud. Once Sèvres had pushed Meissen from the leading position, Mennecy looked towards Sèvres for inspiration.

Mennecy's marks from the start used 'DV' as abbreviation for 'De Villeroy'. This was replaced in 1773 by 'BR' for Bourg-la-Reine.

VINCENNES-SÈVRES

A porcelain factory was started at Vincennes in 1745 by a syndicate led by Orry de Fulvy. The works enjoyed support from the French king in both financial terms and the granting of the necessary privileges.

When the king became directly involved with the business in 1753 it became known as the Manufacture Royale de Porcelaine de France. After the death of

An 18th century Sèvres porcelain gilt and painted powder box.

Fulvy he was succeeded by the renowned chemist Jean Heliot. The true founder of French porcelain production was a man named Bachelier who was appointed to manage the painting and gilding studios. The porcelain from the company – first at Vincennes and later at Sèvres – was soft paste.

The form of the initial tableware was quite original but had much in common with metal tableware. This is due to the court goldsmith, Jean Claude Thomas Duplessis, who put his artistic stamp on the output. The ground colour was much emphasised in decoration and the most important of these was bleu de roi. After 1752, Vincennes pieces characteristically have turquoise glaze. Space was left on the ground for painted landscapes, colourful flowers, birds, and figures. The life-like relief mouldings of flowers are also well-known.

The works moved to Sèvres in 1756 and all the personnel moved too. Three years later the French king took over the remainder of the shares from the private shareholders. Bachelier became charged with artistic management and Duplessis managed the model-making studios, except the relief mouldings which were under Étienne Falconet.

The essential raw materials for hard paste porcelain became available with the discovery of kaolin in Limoges and Sèvres therefore began to make hard paste in 1769. Soft paste continued to be made until 1800.

Sèvres made a wide range of products, including tobacco boxes, tea caddies, chocolate, dinner, coffee, and tea services, inkstands, candlesticks, clock cases, and vases. The works did not change the artistic traditions of Vincennes but after the move developed a wider colour palette that included the clear pink rose Pompadour ground

Limoges porcelain plate, circa 1910.

colour that was produced up to the death of its discover, Hellot. The effect of this base colour was strengthened by gilding, painting, and leaving areas clear of colour.

A very popular decoration form was oeil de perdrix (partridge eye). Colourful flowers were painted by the Sèvres people in the areas left clear of colour, and also harbour views, mythological tableaux, pastoral scenes with shepherds, gallant and war-like tableaux, and birds. The landscapes were occasionally en camieu. Sometimes the gilding was given a smooth finish by using agate, but at other times it was raised.
Around 1770 Sèvres began to produce tableware in a pure Rococo style.

Porcelain childís plate from Sarreguemines, circa 1900.

Two Louis-Philippe style French bridal vases, circa 1840, painted and gilded with 24 carat gold.

Subsequently the Louis XVI era saw a gradual change towards Classicism. Soft paste appeared ideal for relief moulding, which was mainly produced in biscuit. Subjects included busts, mythological and genre groups, and cameos. Initially Falconet, Duplessis, and Bachelier worked on the modelling for these pieces but they were joined in 1771 by Simon Boizot and his pupil Le Riche.

Although Sèvres was owned by the king the business did not cease with the French Revolution. The business was reorganised though in 1800 by the manager Brogniart, with production of soft paste being halted. Because the fame of Sèvres porcelain had been established with pieces using this body, this marked an end to the glory days for Sèvres. Under Napoleon and the Empire though Sèvres did establish a leading role in European porcelain. Both Meissen and Vienna quickly followed the Sèvres lead in producing Empire style pieces.

VINCENNES-SÈVRES MARKS

Pieces were not marked between 1745–1753. After this a pair of 'L's' facing towards each other and interwoven appeared. Pieces made for the king were also sometimes marked with a French lily above this other mark. A year indicator appeared between the letters. This is 'A' for 1753, 'B' for 1754 and so on. Once the alphabet had been completed with 'Z', a double letter series began in 1778 with a double 'A'.

Most of the hard paste tableware between 1778–1793 also has a royal crown above the linked 'L's'. No year letter was used in 1793–1800. Porcelain was now marked 'R.F. Sèvres' for Republique Française. Sèvres porcelain from the nineteenth century has a number of different marks, including 'Manufacture Imperiale de Sèvres', 'M. Imp. de Sèvres', and M.N. de Sèvres' where the change of the 'N' represents 'Nationale'.

ROUEN PORCELAIN

In addition to the famous producers of porcelain, the old tradition of faience continued to be of influence in France. One example of this is the output of Rouen where a porcelain works was established in 1763. Little of the soft paste wares made there have survived. Coloured glazes were applied and fired and ornamentation was derived from the faience styles of Rouen. Rouen pieces are not marked.

ITALIAN PORCELAIN

Porcelain production in Venice began in the 1720's when C.C. Hunger moved from Vienna to Venice. He managed a works established by the Vezzi brothers that operated until the death of Francesco Vezzi in 1740.

Vezzi made high quality porcelain that was decorated either with imprinted motifs or relief mouldings. Pieces were decorated in blue underglaze or with enamel on the glazed surface. Widespread use was later made of iron oxide red.

There was also a soft paste works in Venice from 1754–1812 established by

Geminiano Cozzi. Although Rococo eventually had to give way to Classicism and chinoiserie was slowly depressed, Cozzi's works made identical products to Vezzi.

The Marquis Carlo Ginori set up a works on his estate at Doccia in 1735. He attracted the chemist J. Karl Wendelin Anreiter (also known as Karl Wandhelein) and several other employees from Vienna in 1737. The works was subsequently taken over by Ricardo di Milano. Ginori-Doccia used local raw materials.

In the early nineteenth century the business bought many models from the Capodimonte works of Naples. In addition to this influence, Ginori-Doccia exhibits various style influences closely related to both Chinese wares and the output of other European makers.

King Charles III of Spain, Naples, and Sicily founded a porcelain works within the grounds of his Capodimonte palace in Naples in 1743. The works produced until 1759, when Charles III took the moulds, models, and best workers to Madrid. A new works was set-up at Buon Retiro. King Ferdinand II of Naples re-established the Naples works in 1771.

The Villa Reale works in Portico were initially brought under Naples control but two years later they returned to Naples. Capodimonte was shut down in 1821. Capodimonte tableware is characterised by its rich figurative reliefs. A very wide range of other products were also made. The style was initially Rococo but switched over to Classical. Little Capodimonte has survived and most pieces offered for sale are not genuine.

ITALIAN PORCELAIN MARKS

Vezzi porcelain is marked 'Venezia' in red or blue or with just a 'V' between 1720–1725. Cozzi pieces can be recognised by a blue, gold, or red anchor. The most widely used Ginori-Doccia mark is a six-point star. Eight and twelve-point stars are also sometimes used. The six-point star consist of two triangles in a golden colour. Ginori-Doccia's Capodimonte pieces are marked with an 'N' with crown.

Capodimonte's own production is marked with a lily in blue under glaze or stamped. Figurines and other sculpted products from this works are not marked. The Spanish Buon Retico output has the addition of a double 'C' which later changed to an 'N', usually surmounted by a crown in blue under glaze. The Portico period products are marked 'RF' or 'FRF'.

Lowestoft octagonal soft paste plate.

Lowestoft plate. The Lowestoft soft paste works existed between 1757ñ1802, producing chine de commande type wares, decorated in either England or China.

An extensive 18th century Amstel porcelain tableware service.

English porcelain cup and saucer of unknown maker, circa 1850.

CHELSEA AND DERBY ENGLISH PORCELAIN

Thomas Frey and Edward Heylyn set-up at porcelain works at Bow in about 1745 but it did not prosper and was sold to William Duesbury in 1775 who moved it to his home town of Derby, where he had already established his own works in 1755.

In Derby, Bow made low quality bone china with oriental and German characteristics. A works was also established in about 1745 in Chelsea about which little of its history is known. Chelsea wares were diverse with its designers clearly inspired by several sources.

Duesberry also took over the Chelsea works in 1774 and concentrated production of both the former London works in Derby. The business was sold on to R. Bloor in 1781 and closed in 1848. A very wide assortment of wares was offered by the three makes, especially after Chelsea was added.

Amstel porcelain teapot from the service shown.

Brussels' porcelain Empire style teapot, circa 1800.

The tastelessness of this oil-lamp with porcelain base and dozen dessert plates and dish caused a counter movement.
The items shown are by the maker Bavaria and are marked as imported into The Netherlands by G. Hovig. The reaction to such taste arose as Jugendstil and Art Nouveau.V in 1767

ENGLISH PORCELAIN MARKS

The first pieces from Bow were not marked. From 1760–1765 they were marked with a red anchor and dagger. There is also often the individual maker's mark beneath that of the works. Chelsea bears an oval medallion in which there is a bas relief anchor. The anchor was subsequently coloured. Up to 1782, Derby pieces were marked with a letter 'D' under a crown. After the take-over of Chelsea, the mark became an anchor with a 'D'. After 1782 this changed to a letter 'D' with crossed staves and six dots with a crown. After 1781 most pieces were also stamped 'Bloor Derby'. Derby also produced reproductions of Sèvres and Meissen marks with blue under glaze.

NINETEENTH CENTURY PORCELAIN

The majority of reference works about porcelain appear to stop their descriptions of porcelain around 1800 and indicate that the best output of the various makers ended at about this time or even earlier.

Yet a great deal of porcelain was made in the nineteenth century but it lacks the originality of the previous century. There are several reasons for this. The porcelain works of pre-1800 were really craft industries. These were re-organised or 'rationalised'.
After 1800 the production processes throughout Europe changed radically through the Industrial Revolution. It was now increasingly possible to talk about mass production. This led to a uniformity of products with little opportunity given for innovation. This trend is exacerbated by the lack of a major new style in this era.

This was the time of Eclecticism when porcelain makers looked back to their old forms and decorative styles. There was an increase in the use of porcelain with other materials such as metal, for the production of objects such as lamps.

This situation did not change until late in the nineteenth century. Production of porcelain was given fresh impetus by the arrival of Art Nouveau and Jugendstil. There was a return to hand-crafted methods and new designs were created. Although nineteenth century mass production still continued, the originality of a painted Jugendstil piece is refreshing when compared with pieces from the era that immediately preceded it. The style of porcelain varied in the usual way from country to country.

This porcelain tray mounted in metal with gentian motifs is reminiscent of Jugendstil.

The Dutch firm Rozenburg sold much Jugendstil porcelain.

Hand-painted factory-produced Limoges Art Nouveau by M. Redon.

Early 20th century pale blue glazed Jugendstil Swiss door tile for a ëLadiesí WCí.

French Art Nouveau candelabra of metal and ceramic.

Glass

Glass is distinguished from other materials by its transparency. People like glass because of its shine and the way glass refracts the light that passes through it. Glass is also extremely practical.
It does not allow liquids to permeate it and is a poor conductor of heat. On the other side of course is glass's only disadvantage – its fragility. Glass today is something modern humankind takes for granted. There is an involved process before glass objects reach the consumer.

Glass is formed by heating various metal oxides and quartz. In addition to the raw materials of glass (quartz and borax), there are also alkaline substances (potassium or sodium oxide). These make the silicates indissoluble.
The right composition of substances for glass is the result of centuries of experience. Glass was probably first made about 4,000 years ago – perhaps discovered in ancient Egypt by chance.

The production of glass was then a relatively straightforward process. The glass-makers first smelted glass in earthenware vessels over an open fire. The glowing pieces of glass adhered together and were then plunged into cold water where they splintered.
These shards of glass-like material were known as frit. The frit was then ground between millstones under powdered when it was smelted once more to achieve the desired result.
This principle was in use until some time after 1500. Old illustrations often show two glass furnaces: one is for the initial smelting of the raw materials and the second for melting the powdered frit.

Trick 17th century glass which has small holes that let part of the contents to spill over the drinker.

The production of glass was changed in the eighteenth century in Britain. Coal replaced wood for thc glass furnace but this turned the glass yellow from the sulphur dioxide that is released. This meant that glass had to be smelted in a sealed kiln.
This also made it more difficult to keep an eye on the smelting process. A solution was found by producing softer glass mixtures.

Means of decoration

Glass can be decorated in a number of ways. The most direct method is to apply layers of other glass or to mark the surface during the glassblowing process while the glass is soft. Such results depend on the skill and artistry of the glassblower. Glass has been blown since early times and had reached a state of high art in Roman times.

There are various waysin which glass can be decorated during blowing. One way is to add small pieces of glass or 'prunts'. Another way is to spin the glass of the same or contrasting colour so that it forms a spiral on the glass surface. Many of the varying techniques are based upon centuries old traditions.
An entirely different way of decorating glass is to enamel or paint it.

This technique does not rely on the artistry of the glassblower. This is done with either 'cold' or fired enamel. Glass can also be gilded with precious metals such as silver or gold. Further ways of decorating glass are by cutting or engraving it. Glass is engraved with a diamond which 'draws' a design on its surface and it can also be stippled (a Dutch invention) with either a diamond or softer stylus.

Different effects can be created by making either open or dense stipple marks.

Engraved 18th century wine decanter.

Glass has been cut since early times but etching was discovered by the Swede Sheele who notice that the acidic gases of hydrogen fluoride ate in to glass. Glass can also be 'etched' by sand-blasting. Encapsulation is done by placing objects in glass while it is still soft that then become fixed in the solid glass. This method was especially popular in Europe between 1800 and 1850.

Glass production from east to west

The production of glass spread to other countries from Egypt around 1000 BC. The techniques were extensively improved between the sixth and second centuries before Christ.

A very important discovery was made at Sidon in Syria in the first century before Christ – the glassblower's 'blowing iron'.

This enabled objects to be made of thin glass. It was a technique that spread throughout the Roman empire to Italy and Spain to the west but also to Gaul (France), Britain, and Germany in the north. The major glassblowing centres were established along the Rhine and in Gaul (France).

Production in the east

In common with many other techniques, glass-making was also largely forgotten following the fall of the Roman empire but this was not true in the east. The most important glass-producing region was Byzantium where new techniques were also developed that can be seen in cut and engraved goblets, bottles, ewers, and mosaics of the era.
Arabs were extremely fond of glass embellished with gilt or enamel and major Arab glass centres were Damascus and Aleppo in Syria.

Very fine coloured glass goblets, bottles, ewers, lamps, and dishes were made in these towns between the twelfth and fifteenth centuries. These were often decorated with bright painting.

Persian glass-making took over the leading position in the fifteenth century and Persian glass even influenced Spanish glass. Surviving Persian glass from this era consists mainly of bottles of green or blue glass.

Medieval European glass

Glass production in the former western Roman empire after its fall only survived in Gaul (France), Germany, Flanders, and Britain.

In the early Middle Ages the preference was for decoration with grooves, flattening, and decoration with 'threads' of glass. Several new types of object appeared such as 'trunked' and 'studded' beakers. Otherwise just simple medicine bottles were made from green glass that was far from perfect.
Glass production even went into decline in the ninth century and many in Christian countries regarded glass as a heathen product. After all the heathens used bottles for their 'pagan' burials. Pope Leo IV even banned the liturgical use of glass. Not everyone was of the same opinion.

Bishop Isidorus of Seville in Spain wrote a treatise about glass based on Naturalis Historiae, written by the Roman Plinius. The monk Theophilus wrote an extremely important work about glass – probably during the late tenth or early eleventh century, somewhere along the Rhine.
In a piece about the art of glass he described the constituents of Roman and Asian glass, wrote down many legends, and described the process of glassblowing in great detail.

Venice

Sometime around the birth of Christ, glass was produced in northern Italy. The technique was maintained by cloistered orders and spread from these during the Middle Ages throughout Europe. It was in this region that the one of the most famous glass-making centres was established.
Benedictine monks in Venice specialised in making bottles by the year 1000. Following the conquest and pillage of Constantinople by the crusaders in 1204, many Byzantine glassblowers sought to escape to the powerful trading city of Venice.

They strengthened Venetian glass-making with techniques such as glass mosaics. The first thin and hollow glassware and first glass jewellery were made in Venice in about 1250. Soon afterwards the production of glass became a monopoly of the Venetian state. The glassblowing works though were forced to move outside the city. With their extensive use of fire they threatened the safety of the city and hence were moved to the island of Murano.

The first reports of exports of glass from Venice are also recorded around 1250. They also made optical glass for spectacles and window glass.
A great deal of glass incorporating soda from burnt seaweed was made in the fourteenth century. The Venetians also began to make *latticinio* glass with thin white threads around 1400. The Venetians were also known to make golden coloured glass by chemical means and other colours too with copper and cobalt.

German serpentine glass beer tankard from Eiffel.

They also decorated their glass by 'burning' colours into it. This is very characteristic of fifteenth century Venetian glass. In the sixteenth century the Venetians mainly decorated their glass with patterns of opaque white threads. Vegetal and abstract designs were also created on the thin-walled soda glass.
In addition to clear *cristallo* glass, Venice also made opaque white *lattimo* glass that was translucent but not transparent, *millefiori* containing tiny rods of coloured glass, and frosted glass with a cracked surface. The glassblowers also produced all manner of decorative forms with glass. The chemical composition of Venetian glass was a secret with severe penalties for anyone who revealed the procedures to make it. Despite this, many Venetian glassblowers left for other parts in the early sixteenth century and became involved abroad in the production of imitations of Venetian glass. Excellent copies of glass *à la façon de Venise* were made in Spain, France, and the Low Countries. These are so good that it is very difficult to determine whether a piece is made in Venice or elsewhere.
The main differentiation is that the metal (body of the glass) of the imitations is not so clear, fine, and thin as that produced on the Venetian island of Murano.

Developments elsewhere in Europe

In Bohemia and Germany they also tried to join in Venice's success. The glass works there only flourished after the Middle Ages. Many attempts were made in France employing Italian immigrants to make totally transparent and clear glass. Dutch glass makers began to make diamond engraved fluted glasses in the sixteenth and seventeenth centuries and it was the Low Countries too that made glasses with a characteristic 'winged foot'. It was also quite common for glass made in one place to be decorated elsewhere.

Glass carafe decorated with applied prunts. This is the simplest form of decoration that can be done by the glassblower.

A 17th century Dutch green Römer glass. This type first appeared in the 15th century.

BOHEMIAN AND GERMAN FOREST GLASS

The extensive forests of Bavaria were home to many glass works. The production area lay within an area bordered by the Thuringia and Bavarian forests, and the Alps and Fichtel mountains. Because of iron and potash in the raw materials the glass produced was mainly green.

New types of glassware were created that were primarily functional with the main output being glass beakers but ink pots and alchemists' and apothecaries' jars were also made.

This was often decorated with prunts and molten threads of glass. Glass was also decorated with bizarre relief forms.

All these products were small icrean size in the fourteenth and fifteenth century. Larger pieces were noss bt made until the sixteenth century.

The most widespread of these are so *maigelein:* shallow beakers of blown gas of which the bottom is pressed inwards. There were also much larger *Pasglas* measured glasses, beakers in the form of cabbage stalk, beakers with finger grips, and vertically ribbed cylindrical beakers. The classical slim and tall beakers of Bohemian glass were made in the fourteenth and fifteenth centuries. Their small stems are externally decorated with prunts of molten glass. The *Römer* glass

An 18th century green Römer glass.

was first made in the fifteenth century. These wine glasses were extraordinarily popular in the Rhineland. A bellied glass, shaped like an onion with a curved neck consisting of several plaited tubes of glass also appeared in Bohemia in the late Middle Ages.

ENAMELLING

Every glass works outside Italy strived to improve on Italian glass with their local products but the shape of their glassware is clearly different from that of Renaissance Italy. This is because of different local drinking customs. Wine was drunk in Italy but north of the Alps people mainly drank beer. This caused different demands of glasses. The *Humpen* beer glasses were made from the middle of the sixteenth century.

At first these were conical in form but later only cylindrical *Humpen* were made. This latter type had a low sole and sometimes also had a hinged lid. The style of painting was intended to give the impression of an Italian product and this also helped to mask the imperfections in the glass.

Enamelling was commonplace on sixteenth century central European glass. The best period for this form of decoration was reached in the earlier seventeenth century. The quality of glass was then improved through the addition of chemicals.

Green 18th century Römer glasses.

Another category of glassware was the beakers that bore the owner's crest of arms.

These were also monogrammed and dated. Others, known as 'state eagle' *Humpen* were decorated with the German state arms. Quite separate from these glasses though were the Fichtel mountain ox-head glasses that were painted with pictures of the wooded hills from which the Eger, Main, Naa, and Saale rivers rise. Old and New Testament references, fables, and allegories were also common painted decorations in both the Renaissance and Baroque eras.

Although enamelled glass originally came from Venice it gradually became the speciality of central Europe. This method of decoration was used for more than 250 years.

Spun stem Dutch glass. Spinning a thread of glass of the same or contrasting colour around a glass core is one method of decoration.

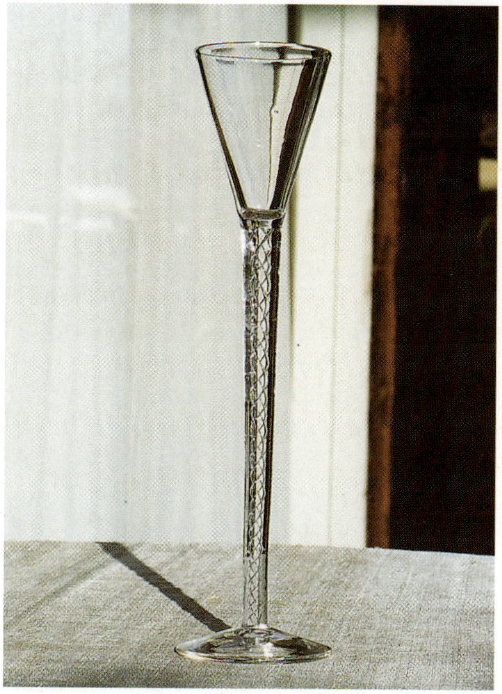

An 18th century French enamelled pill box.

Enamel became less expensive in the later seventeenth century so that 'ordinary' citizens were able to buy it. Finally it became a product for the masses and when applied to *milchglass* became a cheap alternative to porcelain.

Finding out the origins of a piece is no easy matter. There are countless different types with regional and local characteristics but these became less pronounced as glassblowers moved to work at different places.

PAINTED TRANSPARENT GLASS

A new manner of decorating hollow glass objects was introduced in the later eighteenth century using transparent enamels instead of opaque ones. The porcelain artist Samuel Mohn of Dresden was the first to use this technique.

His 'friendship' glasses are painted with portraits, landscapes, allegories, and verses. He customarily signed his work with *Mohn fecit.* His son, Gottlob Mohn, established himself in Vienna in 1811 and signed himself G. *Mohn in Wien.* His first work was the painting of town views.

The Viennese porcelain and glass artist Hothgasser took up this popular subject, working mainly on bell-shaped glasses on long branched stems. He mainly signed his work with his monogram between the 'teeth' of the branched stem.

Dutch 'special occasion' glass of the Dutch East India Company (VOC) of 1741, bearing the words 'Vivat Oranje' on the reverse.

Sometimes though he used his full signature on his glasses. These were given as a present or friendship's token, or served as souvenir. Kothgasser's glasses with playing cards were very popular around 1875. Kothgasser's work was in great demand and hence widely copied but reproductions are easily spotted by the naive compositions and lack of technique.

An 18th century gilded scent bottle.

No-one ever managed to match his quality.

BOHEMIAN ENGRAVED GLASS

The process of engraving was already known during Roman times but the ancient technique was re-invigorated during the sixteenth century in southern German with fresh demand for this style of decoration. This arose because of exports of engraved crystal from Milan. The so-called 'mountain' crystal was rare and hence expensive. This led to people in southern Germany deciding to apply the decorative technique used with crystal on glass. Lehmann One of the most famous engravers is Kasper Lehmann, engraver to the court at Prague. Until recently he was even deemed to have been the 'inventor' or glass engraving.

Engraved ginger glass, circa 1700. Although known since Roman times, it was not re-introduced until the 16th century, in southern Germany. Engraved glass became very popular in the north of the Low Countries.

An 18th century engraved wine glass.

He established himself in Prague around 1600 and in 1609 he gained a monopoly from the king for the engraving of glass. Lehmann had a number of students, including Georg Schwanhardt, the most important of them, who returned to his home town of Nuremberg following Lehmann's death. There were many engravers working in this town but each had his own area of speciality.

Schwanhardt mainly worked with Venetian-type goblets, although Venetian glass itself is not suitable for engraving because it is too fragile. Glass with lime added was used for engraving. This sparkling glass was clear and pure with strong refractory properties. It became known as Bohemian crystal.

Bohemian 'crystal' was discovered between 1670 and 1680 more or less simultaneously in three *glashutten* in southern and northern Bohemia. Knowledge of the process spread quickly throughout Bohemia.

An 18th century glass engraved with 'In Onzen Dagen.

This 18th century glass has an engraved rim and red/white spun stem.

Three 18th century spun stem liqueur glasses

Two 18th century spun stem liqueur glasses.

An 18th century spun stem liqueur glass.

Painting with enamel was depressed here by engraved Bohemian 'crystal'. The first decorations were copies of motifs used in Venice. Because of the high quality of the new material it quickly became a formidable competitor for Venetian glass. Traders not only succeeded in selling Bohemian glass throughout Europe, it was also shipped to other parts of the world.
When the engraving switched to the Baroque style Bohemian glass was even more successful.

SILESIAN ENGRAVED GLASS

The successful formula of Bohemian glass works was also followed in Silesia. The works of Count Schaffgotsch were very important to this region. The *glashut* in Hermesdorf in particular produced some fine pieces. This was due to the engraver Friedrich Winter who engraved a series of friendship goblets and beakers there after 1690.
The engraved glass from the works at Lobkowitz in Wiesau and Warmbrunn were also of exceptionally high quality.
Silesian glass is characterised by the narrowing at the bottom of the drinking vessel. Although Bohemian glass itself was of higher quality, the exceptional Silesian engraving was better than that of Bohemia.
Glass production was advanced following Prussia's capture of Silesia from Austria in 1742. Glass production in Silesia and Bohemia began to become less significant in the mid eighteenth century due to a number of factors. These included a smaller market through European wars that had caused economic collapse and also a reduction in the size of the market through the development of porcelain and lead crystal. Superb glass goblets made way for simple beakers. Both form and decoration were simplified and more suited to the new circumstances.
The Bohemian glass industry searched for a way to emerge from the crisis.

Three crystal wine glasses with spun stems.

One of their developments was *milchglas* that was supposed to compete with the rapidly growing market for porcelain. Entire sets of tableware and drinking services were produced from 1760 to the mid nineteenth century by works at Harrachov in Bohemia.
The opaque 'milk glass' was much cheaper than porcelain but could emulate it in both form an enamelled decoration.

GERMAN DEVELOPMENTS

The discovery of the addition of lime to forest or potash glass in Bohemia was also important for the German *glashutten.*
This was especially true of those works of the electors of Saxony and Brandenburg which bordered Bohemia. Silesian experience in both glass making and engraving was utilised at Brandenburg works at Potsdam, Berlin, and later also at Zechlin. Potsdam attracted Martin Winter, brother of the highly regarded Helmdorf engraver.

The glass specialist and alchemist Johann Kunckel was given the task of researching the best composition for glass. He is credited with discovery of *Zwischengoldglas* or 'gold-ruby' glass. Other gifted engravers also worked for Brandeburg glass makers in addition to Winter.
Glass from this time is solid and heavy. The foot or stem, drinking vessel, and lid were decorated with leaf motifs. Pieces

were lighter after 1720 under the influence of the engraver Elias Rosbach. Zechlin glass though (which had gilt medallions melted into its surface) remained fairly robust.
Knowledge of how to produce Bohemian glass spread via Nuremberg northwards. Important centres were established at Brunswick and Hesse, while the *glashutten* of Thuringia were also important parts of the German glass industry. Just as with porcelain, the electors of Saxony also initiated establishment of glass-works in their domain.

The Saxon works copied Bohemia so precisely that their glassware closely resembles Bohemian glass. Saxon glass though uses slightly different forms, such as horizontal, diagonal, and faceted rims on the stem and underbelly of the bowl. There is a difference too in the gilded relief and gilded engraving

'RUBY GOLD' GLASS

In addition to engraved glass, Bohemian glass works also produced 'ruby gold' glass or *Zwischengoldglas* during the prime era for Baroque style. This type of glass had been known in Roman times but forgotten. Following its rediscovery by Johann Kunckel in Brandenburg, Bohemian glass makers also started to make it. The same type of decoration was employed as was used for Bohemian 'crystal'.

This consisted of engraving, silver gilt or gilt leaf motifs placed between two layers of glass. Only a few pieces were double layered at that time.

English lead crystal and Dutch glass

Around 1750, glass that was stabilised with lead became important in Europe. The heavy lead 'crystal' was well adapted to practically-shaped pieces following

Painted glass box, circa 1850. This type of movingly painted glass boxes were made in Friesland in the Low Countries

Classical lines. Lead crystal has unique properties.

It is absolutely clear and is decorated in an entirely different way. By use of a diamond cutting disc a large number of facets can be created that cause light refraction – acting as a series of prisms. Dutch glass was extensively engraved with diamond cutters and lead crystal became extremely popular there. After 1750, some exceptional Dutch pieces were made by stippling the glass with a diamond.

The solid goblets used for this purpose were partly imported from Britain.

Nineteenth century glass

Bohemian crystal found a strong competitor with English lead crystal cut glass. This was because the lead crystal was ideally suited to the forms of the fashion for Classicism. The Bohemian glass makers reacted by adopting the English cut-glass technique but Bohemian glass was not suitable for cutting. The consequences were therefore limited and the technique was restricted

Painted 19th century German Biedermeier glassware.

so that cutting remained solely an extension to engraving. The subjects for engraving were determined by the current fashion and this can be seen by the motifs used.

Count Georg Buquoy of Neugrätzen in southern Bohemia became very taken with Wedgwood's 'Egyptian Black'. In common with Friedrich Egermann in Haida, Neugrätzen began making black *Hyalith* glass that was mainly decorated in a golden *chinoiserie* style.

The wares included carafes, coffee services, dishes, and vases. Egermann created *Lithyalin,* a different form of opaque glass that resembled jasper and agate. Like these stones it could be facet cut. Egermann's glass works also used a golden yellow glass paint that he invented. This was used on goblets and beakers from 1820. Egermann's greatest achievement though was his contribution to the enriching of glass.
With the help of copper he was able to create cheap imitations of expensive golden-coloured ruby glass. Glass makers sought an ever greater range of colours and forms for their wares. On the one hand they attempted to improve the process of applying coloured glass to a clear glass base while on the other they sought to develop new methods.

This led to a new technique in which several layers of coloured glass were applied to a base. It was a process that had originated in China. By cutting away parts of the different coloured layers, all manner of colour effects could be created. The use of several layers of *milchglas* was particularly popular. With this, when a pattern had been cut out it was further decorated with enamel.

Bohemian glass companies exported lots of this type of ware in the 1850's. Around 1820 the Bohemian glassworks also made glass that was smelted with embedded plaster or porcelain with portraits of famous persons. From 1830 onwards the glass market changed radically because of the major changes in how glass was

German beaker from Kaisersbrun of 1883, decorated with gold leaf.

Swiss or German hand-blown 19th century pot in cobalt glass with gilt decoration.

Hand-blown opaline vase, circa 1890.

made. Until that time each piece was individually crafted by a glassblower. During the nineteenth century factories began to press mould glass. This process made it possible to mass produce glass making.

The artistic level of the output dropped of course but commercial considerations were generally more important than aesthetic ones. Very few managed to avoid this trend. One who did was the Viennese artist Ludwig Lobmeyr, who owned a quality glass making works in Steinschönau. He was one of a group of artists who opposed the levelling down and increasing lack of taste of the mass produced wares.

This group studied ancient and exotic forms of glass and this led to their works making new types of glassware with simple and functional shapes. Before this trend gained wider acceptance though it was consumed in an even more radical movement that swept Europe under the Art Nouveau and Jugendstil names. The artists A. Daum and E. Gallé gave glass-making back its individual power of expression and returned to the old traditions. In the United States Louis Comfort Tiffany was inspired by oriental and classical glass. His work was widely admired and echoed in Europe.

One glass works that copied his lead was the Lütz works at Klostermühle in Bohemia.

Glass and jewellery

Glass paste and beads were used for jewellery back in the age of the ancient Egyptians. Alexandria supplied the then known world with glass beads during the ancient Greek civilisation and during the Roman empire. The strings of beads made with them were of different colours. The

New types of glassware were being created in the 19th century. Brooch of marcasite glass and silver, circa 1900 (60mm/23/8 in high).

Pre 1850 Biedermeier oil, vinegar, and mustard set.

Three silver boxes for reviving scent, circa 1850. One is enamelled.

Silver medallion with enamelled decoration, circa 1880. Various colours of glass have been melted to created the decoration.

Empire style drinks set with silver holder.

Cut glass crystal rose bowl, circa 1900.

English lead crystal fruit dish, circa 1850.

Glass butter dish, circa 1880.

Jugendstil glass vase, circa 1900. The new shape and decoration is refreshing after the Eclecticism of the nineteenth century.

Louis XIV mirror. Mirrors are a different form of glass object in which the main focus is usually on the frame.

Louis XIV style mirror of the 19th century.

glass was decorated with wavy melted threads of lighter-coloured glass. The production of beads spread through Constantinople and the other towns of the Roman empire to Europe.

Venice was an important production centre for glass beads in the eleventh century. Imitation gem stones had been made in Bohemia as early as the fourteenth century. In the eighteenth century they also started to make glass beads. Production of glass beads had started in the German Nuremberg in the sixteenth century followed by the Fichtel mountains area of Bavaria in the seventeenth century, and soon afterwards by Potsdam and Thuringia.
Bead production of importance got under way in France in the seventeenth century.

Tall mirror of the Second Empire period of Napoleon III, 1853.

Louis XVI style mirror.

Tortoiseshell painted French mirror, circa 1890.

Empire style mirror.

Clocks

Humankind has always been able to follow the passage of time through observing the sun, moon, and stars. They saw the seasons come and go and noted the phases of the tides of the sea. The regularity of these was recognised thousands of years ago and calculations of time were based upon them.
Humankind started from those phenomenon that were most readily apparent: the month, the year, and the rhythm of day and night. The month is based on the waxing and waning of the moon, and the year and day and night on the rising and setting of the sun. Other astronomical observation are also useful for measuring time.

Hence the ancient Egyptians made a link between the annual flooding of the Nile and the rise of the brightest star, Sirius.
We still make wide use of units of time that resulted from these observations. The division of the year into twelve months is due to the prior existence of twelve star signs.

The Egyptian year was 360 days because a circle was divided into 360 degrees. The Egyptians had to add five days on to each year to make it fit. Even the division of the day into 24 hours has its roots in antiquity and has held firm since ancient times.

The only attempt to decimalise time happened during the French Revolution. Experts have failed in their attempts to develop a better system.
The western calendar is determined by time and the sun but this is not true of the entire world. The Islamic world has a moon calendar.

Sundial of 1768. Centuries before the invention of the clock, humankind told the time by sun dials.

Measuring time

The attraction of clocks lies in the combination of mechanical and aesthetic form. In our current age we are almost always aware of the precise time and the radio news is generally broadcast precisely on the hour. Because we take the measurement of time for granted it is probably difficult for us to understand its importance.
Well-to-do families by the late nineteenth century probably had a clock in every room in the house and each adult probably had a pocket watch. Before the railways made national time a necessity, every clock was adjusted to local time.
The clocks and watches were mainly set by the local church clock, which was in turn set according to a sun dial.

Measurement of time with a mechanical clock as we know them is relatively recent but there were forerunners of our clocks. The best-known is the sun dial that was probably discovered by the Sumerians who also observed the sun, moon, and stars, just like the ancient Egyptians.

The simplest sun dial is a stick placed in the ground. They also discovered that a sun dial can only provide accurate time when it is known precisely when the sun is due south.
From this followed the discovery that the position of the shadow depended on the position of the sun, which varied at different times of the year. In about 1000 BC the Chinese discovered that it is better to place the indicating arm of a sun dial at an angle and at right angles to the plane representing the supposed daily travel of the sun around the earth.

In reality the indicator is positioned parallel to the earth's axis. Although small errors can occur, these discoveries made the sun dial a very reliable means of measuring time.
This meant that seafarers needed to take account of the place where they were with their sun instrument. The sextant developed gradually into a complex instrument that is still widely used to this day throughout the world. A water clock was used in ancient Mesopotamia to measure time. A container was specially constructed so that the water it held ran out slowly. A scale on this container (or the one into which the water flowed) indicated how much time had passed. It was later realised this could be indicated by means of a pointer and also that the flow of water could be used to power a mechanism.
The hourglass filled with sand is based on the same principle. It may seem strange but the first hourglasses were not made until the fifteenth century. Only then had glassblowing reached such a level in which the hourglass could be accurately made.
The sun dial was the most reliable timepiece for a very long time and the arrival of mechanical timepieces did not instantly make them redundant, since the mechanical clocks were far from accurate. Because the angle of the earth's axis

English 18th century sun dial by F. Barkerson of London.

with the sun varies during the year, sun dials are also not always precisely correct. Hence a mechanism was needed that was entirely independent of the apparent movement of the sun, leading to clock mechanism.
The history of clocks runs through a never-ending series of improvements in order to sub-divide time into increasingly uniform units. All clocks rely upon the creation of a motion that is constant. Considerable effort was required to reach this situation.

Mechanical clocks

It is unknown when the first mechanical clocks were made but it is certain that clocks were being made in fourteenth century Europe. The first clocks probably came from northern Italy.
These were clocks in churches and cloisters that were driven by weights. In

cloisters they were used to indicate the time for prayer. The word *clock* is derived from early German and Dutch *klocke* which actually meant bell that was derived from the French word for bell which is *cloche*.
This indicated the bell sounded by monks (even in the middle of the night) to call them to mass. Wall-mounted and table clocks appeared some time after this in the homes of the wealthiest persons.

The conversion of motion into uniform periods of time was not very precise in these early clocks which had a primitive balance wheel (English clocks) or foliot (Continental clocks) that was a forerunner of the later pendulum. Church clocks were set and adjusted by means of a sun dial and the striking of the church clock was used to adjust clocks in the home.

The first clock-makers travelled around Europe but as demand increased they established themselves in fixed places, choosing towns such as Nuremberg and Augsburg where they established guilds mid-way through the sixteenth century. The German table clock became more common property with the rise in living standards and many such sixteenth century clocks have survived.

Christiaan Huygens and his inventions

The Dutchman Christiaan Huygens made a discovery that was of tremendous importance for the further development of timepieces. Born in The Hague on 14 April 1629 into a family of five children, he received a good education.
His father was the poet Constantijn Huygens (1596–1687). This influential and talented figure corresponded with people such as Descartes, Mersenne, and Diodati (a friend of Galileo Galilei).
His son Christiaan was known principally as a mathematician, physicist, and astronomer.
In the area of physics he made his name with his studies of the motion of a pendulum and in theories regarding light waves. He also constructed a telescope with an improved lens. This enabled him to discover Saturn's ring. His invention of the pendulum was of considerable importance for clocks. Between 1655 and 1660 Huygens devoted his time to seeking an accurate means of determining time. He came upon the idea of using a pendulum in 1656 and patented his idea for a pendulum clock in 1657.
This clock was then made by Samuel Coster, of The Hague. By comparison with other clocks of the age, the accuracy of Huygen's clock was astonishing. This was of importance both for astronomy and physics.

Huygens also wanted to create a clock which would enable seafarer's to determine their longitude. A pendulum was of no use on board ship but he eventually solved this with a balance wheel with clockwork driven by a spring. His invention is utilised in the spiral spring of a pocket watch.

The theory of the pendulum was finally described by Huygen's in his *Horologium oscillatorium* of 1673. In this important book he showed mathematically that the oscillation time of a swinging weight – which has arc-form strips on either side of the suspension point against which the thread comes if it deviates beyond this point – is independent of the maximum swing of the pendulum. In this case the weight no longer describes a segment of a circle but a cycloidal motion. He also demonstrated the relationship between the length of the pendulum and duration of the swing and also the centrifugal force when a pendulum describes a circular path. Huygen's discovery of the pendulum clock was a true milestone in the development of clocks. With this discovery he succeeded in overcoming the irregular frequency of the balance escapement. The regular swing of the pendulum proved to be an ideal regulator for clock mechanisms. Sufficiently accurate for a minute hand to be added to clocks.

The invention of the balance wheel spring mechanism is ascribed to both Huygens and the Englishman Dr. Robert Hooke, a physics and chemistry teacher at Gresham College. He claimed the invention of the mechanism for watches in 1658. A balance is a combination of a mass with a spring that returns the mass to its original position when it moves. Both men used this discovery to improve the accuracy of portable timepieces.

The first pendulum clocks

Dutch makers naturally made use of Huygens' discovery of the pendulum. They were produced in many forms: Friesian longcase and hanging clocks, Amsterdam longcase clocks, Zaandaam clocks, and Friesian, Gronginen, and Drenthe bracket clocks.

Huygens patented his invention and the first maker to produce a pendulum clock under licence to his design was Salomon Hendrikszoon Coster. This clock did not have a long pendulum as in Huygens' design though but a short one.
The mechanism was contained in a small case that became known as a Hague clock. It is a type that can be still seen in many English, French, and Dutch table clocks. Not all Hague clocks have pendulums though. Earlier types have a sprung cylinder or weight.

The knowledge of pendulums was taken to Britain by Ahasverus Fromanteel, a London maker who was apprenticed

LBottom left: Friesian longcase clock from Grouw, made by D.J. Tosma in 1770. The clock not only gives time to the second but also the date, day of the week, month, and moon phase. The mechanism also plays six tunes, has 14 bells and 28 hammers. From the times of water-powered clocks, all manner of mechanisms have been incorporated with clocks.

Bottom right: Bracket clock, circa 1600. The clock has just one hand. During restoration it was found to have several layers of paint on the dial.

Single hand table clock from The Hague, circa 1660. These clocks from The Hague were an example for countless other clocks.

French religious table clock from Paris, circa 1670.

to Coster. Huygens himself took the knowledge to France. Shortly after his patent was granted, Huygens visited Paris where he allowed several makers to produce table clocks with a pendulum mechanism. It was neither the Dutch or French clock industry though that saw the advantages of Huygens' invention but the British who used it extensively. This formed the foundation for the leading role English clocks were later to take.

An Englishman also found a way of improving Huygen's invention. One problem of his design was the inertia created for the pendulum mechanism each time the escapement wheel was released. This problem was solved in about 1670 by the Englishman William Clement who invented the anchor escapement. Countless variations of this invention have been developed in the following three centuries.

The external form of the clock

After the invention of the pendulum mechanism, the cases of most clocks changed from metal to wood. The outward appearance of clocks in the two most important clockmaking countries of England and France went in different directions. A French clockmaker ordered mechanisms in standard sizes which he then incorporated into the case that he built. A consequence of this was that clock cases in France always ran consistent with the major developments of style.

Because the whole process was kept in the hands of the clock-maker in England, the emphasis was far more on the mechanism. For this reason, English clocks tend to run about twenty-five years behind the development of styles. This changed at the end of the eighteenth century through the influence of the great designers such as Adam, Chippendale, Hepplewhite, and Sheraton.

There are other differences between French and English clocks. The French produced large numbers of table and bracket clocks while the English preferred hand-made clocks and watches. The face of English clocks remained fairly rectangular while from 1715 onwards the French stuck to round ones.

A MARITIME CHRONOMETER

At the start of the eighteenth century the British government was aware of the importance of accurately determining position at sea and passed the Longitude Act of 1714 promising a prize of £20,000 to the person who developed a means of determining longitude. The Act required accuracy to with half a degree of longitude. A deviation of two-thirds would be rewarded with £15,000, and one degree with £10,000.

Southern German table clock by Leithener of Dettelbach, circa 1770.

Neo-Gothic English table clock by D. Hill of Rochester, 1820–1840.

The self-taught horologist John Harrison recognised that accurately knowing the time was the secret and he finally developed a chronometer in 1761 that achieved this but had to battle with the government until 1773, when he was 80 years old, to get his money. In order to achieve this precise timekeeping was required. With the necessity of building precise clocks for maritime use, makers at the end of the seventeenth century were able to make clocks that were reasonably accurate. The English in particular made great strives in the early eighteenth century to make ever more accurate clocks.
The French though were not far behind and by 1750 had caught up with the English.

English table clock by Elliot of London.

The most famous French maker is undoubtedly Abraham-Louis Breguet but the English efforts had created the basis of their success.

In the mid nineteenth century, the best clock and watch makers were based in London, with names such as East, Fromanteel, Graham, Knibb, Quare, and Tompion.
At this high-point though there was also a threat for this labour intensive craft.

From the mid nineteenth century both English and French makers faced stiff competition from cheaper mass produced products from Germany, the United States, and Switzerland.

Bottom left: An 18th century Dutch bracket clock from Goor, attributed to Antoni ter Swaek.

Bottom right: Walnut longcase clock by Joan klock, Amsterdam, made between 1680–1700.

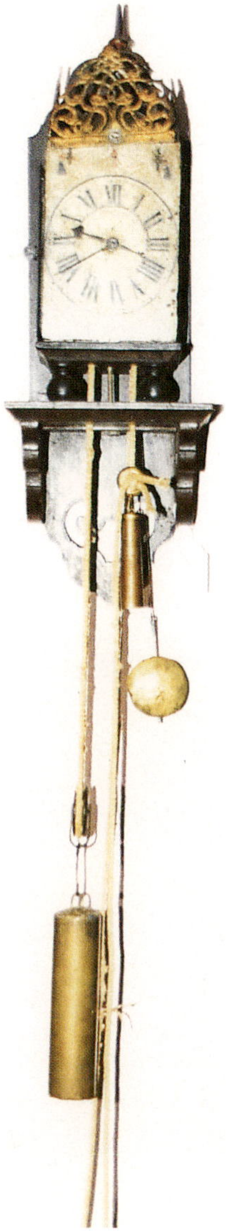

Bottom left: Dutch longcase clock, circa 1750.

Bottom right: This 4 metres(13 ft) high longcase clock is built in to the wall of Zwolle Town Hall, The Netherlands. Built by W. Bramer, 1728.

Mechanism of a Dutch bracket clock by Goslind Ruempol of Laren, 1726.

OIL AND FIRE CLOCKS

Burning substances in order to measure time is a very old principle.

The simplest form is the marked candle which indicates the passage of time as the candle burns down. Central European tin founders made lots of calibrated oil clocks with transparent or partially transparent oil tanks. A scale indicates the burning time of the oil. Such oil clocks served simultaneously as night-lights and simple timepieces but they should not be confused with clocks which had night-lights to illuminate their dials.

Types of clocks

LANTERN CLOCKS

Lantern clocks are among the earliest examples of balance wheel or foliot escapement. From the fourteenth through to the sixteenth century, the early lantern clocks were housed in Gothic style metal cases.

All manner of wall mounted clocks were developed from these simple lantern

Three French comtoise clocks dated (left to right) 1850, 1740, and 1870.

Bottom left: London mahogany longcase clock, circa 1770, with eight-day mechanism, second hand, and date indication.

Bottom right: English 19th century longcase clock.

clocks. Wood and ceramics were also used to make the clock case and the mechanisms also varied. Most were spring or weight driven from the seventeenth century.

LONGCASE CLOCKS

Soon after the development of the pendulum clock the English introduced the longcase clock, designed to protect the pendulum. The first longcase clocks had short pendulums but following the development of the anchor escapement they were able to use longer, second-beating pendulums.

Early longcase clocks were designed along classical lines often incorporating a tympanum and Corinthian capitals. This was quickly reduced to two pilasters that were sometimes turned. Early clocks had opening upper cases for winding the clock but as the clocks became taller after 1710 they had a lower door for this purpose. French makers surpassed the English longcase clocks after 1730. The innate conservatism of the English makers held them back.

The adoption of the pendulum in Britain quickly led to the development of bracket clocks as well as longcase clocks.

Bottom left: Belgian longcase clock from Charleroi, circa 1760. Most such clocks open forward for access but Belgian clocks need to be lifted upwards.

Bottom right: French comtoise clock of 1861.

French wall clock from Neufchatel l'Oise, circa 1740.

Provincial English oak longcase clock by E. Cohen of Redruth, circa 1800. The clock has an eight-day chronometer mechanism that indicates seconds and the date.

English tavern clock by J. Hall of Stourbridge, circa 1870.

A 19th century Vienna regulator in mahogany case.

The cases were made of wood with ebony, walnut, mahogany, and other veneers. Only a few clocks had inlay work but painted examples are more common. Most clocks had eight-day mechanisms. The term 'bracket clock' is derived from the wall-mounting bracket that some of these clocks had even though most were made so they could stand on furniture. Most English bracket clocks that found their way abroad were made in London. Provincial clocks were largely for local sale.

Provincial English longcase clock.

MANTEL CLOCKS

Mantel clocks are similar to bracket clocks but usually both smaller and with less depth. The first examples dating from around 1750–1760 were made in France. English mantel clocks followed on about ten years later.

The first French mantel clocks were developed from French Regency bracket clocks, coming into being when similar

Ceramic cased 19th century clock from Sarreguemines.

French cartel clock by 'Vincenti à Paris', circa 1860.

French 18th century Louis XVI-style clock.

Mantel clock of biscuit by Gavelle of Paris.

Empire style mantel clock c.1800.

Louis XVI clock, Paris circa 1770.

clocks were created in Rococo style without a bracket. It was commonplace to set these clocks on a mantelpiece.

It became customary around 1835 to accompany mantel clocks with a pair of matching ornaments. These *garniture de cheminée* remained popular throughout the nineteenth century. It is easy to distinguish English mantel clocks from French ones. English examples mainly have superb mechanisms and graced studies and libraries.

NOVELTY CLOCKS

It was customary in the seventeenth century to produce novelty clocks with

Empire style clock with classical Egyptian elements incorporated in its base.

English skeleton clock of circa 1870.

Louis XVI style French clock in upright vase.

Carriage clock with single hand.

mechanisms that did more than drive the clock itself. The outward appearance of these clocks was of paramount importance and might take any form from a crucifix with Madonna or animals and even slaves.

CARRIAGE CLOCKS

With the improvements in clock technology it was possible by the early sixteenth century to make clocks that could be taken on journeys.

The mechanisms were more precise to allow for the disturbance of motion and the first travelling clocks were like large watches of 70–140 mm (2¾–5½in) and were known as carriage clocks.

The greatest impulse to the development of portable timepieces was the demand for chronometers that permitted the establishment of longitude. English clock-makers succeeded in creating chronometers that were not affected by the sea's motion The mechanism was mounted in a rectangular casing with the balance and motion unusually situated at the top of the mechanism instead of the rear. Most of these clocks had metal casings with glazed side panels and a small handle at the top.

Carriage clock with travel case produced for the Chinese market, with engraved case and second hand dial. Most Chinese could not tell the time but bought clocks to enjoy seeing them in motion.

Chinese table clock in the English style, circa 1800.

Belgian Jugendstil ladies' watch with stand in form of a chair.

WATCHES

When the mainspring was developed around 1500 this quickly led to the invention of the first watch. These small portable clocks were worn on a cord around the neck. The casings were generally of very luxurious and fine style with the main function of these watches being decorative.

Silver, gold, or gilded watches were engraved and from 1630 onwards were also decorated with polychrome enamel. These watches were not very reliable until the development in 1670 of the balance wheel. After this date the watch's function became more important in its design. Minute hands were added and dials with the hours marked in figures became more prominent.

French watchmakers fitted wholly enamelled dials from 1725 on and within a few decades the rest of Europe followed this example. Nineteenth and twentieth

The case is superbly decorated.

The opened watch.

Silver-plated ladies' watch with diamonds by l'Epaule of Paris, 35mm (1_in) in diameter.

Silver 19th century ladies' watch.

century pocket-watches were generally devoid of expensive enamel decoration and their metal cases were plain metal that was sometimes embossed or engraved. Enamel's place was sometimes taken by cheaper painted horn.

The invention by Thomas Mudge in 1755 of the anchor escapement was very important to the development of the watch and made them much more accurate. Although this invention was ignored for almost 80 years it replaced virtually every other type of movement in the period 1830–1850 and has been used in virtually every mechanical watch mechanism since.

Abraham-Louis Breguet is regarded as the spiritual father of the modern watch with his invention of a mechanism that counteracts the detrimental effect on accuracy of wearing of a watch.

UNUSUAL MECHANISMS

Clockwork can of course be used to drive other mechanisms such as striking

Watch with separate watch case and key. This is a series production watch, indicated by its serial number 77489.

Modern form of clock by J. Boucher of Auxerre, with bone dial.

or chiming mechanisms to signal the hour and parts of the hour. Some clocks have chiming mechanisms that can play one or more pieces of music. Alarm clocks also have a striking mechanism of course and other functions found include indication of the date and the phases of the moon. Some clockwork mechanisms even have a solely astronomical function, incorporating a complete planetarium and universe.

WRIST WATCHES

Wrist watches date from around 1865 when the first ladies' bracelets incorporating a watch were made.
Almost no men's watches were made before World War I and the rise of the wrist watch coincided with Switzerland gaining a leading position as watch and clock-makers.

ELECTRIC CLOCKS

Alexander Bain is regarded as the person who invented electric clocks. He acquired a patent in Britain in 1841 that incorporates virtually all the principles on which subsequent electric clocks were based.
One of these is the use of electromagnets to operate clocks. Many electric clocks still use the ever reliable pendulum.
Subsequent electric clocks incorporated a means of winding up a spring.

IMPORTANT EVENTS IN THE HISTORY OF CLOCKS

3000 BC: first sundial in Sumaria
1300 BC: first reports of water driven timepieces in Egypt
1500: first wheel escapement mechanisms. The first town halls and churches were equipped with clocks that struck the hour.
1300–1350: Metal clocks become increasingly in vogue in prosperous homes.
1425: first modern sundial with upright parallel to the earth's, axis (Germany).
1450: first spring driven clocks originating from Flanders and/or Burgundy.
1500: Details such as fusees, striking mechanisms, and porticos were in wide use
1500–1550: Development in Nuremberg of clock mechanisms with the possible invention of features such as asymmetric spinning 'spoons' to correct inertia.
1657–1658: discovery of the pendulum by Christiaan Huygens
1670: invention of the anchor escapement by William Clement.
1755: development of the balance wheel by Thomas Mudge
1800: Abraham-Louis Breguet develops a number of improvements for watches.
1841: Alexander Bain is awarded a patent for an electric clock mechanism.

Mass production

DThe Americans were the first to take the steps necessary to mass produce clocks. A flood of inexpensive clocks were exported to Europe in the 1840s, resulting in the demise of the English clock-makers. In continental Europe though makers managed to survive in southern Germany and Switzerland by switching to mass production.
The Swiss led the watch industry until the 1960s when the Japanese flooded the world market with cheap watches.

Other antiques

Antiques are dealt with in this chapter that cannot be ignored but for which there is insufficient space to deal with them in great detail.
Firstly their are the *country pieces* that can still be readily found and which are well suited to modern interiors with their simple lines.
Antique *toys* are highly desirable objects and unfortunately there is only room here to deal with dolls and trains.
Sculpture is an area of collecting that has grown considerably so we include a brief summary about antique *statues and busts*.
A new area for collectors of nostalgia is that of *antique stoves* and *fireplaces*. In spite of today's centrally heated world the value of the fire as a focal point of a room has regained its place.

Painted Moldavian cabinet, circa 1900.

Painted objects are commonplace in folk art. Painted pine chest from Prague, 1885–1895.

Furthermore cast iron stoves can be so attractively designed. With a reduction in religious life in many European countries increasing volumes of *religious curios* are coming onto the market.
Arms and armour interest a special area of collectors but we include a brief summary for the interested non-specialist.
Collecting *jewellery, gold, and silver* covers a wide field of both objects of adornment worn by our forefathers and domestic items that were once in everyday use. *Nautical* objects encompass everything related to the sea such as navigation instruments, ship's models, and telescopes. *Books* have a long history which is summarised in this chapter.

Country pieces

These are sometimes referred to as rural or rustic antiques, but this does not fully encompass the scope of country pieces. These are not solely simple pieces from the rural peasantry but include provincial pieces from larger villages and smaller towns and objects from areas with other backgrounds than agricultural, such as

Hungarian painted cabinet of 1836.

fishing communities or mining villages. The rural population included a broad diversity of occupations in addition to farmers and farm workers, including shopkeepers, merchants, seamen, and the barge men on the canals and rivers. Of course there were also the gentility, richer landowners, and merchants.

Country pieces include once commonplace objects from homes that were used for special occasions and for weddings, feast days, christenings and funerals.

Many are traditionally decorated in folk art styles. This is an anonymous form of art that leans heavily on traditions, making them not unique and difficult to date.

Dutch 18th century fire screen from Hindeloper.

Expressions of folk art are influenced to a greater or lesser extent by thc great style trends.

Pieces that were made for the former local nobility of a rural community exhibit the greatest influence by these styles. Objects which clearly demonstrate that they form part of a specific style gave its owner a certain reputation for good taste and refinement. Elements were borrowed over the years from all the major styles but the characteristics of these styles were simplified.

Neither the rural craftsman or his client probably had a good example of the style available and even if they did, the insight or background knowledge was perhaps missing to interpret the style correctly.

Folk art

Folk art here is intended to mean the artistic creations of groups and sub-cultures within the population, including the decoration of tools and household effects. Entire industries have grown up around folk art such as the production of folk art furniture from the small Friesian town of Hindeloper in The Netherlands. Establishing the line between folk art and the other applied arts is very difficult. Many regard naive art forms as part of folk art. General characteristics of folk art include a preference for pure decoration and use of bright colours. Symbolism is common in folk art ornamentation and geometric patterns.

It is not uncommon for extremely old forms and modern to co-exist and folk art reflects a timelessness and an apparent lack of interest in or respect for perspective and anatomy.

All manner of lamps have illuminated houses. This 180mm (7in) tall oil lamp is circa 1880.

A genuine 19th century farm interior. The family lived, cooked, and slept in one room. Sometimes there was also a 'front room' kept just for Sunday use. They slept in a 'box bed': the cupboard on the right.

Once elements from a style were incorporated into country pieces they remained in use much longer than in the towns. Rural inhabitants were less exposed to cultural developments and so there was little pressure to move with the times or the fashion of the day.

Once country people adopted a style they saw no imperative to follow a new one so quickly.

Elements related to their daily life and sphere of imagination were far more important for country people than the various styles. Ready use was made of prints or illustrations in books for paintings, woodworking, and metalwork. Major political developments did cause reactions among country people and these can be found in particular in painted decoration on furniture and earthenware. Country people who made

Tin coach lamp, 19th century.

A Spanish brocero of circa 1850. Farmers sat around this stove, putting their feet on it and covering their knees with blankets.
The underside shows fine construction.

objects themselves in their spare time often copied old examples and so the motifs they use vary little..

RELIGIOUS INFLUENCES

Another source for decorative images was the Bible. Sometimes these may be direct illustration of Bible stories or incorporation of symbolic Christian elements. These include a lamb to depict The Lamb of God (Christ who was led like a lamb to the slaughter on the cross), a fish (sign of the early Christians), and dove (symbolic of the Holy Ghost). Typical Roman Catholic symbols include the *arma Christi* or means of causing Christ's suffering: the cross itself and the nails with which he was fastened to the cross, the crown of thorns with which he was mocked, and the whip with which he was scourged. The letters 'IHS' often appear at the centre of such representations. These are the Greek capital letters that form the equivalent of 'JES' as an abbreviation of Jesus' name.
Others say that IHS is an abbreviation of *In Hoc Signo (vinces)* which means 'in this sign (they will conquer)'.

Iron stable lantern, 19th century.

Legend has it that Roman Emperor Constantine dreamt of the cross and these letters before a battle. He won the

Painted Dutch canister from North Holland. Biblical scenes are commonplace. This rural handicraft of the 18th century would have hung in a corner.

Fire hook that hangs above a fire from the 17th century.

Metal decalitre measuring beaker with levelling stick, late 19th century

battle against his opponent after he had these letters scratched on the shields of his army.

ANTIQUES FROM THE COMMUNITY

Country antiques come from the entire community: their makers are farmers and peasants, fishermen, local craftsmen, and other rural inhabitants.

Generally throughout western Europe only the craftsmen in the towns were formed into guilds. For this reason there is often little known about the working practices of rural craftsmen. Motifs, symbols, and other decoration in folk art were passed from master to apprentice, mother to daughter, and father to son down the generations.

The various trades have their own characteristic traditional designs that may be specific to a particular country, region, or even small town or village.

GEOGRAPHICAL AND CLIMATE SITUATION

The form of rural antiques are not influenced just by the era, character of folk art, trade or profession, and social status. The climate and geographical position are also of great importance.

The climate determines the way in which people cope with the weather and this has a major effect on their life-style

Common objects are found in country households. These are 19th century wooden tea caddies.

Table-top press of the 18th century.

Oak bread cupboard, 18th century.

Chestnut bench/table of circa 1880 from Northern Spain. The bench can be closed to form a table

and the objects they produce. You will not find horse-drawn sleighs in southern Italy nor a wine press in Norway. The climate also has a bearing on the raw materials that people use – particularly the type of wood they use. The trade in raw materials blurs this distinction though.

The geographical situation, together with the climate, determined the potential for the local community and was of considerable influence on the agricultural scope, the availability of natural raw materials, minerals, population growth, and other factors.

Spanish corner cupboard from Lugo, circa 1890.

Friesian earthenware fire-pan. This food warmer dates from circa 1700.

Late 19th stove with fire-pan. Stoves were used to warm the feet.

Oak church stove (with tongs for the coal) of 1745. This stove was taken to church to keep the feet warm.

Late 19th century coach stove of wood and metal.

Wooden tobacco jar, 1898.

Geography also determined the extent of contact with other people and the influences of other cultures and styles.

Late 19th century ice-skates.

Four 19th stamps for sealing wax. Letters used to be sealed in the past with wax to ensure they were not opened.

LOCAL CUSTOMS

The beliefs and customs of a village, small town, or area sometimes directly cause certain forms of applied art. For instance in the Dutch provinces of Friesland, Groningen, and Holland people like to show their wealth.

It was therefore customary during festive occasions to serve raisins in brandy in a bowl which was passed around the entire company. The poor used earthenware or pewter but the wealthy liked to show off their superbly decorated silver brandy bowls. Another examples comes from Graubünden (Grisons) in Switzerland where the sitting room of the Roman-speaking people often had a small hatch to the outside.

This was only opened when a dead person was lying in the sitting room. People believed that the soul needed to escape via the hatch.

Almost every country in Europe has customs related to courtship, betrothal, and the wedding, and also surrounding pregnancy and giving birth.

The newly born infant is often given traditional presents such as a silver cup or spoon. Special food and drink is often offered to guests when the pregnancy is announced or following the birth.

In many countries there was a marked difference between the plainness of the week-day clothes of the ordinary people and their Sunday clothing. Sunday clothing was often strikingly rich in style and quality. All manner of jewellery would indicate the position of the owner.

Rotating seal, circa 1720.

Windows were cleaned with this late 19th century window sprayer.

Silver-plated tilting kettle on a pewter pot warmer, circa 1900.

Late 19th century coffee grinder that was found in most kitchens.

Metal pot warmer, 19th century.

Brass spirit stove, circa 1890.

Copper kettle with bone handle and knob, 19th centu

Copper kettle with valve on the spout, 19th century.

Early 19th century brass smoothing iron and stand for heating with hot coals.

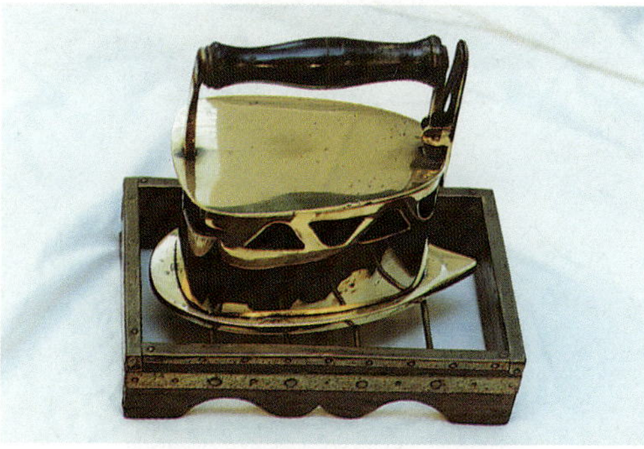

INTERIOR FITTINGS

In addition to antiques that arise from a desire to display wealth or that are associated with special occasions, there are many other types of country pieces. These include objects related to the fitting out of a home. Country style furnishings are generally simple with somewhat crude and heavy forms.

As a rule they are plain or otherwise decorated with simple folk art motives and paintings.

Wall-mounted furniture is often decorated with paintings because painted pictures are beyond their scope.

Nest of 18th century brass weights. The middle weight of the range is missing, as is often the case.

Nest of 19th century weights. Remarkably the middle weight is still present

HOUSEHOLD EFFECTS

Metallic objects served both their functional purpose and acted as decoration. The main emphasis though was on the functional use so that decoration and other characteristics which would help to date them are absent. Because of their functional design these objects also remained more or less unaltered for a long time, making it further difficult to date them.

Iron is more common among country antiques because it is cheaper than copper, brass, and pewter. It is also robust and easy to maintain. A further disadvantage of copper, brass, and pewter is that pewter was expected to have a silvery lustre and brass and copper to shine.

Most more lowly homes had no time or staff for the additional work this meant. Despite this though pewter and copper

Early 19th century Pewter inkstand. Pewter was used brass and copper for metal objects.

Pewter washing set]

Pewter mug, 18th century.

could be found in country homes with copper used for cooking pots and pans. Those who could afford it ate and drank from pewter tableware.

It can be difficult to ascertain if pottery originates from the country or town. Simple earthenware with a lead glaze was widely used until well into the nineteenth century.

Pewter coffee pot, 17th century.

Late 19th century pewter funnel.

This earthenware was locally produced in large volumes but large exports of lead-glazed earthenware were also made from potteries along the Rhine.

Fine decorated earthenware encounters the same problem. Decorated tin-glaze pottery wares (such as those from Delft) and Chinese porcelain were found with the wealthy both in the country and town. The best that can be said is that they originate from rich homes rather than penniless ones.

Pewter jug, 18th century.

TOOLS

Country antiques include objects related to work. This includes above all those farming implements and objects such as scythes and butter churns to wine and cider presses but there are also objects from the fishing, mining, and quarrying industries. It is impossible to say whether the tools once used by craftsmen originated in the town or country.

This 19th century silver sewing set has scissors, thimbles, needle cases, and bobbin for the thread.

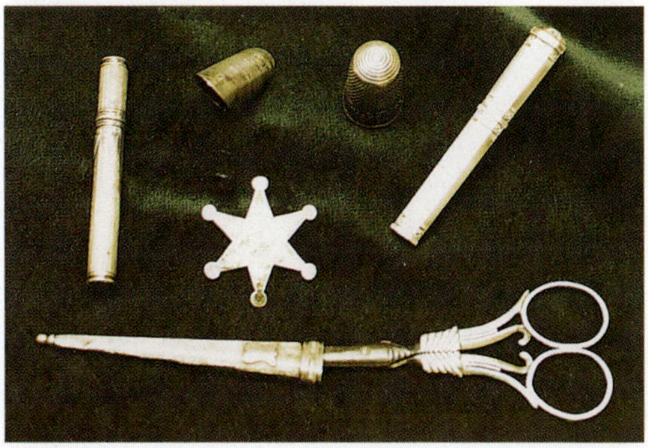

Some sewing boxes were extremely fine and passed down through the family. Tortoiseshell sewing box, circa 1860.

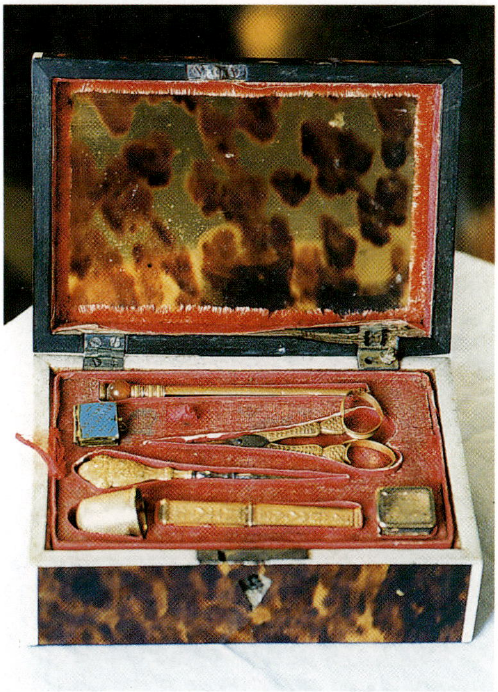

Gilt sewing accessories in a tooled leather case with glass base, 18th century.

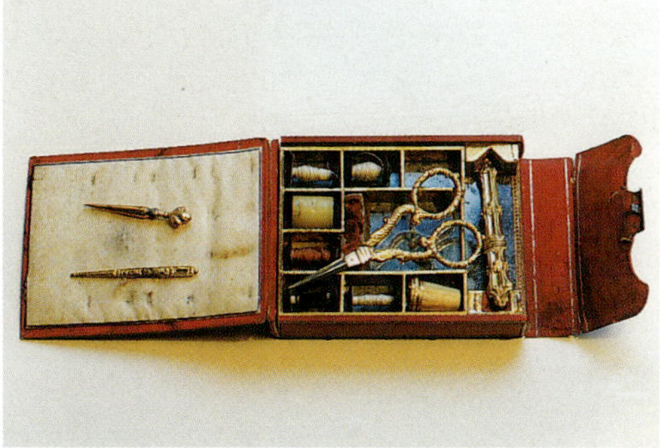

A 19th century bone yarn holder of wood and bone.

Interest in both genuine and false country objects

Considerable interest grew in certain lands for country objects towards the end of the nineteenth century and so objects have also been reproduced since that time. These were often made by good and genuine craftsmen but were then given 'antique' provenance by dubious dealers and some are still wrongly identified.

Wooden Friesian school case of 1830.

Travelling trunk, 18th century.

A wooden horse 'shoe' from the late 19th century. This spread the load on the horse's foot to prevent it sinking into marshy ground.

WOOD

Here are a few pointers to tell the genuine from the reproduction. Generally old timber feels quite different to new and has irregularities.

Scoops were used in many trades. This is a 19th century baker's scoop with iron fittings used to remove bread from the oven

Late 19th century wooden malt scoop with iron fittings

Late 19th century peat cutter's wooden spade with iron fittings

The carving and moulding is smoothed and worn by a great deal of use and polishing.
No screws were used in genuine seventeenth and eighteenth century furniture.

Butter traders used the tools in the upper photograph to probe deep into a barrel of butter to check the quality.
The hooked knives below were used by them to mark the casks they wished to buy. One is marked '1869'.

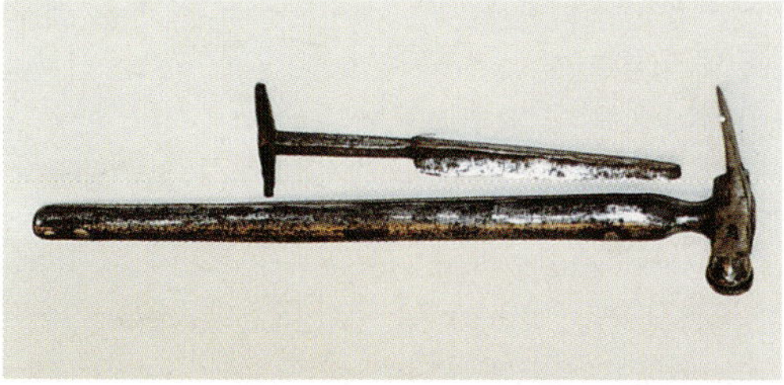

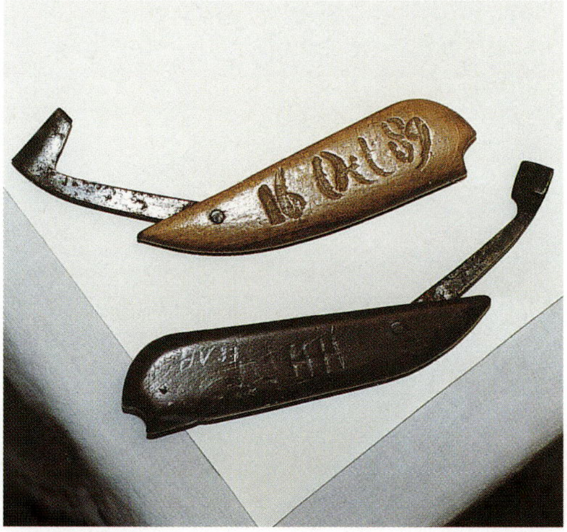

French butcher's chopping block from Normandy, circa 1900.

Spanish baker's trough, circa 1800.

Carpenter's 19th century wooden clamp.

When the nails have been replaced during restoration the holes left by the original ones should still be apparent. Chests have always been popular antiques but for the convenience of their customers the trade often replaced the curved lids with flat ones and the tray for trinkets is usually missing. The means of fastening the chest should always be apparent with a genuine chest.

COPPER, BRASS, PEWTER, AND SILVER

There are plenty of pewter, copper, and brass objects to be found in antique shops. Evil minded traders offer lots of reproductions. Reproduction copper and brass items are often heavier than the authentic ones because a lesser quality alloy has been used.
Genuine copper and brass is smooth and rounded through constant use and poor finishing often gives reproduction pieces away. Parts such as spouts, handles and hand grips are often poorly soldered. Old copper and brass jugs and kettles were constructed from horizontally arranged pieces and hence always have horizontal seams whereas reproductions almost always have vertical seams.

Reproduction of pewter objects is often done to a high standard. It is worth following up on any marks there may be. Modern pewter objects can often be recognised by their inferior alloy. When tapped they give a dull sound while old pewter gives a brighter sound.
With pewter too the jugs were made from horizontal rather than vertical pieces. One new piece is sometimes created from several old objects. Often these look right but instincts suggest something is wrong. It is then worth checking if the proportions are appropriate. A further trick is to press old pewter plates into a new shape because plates with broad rims are more popular than those with small ones.
It is not forbidden in some countries to use old marks on new pieces. This can be very misleading. Even when pieces have been melted down and recast they have acquired old marks. New pieces should of course acquire new marks but these are sometimes then removed by fraudulent persons but traces of this can usually be found. It is certainly worth checking out marks on silver. Forged marks rarely make sense.

Iron 18th century cleaving axes.

Brass 19th century spirit level.

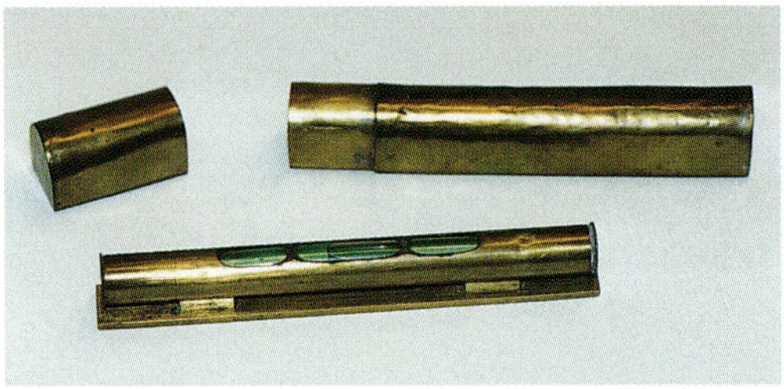

JEWELLERY

Traditional jewellery is still made and sold by jewellers in some areas. Fraudulent traders sometimes sell them as antiques which fetch a higher price.
Because the jewellery has been made using traditional methods it can be difficult even for experts to separate the new for the old. Most old jewellery has been altered or repaired over the years and the traces of this can be seen on the back of jewellery in the form of solder.

Toys: dolls and trains

Toys have existed as long as children. Toys are extremely important for children. They help to create a space within which the child can use its imagination and creativity and learn to interpret the world. The earliest forms of toy were made of clay but by the time of the great early civilisations they had already

Hand-made 19th century domino set.

Jack stones or dib stones and local variants are very old games. These are formed from sheep's vertebrae. The various games require the player to successively pick up a stone while catching the others.

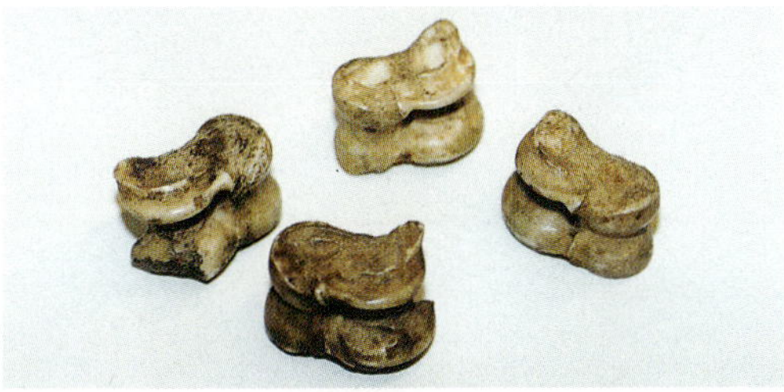

developed further. Some toys from the early Middle Ages remain popular to this day: soldiers, dolls, tops, and dice etc. Toys are depicted in many paintings and toys should not be regarded as objects merely for children since adults also play. There are two types of toy: the first consists of games and other forms of amusement such as dice and card games. Jack stones or dib stones are included in this category. Sheep's vertebrae were use for this game in some countries.

These various games all required the player to gradually pick up stone while catching one or more of the others.
The second types of toy originates from children's needs to mimic their world. These include toys such as toys shops, and model trains, but also dolls. It is impossible to deal with every type of toy here so we give a few examples.

Children do not only play but also go to school. Friesian wooden school case, circa 1850.

Dolls

Children have played with dolls for thousands of years. Little figures can be found in museums throughout the world from early civilisations. It is certain that they were not all of religious significance but rather that some were toys.

Through the ages dolls have been made of wood or clay, or a combination of both. For a long time dolls represented adult figures with baby and child dolls first appearing in the nineteenth century.
As standards of living improved the demand for dolls also grew, and also for better quality. The rigid bodies of the earlier forms were replaced by dolls with movable arms legs, and head. Doll making was so important that the guilds dur-

Late 19th century child's desk.

Doll's house chest of drawers, circa 1880.

ing the eighteenth century in some countries banned unqualified people from making them. It was only permitted for established wood turners and carvers to make dolls. The same applied to the clothing and painting of the dolls.
The well-known doll makers were often unable to meet the demand and they put their entire families to work in making dolls. This was certainly true of Germany in the nineteenth century.

Doll's chair, 1909.

An unglazed porcelain doll's head with stereotypical expression, circa 1875

After 1700 dolls acquired glass eyes and real hair. The form of the hands was also greatly improved. Furthermore a great deal of care was paid to the painting of the dolls' heads. Even the makers of papier mâché dolls were controlled by

A wax doll with implanted hair in original condition, circa 1870.

An early wax over papier mâché doll of circa 1875.

the guilds. These rules were so rigid that girls were even forbidden to make papier mâché dolls around 1700.

The production process with wet paper was so messy that the guilds considered it damaged a woman's dignity. Many dolls heads were made of papier mâché up to 1810 but Germany in particular then switched over to composition moulding on oiled forms. This was time-saving and permitted much greater production levels. Mass produced dolls from Sonnenberg flooded the market leading to fierce competition between German and French makers. This led to the French doll makers forming together in an association in 1900.

In the nineteenth century doll's heads of other materials were also popular. This included biscuit porcelain and the individually modelled wax heads made in London by the Montanari family which were renowned. Around 1850 doll's faces became almost life-like with eye-lashes and brows, painted mouths, glass eyes, and real hair.

The nineteenth century porcelain heads are less life-like and often possess a stereotyped smile. Only a few of them possess a portrait-like character.

Model trains

The first wheel was used some 5,000 years ago. In the second half of the eighteenth century coal started to be transported from English coal mines along tracks. At first these tracks were made of wood but soon they began to lay metal rails.

In 1769 James Watt applied for a patent for an important improvement for the steam engine, making it possible for wag-

Stations form a part of a model railway such as this 1902 Märklin example, catalogue no. 2641. Unfortunately the side roof is missing

ons to be moved along the rails by steam traction. It was not until 1825 though that George Stephenson made this happen. The world's first steam railway was opened between Stockton and Darlington in that year. In the rest of that century the railway network was extended throughout Britain and also in continental Europe.

Soon after the first railways were opened in continental Europe they became the subject of artistic output. The train was regarded as something of a wonder in its early years and various artists saw commercial possibilities in this.

Hence shortly after the opening of the line between Leipzig and Dresden a map with thirteen engravings was published to immortalise the occasion.

Tinsmiths also saw an opportunity and soon brought out three dimensional and flat pewter representations of the train.

Soon afterwards toy makers started to produce the first toy trains. At first they were made of wood with rails being considered unnecessary. The train and wagons made excellent toys to pull around.

The wooden toy train then was the equivalent of today's model railway.

The toy industry became more deeply involved with trains and began to make trains of tinplate that ran along the floor. They were powered by steam or by a flywheel; clockwork motors were added later. By 1870 there were manufacturers making complete train sets. Some of these had rails that were pressed from a single piece of tinplate but most quickly made separate rails soldered to tinplate sleepers.

The first model railways had a track width of 48mm (1.89in) which was named 1 gauge.

When people began to make wind-up and steam locomotives with a narrower track width it was called 0 gauge as it was smaller than 1 gauge. This too proved to be too wide and led in the twentieth century to the creation of 'half 0' or HO (OO in Britain and the Empire/Commonwealth). The German firm of Märklin offered trains, rails, crossovers, and points in various track widths at the 1891 Leipzig Fair. The prototypes were by the firm of Lutz that Märklin had taken over. This promised much. Märklin (founded 1859) though was not the only company making model railways. Other leading names (with their year of establishment in brackets) were Basset-Lowke (UK), Bing (1866), Karl Bub (1851), Schoener (1875), Cerette (1866), Fleischmann (1887), Kibri (1895 for model railway accessories). The firm of Lionel is a well known US name.

An attractive scenery item: a 1930 news stand complete with miniature newspapers by Märklin, no. 2628.

A fine example of Märklin no. RS 13030 electric locomotive of 1926.

A fairly late electric-powered Märklin locomotive of 1938, no. 12880.

These makers produced trains in the following gauges, of which III, IV, and V are extremely rare.

Gauge	scale ration	track width
O	1:45	32mm ($1^{1}/_{4}$in)
I	1:32	45mm ($1^{9}/_{10}$in)
II	1:28	51mm (2in)
III	1:20	72mm ($2^{8}/_{10}$in)
1935 HO	1:87	16mm ($^{6}/_{10}$in)
1938 OO	1:76	16mm ($^{6}/_{10}$in)

There are also TT, S, IIm, HOm, HOe and other gauges. Besides making the locomotives and rails firms also quickly started to make all manner of accessories related to railways such as stations, level crossings, lamps, signals, and model people.

The young Briton Basset-Lowke visited the World Exhibition of 1900 in Paris where he became very impressed by the work of the German firm of Bing from Nuremberg, which had a major stand there. Both men were good friends and they were joined by the renowned constructor Greenly who designed superb models. Bing built these models and Basset-Lowke sold them in Great Britain with great success. Basset-Lowke also soon began to sell products in Britain by Carette of Nuremberg, which mainly supplied wagons but also the occasional locomotive.

Goods trains were also made with great imagination such as this 1933 Märklin wagon, no. 1985.

British model railways were quite close to scale from the beginning of the hobby while the concept of scale seemed quite unheard of in continental Europe. After the start of the twentieth century the two most important makers of model railways were the German firms of Märklin of Göppingen and Bing of Nuremberg. The competition between them caused both companies to produce a number of different systems.

Bing developed what became known as the Nuremberg style. Mass production and far-reaching rationalisation kept their prices low and many smaller manufacturers followed Bing's example. Märklin though chose a different route. Hand craftsmanship remained important with Märklin for many years which kept their prices quite high but then so was

Märklin did not just make German trains. This 1934 electric locomotive no. 12920 is based on the Swiss railways prototype SBB Ae 3/6.

Märklin were not alone in making 'toy trains' of course. This Bing model 11/463 of 1927 of a steam locomotive shows what can happen when a toy is played with extensively

their quality. Märklin established its own sales organisation in the Great Britain and around 1900 they produced a wide range of British wagons and locomotives for the United Kingdom market with the liveries of the various railway companies. These British models never appeared in the main Märklin German catalogue.

Märklin produced many models for its home market and for the rest of continental Europe. These models varied significantly from those for the British market and appeared in a separate catalogue.

It was not until the 1920s that European models were built to scale and with the correct liveries. Model locomotives are extremely desirable collector's objects and the prices reflect this. Some models have fetched more than 10,000 Deutschmarks on the German market.

Sculpture

By sculpture here we mean all three-dimensional forms of artistic expression in wood, stone, clay, and wax and other materials, including those who model in clay or wax in order to cast their work in metal. Works of sculpture have been found dating back to prehistoric times. Their function is uncertain.

They may have had ritual purposes or even been early toys. In any event, sculpture is found in every culture. In terms of styles, sculpture generally runs in parallel with the pervading style of the era found in paintings.

When considering a piece of sculpture one needs to remember that it was originally created for specific surroundings and that the artist has taken this into account. Sketches of the ideas have often been made first on paper, followed sometimes by studies in clay, which on occasion may also be cast in plaster.

These would have been used as a guide during the working of the final piece. Some sculptors used a system by which they established fixed points on a scale model which could then be transposed to the final sculpture.
Sculpture includes both individual or free-standing pieces and reliefs which are fixed to a surface. Free-standing pieces may stand alone or have formed part of an overall architectural design, making them subordinate to architecture.
Sculptors in past history almost always used colour. It was not until the Italian Renaissance with its use of marble that painting of sculpture ended. It was wrongly assumed that this was the tradition in classical antiquity The separation of sculpture from architecture was a fairly slow process in virtually every culture.

Often it has also been necessary to break free from the prescription of painted and drawn art. Reliefs logically precede free-standing sculpture and it can be quite late in development before sculpture breaks free from its place on walls.

This occurred through the transitional stages of *bas-relief* and *haut-relief*. The earliest free-standing sculptures are therefore somewhat constrained, not really breaking free from the wall, and are to be viewed solely from the front.

A simple figurine from the 3rd century. This Hellenic mother goddess originates from Aleppo in Syria.

Not all of the early major styles of art saw sculpture break its architectural bounds. This is certainly true of Middle Ages Romanesque and Gothic sculpture. This was not achieved until the arrival of the Renaissance and then Baroque.

DIFFERENT USES FOR SCULPTURE

Sculpture in classic antiquity was solely of a religious nature but sculpture as portraiture gradually became popular. Sculpture was also used ornamentally both indoors and out.

Things reverted in the Middle Ages and sculpture was once more principally of a religious nature: Romanesque and above all Gothic churches were decorated with images of Jesus and the saints. Sculpture noticeably became more free-standing during the Gothic era but was still subordinate to architecture. As the Middle Ages progressed, sculpture

This series of five late Gothic carvings was made shortly after 1450 in the north of Holland. They were originally bearers for beams fixed by wooden dowels that faced downwards (they are in the wrong position here). They illustrate how late Gothic sculpture slowly started to shake off its architectural constraints.

South American 17th century polychrome Pietà.

Madonna and child in lime wood, 19th century.

Southern German 18th century cherubs.

came increasingly to gain independence from its background. One remarkable use of sculpture was the effigy of dead persons on the lid of their tombs with their head laying on a 'cushion' or as upright figures with their feet on apedestal. The Italian Renaissance gradually came to bear on sculpture which regained the position it had once enjoyed.

As a result we find classical portrait busts in marble, statues of gods and goddesses for both indoors but especially the garden. These statues remained unpainted because it was thought that the sculpture of classical antiquity was also unpainted.

Cast iron fires and stoves

Cast iron was widely used in the nineteenth century. It is iron with three to four percent carbon and up to six percent silica that is cast in moulds. The desired consistency of cast iron is varied during the production process through carbon and silica, and oxidisation.

Before the arrival of cast-iron fires and stoves, the rear of a fireplace was protected by an iron fireback. These examples originated in the 17th or 18th centuries.

Further treatment with heat can follow the casting process during which any excess of carbon can be converted to graphite. The extent of this has significant bearing on the mechanical properties of the cast iron and there are many different qualities of cast iron ranging from very brittle to extremely hard. Cast iron was used to make parts for machinery, to build bridges, and manufacture of household appliances.

Many of these uses only vanished with the arrival of steel in the twentieth century. Mid-way through the nineteenth century cast iron fireplaces and stoves entered the home. Cast iron fires are somewhat strange objects for the antique collector since they were mass produced

Cast iron fireplace, circa 1870.

This Parisian stove made before 1895 was used by market traders in Les Halles to keep themselves warm.

in foundries on industrial lines and hence do not have the craftmanship normally associated with antiques. On the other hand their designers gave much thought to their appearance and many cast iron fires are of very fine and striking appearance. This attracts many collectors to them, making them well worth considering. Trade buyers are always eager to acquire them because of their ready sale.

Norwegian Ulefos cast iron stove, circa 1990.

There were makers of cast iron fires throughout western Europe from Ireland to the former Czechoslovakia.
The appearance of their products vary widely. Most European makers though remained several decades behind the renowned French maker Jean-Baptiste André Godin (1817–1888).The 23-year old Godin started his business making fireplaces in the hamlet of Esquehieres in the centre of Thierache in 1840 with 4,000 francs from his parents. Godin quickly recognised the advantages of cast iron for the production of fireplaces in Esqyehieres.

His success was so great that he established a foundry in a small shed in 1842 but this quickly became too small. The works soon moved to Guise where 30 people were employed. In spite of fierce competition and the unremitted and unpunished copying of his patented

An original Musgrave Franke. German cast iron stove made in Mannheim following an Irish style.

products, his business grew rapidly. The most important reason for this was his innovation. Godin applied for many patents for his products and concentrated on continually improving them both aesthetically and technically.

This helped his factory to be the leading manufacturer. Godin conducted many experiments and was a very good business manager. One of his achievements was the mechanisation of the casting

1905 German stove.

process. His modest works had grown by 1880 into a factory with 2,000 employees. The success of Godin was a great surprise to many of his contemporaries.
This scepticism was founded on the poor economic circumstances of the department of Aisne which was far removed from the many traffic routes and urban markets and raw materials. Godin chose it though because of a ready supply of labour that was less demanding than in the urban areas. Much of Godin's success was due to the input of his employees.

Godin was a utopian socialist who was remarkably interested in his workers. Godin paid wages that were relatively high for the region and successfully sought to raise the living standards of his workers. The socialist measures he undertook through his company created an unparalleled community. He had houses build for his workers, for example, to high standards of safety, hygiene, and

This French 'La Salamandre' enclosed living room fire for coal and wood was made between 1870–1895.

Dutch clover-leaf or IJhorster stove (from near Staphorst), between 1850–1900.

Belgian cloister stove of 1895 in original condition. These stoves were made to order.

French dining room cast iron stove by Godin made circa 1900. Food could be kept hot in the cupboard on the right.

Not everyone could afford a cast iron stove. A simpler version was the tinplate oil stove, made circa 1900.

Godin cast iron stove no. 40, circa 1870.

comfort for their time. Alongside this he founded a unique system of social insurance, established schools, stimulated the organisation of out-of-work activities, and even developed a profit-sharing arrangement. Eventually, at his initiative, the company became a worker's cooperative. The business ran for 90 years until 1968.

For many the Godin name evokes stoves that were still in use until after World War II but he was also a leading figure in his branch of industry and known too for his forward-looking social ideas. It is therefore such a pity that little is to be found about his work in books.

Religious curios and Church antiques

Religion is the veneration by humankind of a deity. This may include one or more gods, spirits, powers, or natural forces. The experience of religion varies from immediate and personal contact to a shared experience with a group. Holy scriptures can play an important role in this process.

Objects or relics were formerly used in particular in group religious experiences as intermediaries between humankind and their deities. These objects themselves can also be the subject of direct veneration and may be central to a ritual. Other types of objects are used to decorate a holy place.

In the European and North American context religion primarily means the Christian church. The interior style of churches down the ages has largely been a matter of a plethora of different

Church chandelier of 1670 from Friesland (Holland). It was converted to gas in the late 19th century and later to electricity.

A 17th century Roman Catholic relic receptacle containing relics of the crucifixion.

An 18th century Italian church candlestick.

A 19th century brass church candle-holder.

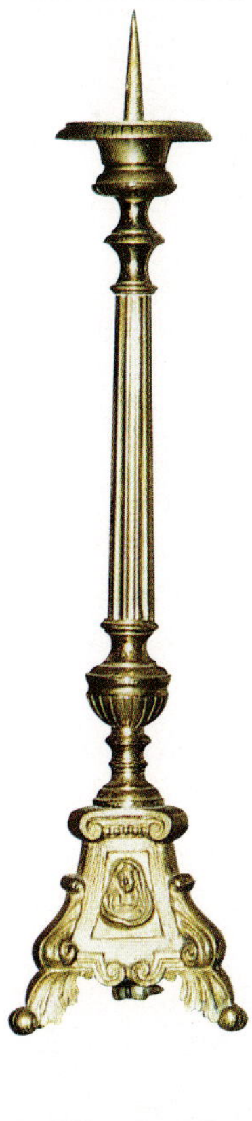

Simple parish church offertory box, possibly 18th century.

Church sconce, 18th century.

styles. These are often intertwined with traditional elements from Christianity. Generally those objects from the Roman Catholic and the Orthodox Churches are more luxurious than those from Protestant churches. Some of the objects from Protestant churches are remarkable for their powerful simplicity.

It is not just the matter of pomp and ceremony or absence of them that dictates the interior of a church but far less consideration was given to such down to earth matters as the general lighting and the pews for thoughts were always directed towards the services themselves. Consequently the form and decoration of church interior fittings and fixtures are subordinated to the church services.

Jewish objects

Jewish people have established themsel ves over the centuries in many different countries. In each place where they have settled they have absorbed something of the local culture into their own Jewish culture. Despite this Jewish culture remains distinctive. For readily apparent reasons fewer antiquities have survived from Jewish culture than one would wish. Most Jewish antiquities are of a religious nature.

The Jewish religion is founded on the five books of Moses that form the Pentateuch which are set down in the Torah or

Silver yad used by Jews to read the Torah scriptures, 19th century.

parchment scroll that is rolled onto two staffs that are embellished with *rimmons* – decorative silver finials.

In order that the Torah is not touched with the hand while reading, the reader uses a silver pointer or*y ad* to mark the place in the text. When the Torah is rolled up it is protected by an ornate embroidered covering over which a silver breastplate is placed with a depiction of the two tablets of stone containing the ten commandments of the Mosaic Law.

In addition to those objects associated with the Torah there are numerous objects that are typically Jewish such as the cedarwood dishes uses to eat *matzah* at Passover and the well-known eight-armed *menorah* candlestick that is lit at Hanukkah by means of the ninth server or *shammes* candle. The Sabbath candle or lamp is lit on the eve of the Sabbath.

This is a silver or brass candelabrum or (rarely) chandelier. The Sabbath meal commences with the *kiddush* goblet in the hand and wine is also drunk in a goblet to mark the end of the Sabbath. Sometimes this is also marked by burning incense in a spice.

ICONS

Icons are painted representations of Biblical figures and the saints. They form an important place in the religion of Eastern Europe, the Balkans, and Greece. These stylised representations are intended in the first instance as cult objects and they form an important liturgical role.

The Neo-Platonic philosophy was central to the development of icons from the middle of the fourth century. This held that humans could contact invisible religious entities through a visible image. There was a major struggle in the Byzantine empire in 726 over idolatry and Emperor Leo III decided for political reasons to ban the worshipping of icons. His soldiers entered the churches and destroyed the icons, bringing the word iconoclasm to the language (meaning destruction of icons).

The iconodulists (those who revered icons) gained the upper hand in 787 and the worshipping of icons was restored. Soon after 800 the iconoclasts started a second wave of destruction. Icons are typical of the Orthodox church (with its origins in Greece). Major Orthodox

Late Novogorod school Russian icon, 17th century.

The metal guard that protects the icon from mistreatment.

church countries where icons were (and still are) made include Greece and Russia. There are specific considerations in iconography and this means that the image is not a precise likeness but a representation.

The icon's purpose is to reproduce the hidden. A believer who venerates an icon does not worship it but the original image behind the icon (such as Jesus or a saint). The Greek word eikon means illustration or likeness. The production of icons is solely according to strict written rules. The painting of an icon is not considered profane, rather it is a sacred task. The icon is painted onto a wooden board by a complex process. This method of painting probably originated in ancient Egypt. There are portraits of mummies painted two centuries before Christ that resemble icons.

The central part of the icon is hollowed out to form a small rim or frame and small grooves are cut in the rear into which strips of wood are fixed to prevent the icon from warping.
The story of the holy robe or mandilion is linked to icons. This starts with the legend of Saint Abgar who was the king of Edessa during Christ's time on earth. He was ill and asked Christ in a letter to heal him. The request was sent to Jesus by a messenger named Ananias who was also to present Jesus with a present of a robe or mandilion.

Christ said he could not go with the messenger for his purpose in Jerusalem was not done but he pressed his face into the cloth whereupon Christ's face became imprinted. Jesus sent Ananias with the cloth back to Abgar. The image on the cloth is known in Greek as *vera ikonika* or the true image or as the mandilion. When the town of Edessa was conquered in 944 by the Byzantines the siege was lifted in exchange for 12,000 pieces of silver and the mandilion.

The cloth was borne in triumph to Constantinople and the first icons were created as representations of the mandilion. The crusaders invested Constantinople in 1204 and took the mandilion as booty. Meanwhile the cloth turned up in Paris, Rome, Genoa, and ...
The iconographer's art spread to Russia and was found in such major centres as Kiev and Novogorod.

A style of iconography developed in Novogorod with specific characteristics. The body was graphically outlined, the colours were used without mixing them, the composition was straightforward and figures are powerfully portrayed.
The Russian icon shown on page 191 is a late example of the Novogorod school of the seventeenth century. The typical Novogorod style remains although in a modified form. Believers were and are accustomed to kissing icons. The metal part surround the icon is meant to protect the icon from mistreatment.

The icon with its protective guard.

Arms and armour

It is impossible to consider the history of mankind without arms or weapons. Their first function was for hunting but humankind quickly discovered of course that they could be used against other humans and weapons were used to fight in major conflicts.

The comparatively benign western world of today was once not so safe and people carried arms to defend themselves alongside officials such as the bailiffs or sheriff, and his constables who were charged with protecting the community and were therefore armed. Very few of the enormous numbers of weapons that have ever been made have survived. Arms were tools which were replaced by new ones when they became unserviceable, quite apart from ornamental swords and daggers which were heavily influenced by fashion. Technical improvements in arms progressed rapidly following the Middle Ages.

The purpose of arms

The making of arms quickly became work for the specialist armourer even long ago because he had knowledge of the special handling required to make weapons from metal. Armourers kept the knowledge of how to impart metals with sufficient harness to themselves and they ensured that they supplied work of the highest possible standard. Those who knew the secrets of making arms therefore held leading positions in society.

The form of a weapon is only in part a result of its function. Bearing arms also conveys status to the bearer and he often chose to emphasise this by having his arms embellished with precious metals. The only purpose of some arms was that of status symbol but the owner can have had little enjoyment from his possession in battle. Psychological factors also play a role in both the form and decoration of arms. Despite the fact that they were impractical they have performed an important role.

Elements are incorporated into arms that establish the courage and manliness of their bearer and this is not just to impress

Late 18th century shackles and chain. Such items formed part of the equipment of those who kept order in addition to arms.

his opponent. The bearer often derives the necessary courage from this too. The fact that the psychological factors are so difficult to describe gave great scope for an armourer. Some of them were extremely creative craftsmen. Psychological factors also play a role in battle.

Think of the red coats that British soldiers wore in the seventeenth and eighteenth centuries. The choice was quite intentional. A mass of soldiers in red always look bigger at a distance than they actually are. This is an optical illusion.

The drum was also a psychological weapon. The manly rhythm stiffened the resolve of the soldiers and created a sense of unity. The fact that arms were also status symbols made them very much subject to fashions.

This is particularly true of armour that is heavily influenced by the style of clothes of the day. Armour is really nothing more than an iron suit of clothes.

For those condemned to death: a guillotine in the sheriff's court of Zwolle town hall, Holland.

Drum of the local militia of Grouw, Friesland, Holland, circa 1830. The drum served a psychological purpose by creating a manly rhythm and sense of unity.

The craftsman made arms are highly sought after by collectors and those in particular that exhibit the craftsmanship of a jeweller are found in major collections and museums. The best pieces are outside the pocket of most collectors but for those prepared to seek further afield there is much still to be found.

Offensive and defensive arms

Arms can be divided into whether they are used for offence or defence. Defensive arms are solely used to protect the bearer and these include helmets, armour, shields, and chain mail. Offensive weapons are those intended to physically harm an opponent, such as swords and daggers, arrows and lances, pikes, guns, and cannons.

Offensive arms can be further subdivided into those which use projectiles and those used at close quarters.

With a projectile the fight can be taken to the enemy whereas other weapons can only be used in hand-to-hand fighting.
In the course of time a considerable variety of both offensive and defensive arms have been developed and to describe them all would require an entire library. Here we must limit ourselves to describing some of the important aspects of arms.

DEFENSIVE ARMS

All the means of protecting the body against attack were developed in the earliest days of civilisation. Shields and helmets have come and gone and come again down the ages. The first helmets were fashioned from bronze and leather and later these were entirely made of iron that offered better protection.
To afford still more protection helmets were equipped with protection for the neck, a visor, and protection for the ears. The crest of many helmets was decorative but also helped recognition during battle. Both these functions can sometimes be recognised in shields.

The nobles in particular bore their crest or arms on the face of their shield. This gave them pride and also made them recognisable in battle. Protection of the body was also provided with chain mail, full armour, or cuirass (consisting of breastplate and backplate). There are three types of armour. One consists of smaller metal plates joined together by cord which was flexible but did not protect well against stabbing thrusts.

Chain mail does protect against stabbing. It consists of small chain links forged together closely and enables the wearer to move fairly freely but does not protect so well against chops and blows. Other armour was 'tailored to fit' the wearer, consisting of fewer and larger plates that were joined together. This provided good protection but restricted the wearer in his movement.

Ladies pistol, circa 1800.

OFFENSIVE WEAPONS

Edged weapons have a sharpened cutting edge and or point to their blade. This does not just include shorter arms such as daggers, swords, and sabres but also lances and spears. The sword has been regarded since early times as a symbol of authority and power. This is because it is heavy enough to inflict injury while being light enough to wield. High technical demands were made of swords which varied between different cultures.

This can be seen during the crusades when the western knights were equipped with hard swords that were mainly intended for thrusting and which broke more easily than oriental swords.
This resulted from the development of armour within Europe. The swords of the Muslims on the other hand were made of damask (or Damascus) metal and their method of waging war relied primarily on chopping and hacking for which the damask blade was more flexible.

This resulted from repeatedly double forging their metal until a whole series of very thin layers were formed that was more resilient. The damask blade by contrast was less suitable for stabbing thrusts. The earliest form of projectile weapons include the javelin, the bow, and the sling.
The crossbow was a later development. The discovery of gunpowder increased

Set of pre-1830 duelling pistols by J. Montigny of Brussels, supplier to the Dutch throne.

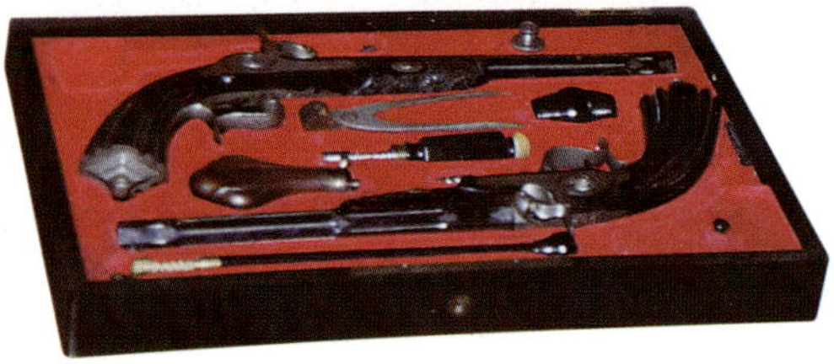

the role of projectiles and brought about a revolution in the style of warfare. Early cannon caused the fall of the previously invincible Constantinople. The Turks had been unable to breach the city's walls before they acquired cannon. The first firearms were cannon but during the late Middle Ages men were striving to develop personal and portable firearms.

The first of these were extremely heavy and were not carried but dragged along. These early muskets had metal plates on the butt of their stocks to protect them from wear. The first hand-held firearms were fired with a fuse and the necessity of first lighting the fuse was extremely inconvenient.

The development of the wheel-lock in the late fifteenth century was therefore a major advance and the flintlock was an even better improvement. Firearms come in myriad different forms. The story is one of continuous improvement with better types and improvement in their projectiles.

A major advance was the development of the cartridge cap which made rear loading of their weapons possible but this also marked the end of individually crafted guns by the gunsmith and introduced the era of mass production for the majority of arms.

Gold and silver smiths

The work of the goldsmith and silversmith includes the artistic creation of objects from gold, silver, and other fine metals.
It was soon discovered that gold and silver could readily be worked and in ancient Egypt and other early civilisations it was preferred to fashion the soft metals of gold, silver, and copper than bronze and iron.

Silver thimble with inscription in 1632 for Antje van Andringa.

Silver brandy bowl, circa 1640. It was customary among Dutch farming communities to pass around a bowl with raisins in brandy on festive occasions. The rich like to ensure they sent a richly decorated silver bowl around the gathering.

Gold and silver have unique properties. They are extremely resistant on the one hand yet can be easily worked by a number of techniques including enamelling and insetting with precious stones.

There are two main types of products from the gold and silver smith: decorative pieces (including jewellery) and useful items (mainly serving ware). Useful does not mean utilitarian of course and precious metals have always been used to denote status and wealth of the owner.
Useful pieces therefore have been made down the ages in precious metals and richly decorated.

German travel cutlery in leather case. Silver gilt, circa 1650.

Gold, silver, copper, and brass

Gold is regarded as one of the most precious metals in virtually every part of the world with its intense lustre and attractive yellow colour.
Gold can be rolled out easily and is elastic but it is also resistant to acids and is indissoluble by most substances. Gold is a mineral found as nuggets and dust that can also be sieved from sediments and this is probably how the ancient myth of the Golden Fleece arose.

Gold was found in ancient times by laying a sheep's fleece in a river. Lighter sediments washed through the hairs of the fleece but the heavier gold remained trapped. Silver is a white and very shiny metal that retains its colour for a long time in exposure to air and only tarnishes to black when exposed to sulphur vapour or hydrogen sulphide.

For this reason silver was often coated with a thin layer of gold in the past. Silver ore is mined. Silver is less heavy than gold and also less valuable. Pure gold and silver are too soft for practical purposes and so they are alloyed with other metals. Silver is mixed with copper and gold is mixed with copper and silver. This makes the metal sufficiently hard for use.

The addition of other metals particularly influences the colour of gold.In addition to gold and silver, both copper and brass are also used to make decorative items with copper being easily gilded

Metal working

The two precious metals plus copper and brass can all be worked in the same ways. The first of these is to melt the metal and then to cast it in a mould of copper, lead, wax, or sometimes of wood. Complex objects are cast in several pieces which are then joined together with screws or solder.

The more difficult technique is forging or beating the cold metal with a hammer until it is thin. This can be done with gold, silver, copper, and brass without losing its elasticity and resistance. The metal is repeatedly hit with blows close to each other while it is turned and pressed until it assumes the desired shape.

It is easiest to make a piece from several pieces and then solder them together. Objects made from a single piece of metal are of the highest quality.
The decoration is also produced using chases, punches, and hammers. It is also possible to fashion gold and silver by beating it over a hard metal form.
A similar technique is to emboss the metal by beating it into fixed dies of bronze, iron, or stone.

This causes an indentation on one side and raised relief on the other.

Silver Louis XIV coffee pot of 1716.

A related technique enables the design to be struck or stamped into one side of the metal as in the case of coins and medals.

Silver ewer and large dish made as a display piece in the 17th century by Rintie Jans of Leeuwarden, Holland.

Silver Louis XIV tray of 1752 engraved with the arms of the Dutour de Beaufort family.

A gentleman's grooming set of 1716 made in Amsterdam, including powder boxes, candlestick, wig brush, and pin cushion. The mirror is missing.

Decorative techniques

The most widely used technique for decorating gold and silver is filigree. Small beads of gold and silver are soldered to the surface and this can also be associated with open work executed with thin threads of silver to form grills, stems, or spirals.

In addition to being cast or forged, the metal is also chased and burnished which gives it an animated and artistic appearance. A sand-bag or lump of pitch is placed under the surface being worked on and the smith then chases or punches scrolls, lines, and small patterns into the metal. For a smooth finish the underground is punched.

Engraving is really related to chasing, with the smith drawing designs with a sharp scribe in the soft metal. So that the engraved lines stand out better they are filled with a soft composition of sulphur and silver and or copper known as niello. In the late eighteenth century

Silver 18th century Louis XV tray.

a method was introduced of machine engraving that enabled uniform engraving including long lines, waves, circles, and bows. The technique was mainly employed for engraving clock and watch dials and boxes. Etching is a technique used to apply graphics in which the piece is covered with a layer of resin or asphalt with honey. The design is then scratched in this layer after which the piece is immersed in the etching solution.

Only the areas scratched away are eaten away, leaving their surface matt. The

Louis XVI style table bell, circa 1780.

silversmith can also created open-work areas by cutting or filing metal away. Silversmiths also used to apply enamel which formed an extremely important decorative technique.

This meant that they also needed to be adept at painting pictures. Enamel is a layer of glass that is melted or fired on the surface. Powdered glass with a

Silver 18th century Louis XVI tray.

This 18th century silver tobacco jar on wooden base is a country piece.

plant-based binding agent is used to create enamel and this is melted on the surface of the piece to be decorated at a high temperature. The enamel bonds closely to the surface.

The artistic effects are achieved by using different colours of glass. A related form of decoration to enamelling is niello in which a mixture of borax, copper, lead, and silver are applied to engraved lines. The mixture is burned into the piece using a gentle flame. There is a variety of enamelling techniques.
With *émail cloissonné* golden thread is soldered to the metal and then different colours of glass are applied between these threads before the glass is melted to form enamel.

With *émail champlevé* the fields to be raised are first recessed before being filled with a glass mixture. Transparent glass is used for the process of silver enamelling. The design is first chased or engraved in the silver before being covered with transparent molten glass. A delightful play of light is created by the reflection of light from the silver. With gold enamelling, figures that have been cast are partially or wholly covered with either transparent or opaque enamel.
With Limoges enamel or enamel paint the sheet metal is covered with a melted layer of colour.

A bit of late 18th century propaganda: cameo of Willem V of Holland (1748–1806).

This is then covered with a painted picture or design in different colour enamel paints which is then fixed by firing. These representations in enamel are often framed in gold. During the Middle Ages and the Renaissance a single colour enamel base was used with cold enamel.

Unique fer de Berlin *jewellery made of cast iron in Berlin. Silver was given to the state in Napoleonic times for war funds and ladies wore cast iron jewellery.*

The paint has flaked off most of these pieces. The technique of painting with enamel is far better. This process uses paints based on metal oxides which are applied to an enamel base (usually white).In the eighteenth century it was fashionable to decorate objects with several different colours of gold. This was also known as *argent à quattre couleurs.*

Decoration with precious metals

Bronze or iron can be encrusted with gold or silver by two different methods. The design can be engraved into the hard metal and then filled with gold or silver wire beaten into place or gold or silver leaf can be placed on the surface of the metal to be decorated and then struck into the surface whereby it binds to the background.

Cheaper metals can also be gilded to given them the appearance of gold. The earliest method of this is that already described of striking gold leaf into the surface of the base metal. This is known as cold gilding. A variant of this process was used for making silver plate. Silver plate or Sheffield plate was invented in Sheffield in 1743 when it was discovered that a layer of silver could be made to adhere to copper with use of solder by pressing them together.

Silver Empire tea caddy of 1831.

Dutch Empire-style mustard pot of blue glass and silver.

Perhaps the finest gilding process was to dissolve gold in mercury before coating the mixture on the item to be gilded.

The surface was then fired but since this released poisonous mercury vapour the process is extremely harmful. This was resolved in 1805 when electro-plating was discovered, using a galvanising process.

Empire-style salt, pepper, and mustard set.

Late Empire style Dutch silver tobacco jar and pot warmer.

History of gold and silver smithery

The earliest items made of precious metals have been found in prehistoric graves. Many other items have been made in the thousands of years since then. The gold and silversmith's art reached high levels during the Roman empire.

When the western part of the empire fell into decline these techniques were upheld in the eastern part of the empire and the Byzantines extended these.

There are surviving examples though of early Middle Ages craftsmanship in precious metal from western Europe. The emphasis during this period was on sacred items with non-sacred pieces being increasingly made in the late Middle Ages.

These items were made not just for the nobility but also for well-to-do citizens, town aldermen and the guilds. While Gothic continued to hold sway for a long time to the north of the Alps, goldsmiths and silversmiths in Italy were strongly influenced by the Renaissance. Their art was largely concentrated in Rome, Florence, and Venice.

These craftsmen sought to use classical forms of deco-ration from ancient antiquity. Even great artists such as Michelangelo kept these craftsmen busy.

They did not make pieces themselves but supplied designs for the smiths to make. The effects of the Renaissance slowly pushed north of the Alps and reached its heights around 1600.

BAROQUE AND ROCOCO

The Contra-Reformation was the Roman Catholic church's reaction to the Reformation. This placed great emphasis upon influencing the ordinary believer and the goldsmith and silversmith had a key role to play in this. The style which relates to the Contra-reformation is Baroque. Catholic churches were excessively decorated, including work of gold and silversmiths.

Non sacred pieces in gold and silver were also created in the Baroque style of course. Just as they had taken a leading role in the art of painting, the Dutch also became notable goldsmiths and silversmiths. German smiths were influenced by the Dutch from the late sixteenth century but the best period for the Dutch master craftsmen was in the eighteenth century.

Display pieces were extremely popular at this time and most of these were made of silver. Superb pieces were made for the guilds in the sixteenth and seventeenth centuries and also pieces for special occasions such as the silver boxes the bridegroom gave to his future wife, containing traditional tokens or coins. Silver also found its way into the wealthier homes resulting in superb eighteenth century silver tea caddies and bread baskets.

Two silver biscuit barrels, circa 1820.

Silver wool basket, 1824.

FRANCE

All the arts in France were controlled by the life at court including the crafts of gold and silversmiths. A number of leading artists and craftsmen worked in the court of Louis XIV, some of whom also occupied themselves with making objects of precious metals.

Architects such as Jean le Pautre and Jean Bérain published engravings of their work in this area and these were spread throughout Europe where they were of great influence. The most famous French gold and silversmith was Claude Ballin who had many commissions from the court at Versailles.

In the late seventeenth century gold and silver objects were of large proportions and richly decorated with egg and tongue and parallel mouldings, with pediments and ribbons and acanthus leaves.

Enamel decoration on silver was also extremely popular. Between 1715 and 1735 the decorations became lighter in touch and more informal. Eventually the asymmetric forms of Rococo took over. Serving dishes and tableware became lighter and more elegant. Medallions were widely used as a form of decoration. The most famous craftsmen were Pierre Germain and Juste Aurèle Meissonier (who was also an architect), who created more than 1200 designs. The greatest volume of silverware stems from the period 1735–1770 of the Louis XV style. His court had precious metal craftsmen such as Thomas Germain and his son François working for them. Their work reflected the playful and curvilinear style of Rococo.

GERMANY

Augsburg in Germany was an extraordinarily important centre for working in precious metals at the end of the eighteenth century. The number of silversmiths in the town grew from 190 in 1696 to 275 in 1740. The Augsburg craftsmen were strongly influenced by French examples. Augsburg silver was exported throughout Europe as far afield as Russia. Master silversmiths were attracted to Augsburg from throughout Germany. Well-known names among these include Elias Adam of Zilchau, Bernhard Heinrich Weyhe of Osnabrück, and Salomon Dreyer of Elbing. There were also families that produced a succession of Augsburg craftsmen such as the Biller, Busch, Meitnacht, Pfeffenhauser, and Thelot families. The Drenthwatt family worked as silversmiths from the early seventeenth to the late nineteenth century.

Two silver Biedermeier teaspoons.

A 'young Biedermeier' silver tea and coffee service from the Black Forest, circa 1820.

CLASSICISM

During the reign of Louis XVI all forms of applied arts turned towards Classi-

Three eau de la Reine containers and a nutmeg case (the taller one).

Early 19th century silver tobacco box.

cism, including that of gold and silversmiths. Famous craftsmen in precious metals at the French court included François Thomas Germain and Robert Josephe Auguste. French silversmiths used classical household items that were excavated at Pompeii and Herculaneum as their examples.

Early 19th century silver shoe buckles worn with traditional costume by men in Friesland, Holland.

Early 19th century ladies' handbag embellished with.

Silver bottle stand with fine open-work, circa

Silver fish knife and fork, circa 1850.

During the French Revolution a great deal of French silver was stolen or lost. Shortly after this the production in Britain of Sheffield Plate started to depress the work of silversmiths. Products had to be less expensive and greater emphasis was placed on ease and speed of manufacture. Consequently the craft skills of hand forging were lost and products were pressed as in Britain.

The Rococo style held sway until about 1775 in the main German centres for

Country style silver tobacco box, circa 1860.

Two silver fish servers. One has a beaded border, the other has an ivory handle.

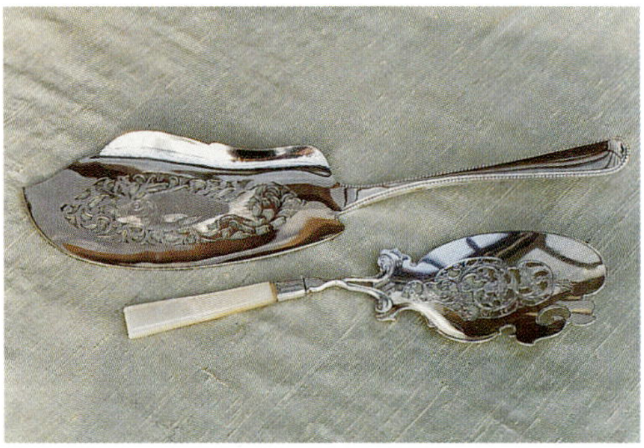

silversmiths with Classicism not making inroads into Germany until about 1780. Pressing also pushed the craft skills of forging into the background here too.

English silver

English silver developed quite independently from the continent. Early English

Silver knitting needle holder, circa 1870.

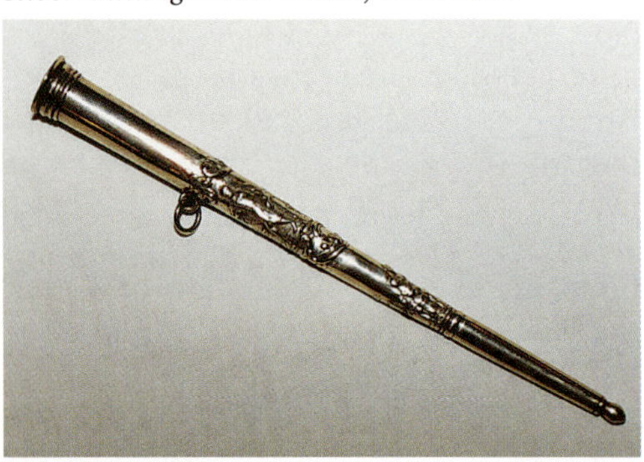

Silver matchbox marked 'Juni 1878'.

Silver number set for persons with large numbers of visitors. This set is unusual: most sets only ran to 12.

Two silver sugar scoops, circa 1890.

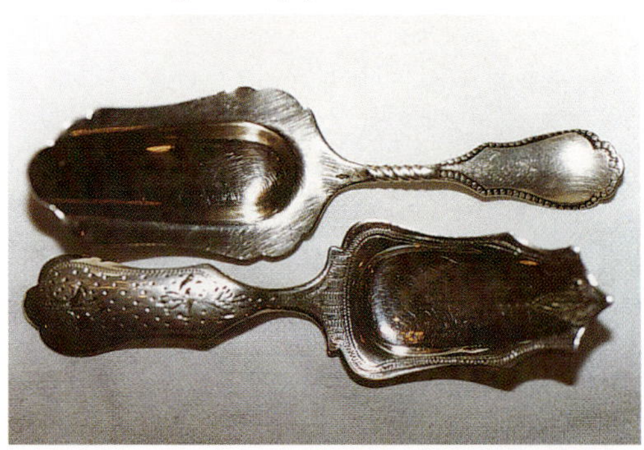

This late 19th century silver hat pin was used to hold the hat brooch of Friesian traditional costume in place.

Late 19th century Friesian gold hat brooch.

German 19thC water boiler.

Silver 19th century Delft tray with beaded border. The open work (see detail) is very fine.

silver was collected from early times so that many examples have survived. England's wealth as a trading nation attracted many craftsmen from Europe.
A large group arrived in England from France following the revocation of the edict of Nantes (1685). The most important centres were London, Birmingham, Exeter, York, Newcastle, and Sheffield. In Ireland the centres were Cork and Dublin and the Scottish centres were Edinburgh, Dundee, and Glasgow.

The high-point for English silver was during the period of Queen Anne from 1689–1727. Silver from this period is tasteful, simple, and of fine style. The decoration is generally limited to gadrooning although some acanthus motifs in the French style of Le Pautre also exist. A common form of decoration is the monogram of the owner or heraldic representations. Although English silver retained its own character, mid-Georgian silver of 1727–1760 shows the most influence from decorative styles used on the continent. Silver produced in the style of architect and furniture maker Robert Adam is an example of Classicism.

He designed tea and coffee pots, dishes, terrines, tea caddies, slender vases, and urns that were inspired by classical examples. Candlesticks of this style, with vase and goblet-shaped column on a square base are typical of Sheffield. English silversmiths in turn greatly influenced continental silversmiths.

The nineteenth century

The market for silver changed radically around 1800. The emphasis shifted to cheaper silver plate from factories in Sheffield and Birmingham. The Empire style in Europe and to some extent the Regency style in England kept some craftsmen going a while longer and large and pompous items of silver for display were essential for the court ceremonial of Emperor Napoleon during his rule.

The Empire style silversmiths derived their ideas from the age of the Roman Empire. Another source of inspiration was Egypt where the French were carrying out excavations. Important silversmiths of the time included Guillaume Biennais, Jean Baptiste Claude Oriot, and also Robert Joseph Auguste who had already made pieces based on a classical past.

After the fall of Napoleon the silversmiths came under the influence of the Romantic style and much earlier work was also copied. In the 1830 there was a Rococo revival in silver.

Silver 19th century angostura jug.

Early 20th century silver brandy bowl.

Oriental silver butter dish made in the Dutch East Indies circa 1900 for the European market.

Oriental silver peanut dishes, circa 1900.

Shell cameo in silver mount, circa 1900, 45mm ($1^{1}/_{2}$in) high.

Set of teaspoons in the Dutch Nieuwe Stijl, of Van Kempen and Begeer.

The style was first popular in France but quickly caught on in England, Germany, and Austria. Vienna had become an important centre for silversmiths from the beginning of the nineteenth century.
After the Rococo revival hand forging of silver virtually came to an end as the making of silver objects became mechanised. Presses flooded the European market with inexpensive in all manner of – often mixed – styles. Only a few pieces can be found that were designed by leading artists.

There was little sign of craftsmanship until the temporary resurgence of craft production around 1900 as a result of the influence of the Arts and Craft, Jugendstil, Sezession, and Art Nouveau movements which is clearly apparent in silver of the time. These movements arose out of the other visual arts and are striking for their use of the naturalism found in Japanese art. This is most apparent in the floral motifs and patterns.

Set of silver teaspoons, circa 1900.

Close-up of a Jugendstijl strawberry spoon.

Dutch Jugendstil lobster spoon.

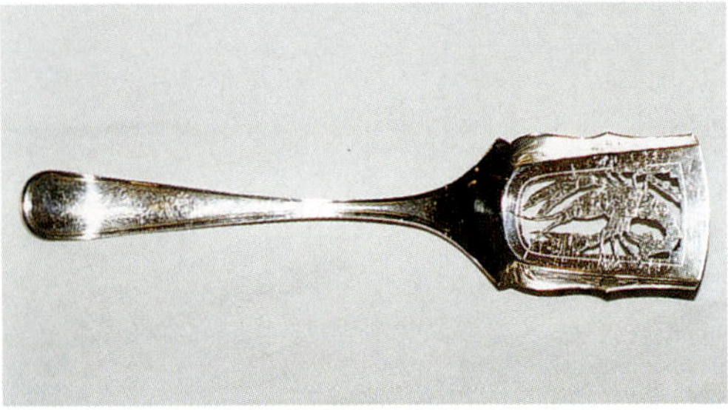

French Art Nouveau silver bonbonnière.

Hallmarks

In comparison with other antiques, silver usually has the advantage of being marked which enables fairly accurate dating and identification of the maker. The countless marks can be found in a host of reference books. Problems arise when the mark is illegible, not found in published lists, or is not present. This indicates the likelihood that the piece is of dubious origin or was made outside the various controls of the authorities, guilds, court, or cloister workshop.

There are various types of mark. The first of them is the assay mark. The town of the assay office is generally denoted with its initial letter or its arms.

The content of precious metal started to be indicated from the seventeenth century onwards. Years used to be indicated with letters but this system was not uni-

Late Jugendstil silver vases, 1922, 100mm (4in).

French Art Nouveau silver handbag fittings.

Two French Art Nouveau silver mustard pots. Unfortunately the glass inserts are missing.

Russian silver gilt liqueur set in original box. It is transitional between Jugendstil and Art

formly introduced in every country. This occurred in France in the fifteenth century but did not occur in Germany until the eighteenth century.

In addition to the assay mark the maker's mark is also stamped, introduced in England, France, and Germany in the fourteenth century. This did not happen elsewhere until the sixteenth century.

Late 19th century bonbon dish.

Six 20th century bonbon dishes. These pieces show how difficult it is to spot reproductions on sight alone. Top left: repro Biedermeier, cast circa 1950; top centre: dishes of 1930; top right, and bottom row: newly cast reproductions of Biedermeier designs.

The maker's mark is generally in the form of a monogram or house mark. The silversmiths were required to lodge their mark in the guildhall or town hall to prevent its misuse. Pieces may also carry other marks indicating importation or repair. It was always essential with repairs to be able to show that a piece was not new and that duty had been paid.

Nautical objects

There is considerable interest in objects that are related to the sea and shipping. These antiques take many forms.

Boat's compass, circa 1810.

Maritime chronometer, Amsterdam 1890. Chronometers were essential to determine longitude.

Apart from the Asian objects dealt with elsewhere in this book, antiques from exotic countries are not really dealt with in this book although seafarers often collected them. They fall outside this book's scope.

Other objects are directly related to shipping itself such as ship's models, but also objects that indicate how satisfied a shareholder or shipowner was with the prosperity of his company or ship but maritime misfortunes were also sometimes marked.

Maritime ornaments

Many fine objects originate from boats and ships themselves, falling broadly into two categories: those that were used for decoration and those required for navigation. Once humankind started to make longer voyages they started to decorate their vessels. This is true both of vessels plying the inland waters as those at sea.

English 19th century artificial horizon.

Because most vessels were made of wood, woodcarving was the main form of ornamentation. Such carvings were often also painted or even gilded.

Navigation instruments

Learned Portuguese and their seafarers made considerable contributions in the sixteenth century to the development of navigation instruments.

They were the first to use the astrolabe among other advances. This was a metal ring that was marked with degrees. A moving pointer in the centre with

Early 19th century telescope.

shadow fins was attached to the centre. This was used to sight the sun and when the shadows converged at a point he was able to read of the angle of the sun which enabled him to ascertain latitude. The Jacobs' staff was an improvement on the astrolabe and was used until well into the eighteenth century to determine latitude. It had a movable diagonal staff that was moved to and fro until the sun and the horizon were aligned with respectively the top and bottom of the Jacob's staff. The Davis quadrant of 1594 was an improvement on the Jacob's staff and this was followed in 1717 by the sextant and 1731 by the octant.

Both these instruments allowed more accurate calculation of latitude. The determining of longitude was at first done by means of sand timers but this was not sufficiently accurate. Precise measurement only became possible when a maritime chronometer was developed (see chapter on clocks).

Model ship's stove based on a real galley, made in the 19th century on board a Dutch freighter.

Other tools and charts

There were many other objects on board ship in addition to navigation instruments, tools, and other typical maritime items. These include charts, compasses, and dividers to help determine a ship's position, ordnance, telescopes, barometers, sea chests, bosun's whistles, and many other things.

Riga jars, 19th century. Seamen brought these jars from the Baltic.

Books

The word book used in the Germanic languages as book, *Buch*, and *boek* is derived from *bôk* which relates to the origins of a surface of beech wood into which letters were carved. This is similar to the Latin *liber* which originally meant bark of a tree but came to be associated with books.

Even the Greek word *biblion* has a similar derivation in that it is derived from the Syrian harbour of Byblos through which the Greeks once shipped large volumes of papyrus on which to write. Papyrus is a kind of paper made from reed stems that has been used in Egypt since ancient times.
Even the name of The Bible is derived from the town of Byblos. Books were written in the early civilisations of Assyria and Babylonia. The letters were impressed in tablets of clay. A similar

Illuminated 15th century manuscript on parchment. It lies open at a page that is clearly much used. The priests have laid their hands on the pages and their sweat has damaged the calligraphy and illumination.

method was used in western civilisation with wax. One advantage of the wax method was that the wax could be reused.

The most widely used writing material of the Hellenic empire and first centuries of the Roman empire was papyrus. Sheets of papyrus were about ten meters (33 ft) long and they were rolled up. A book consisted of a number of papyrus rolls. The Latin world for these roles is *volumen* and the word survives today for a part of a book.

Parchment started to be more widely used from the second century BC. This

The founding deed of a funeral fund of Groningen, Holland. The participants names were added between 1318 and the reformation.

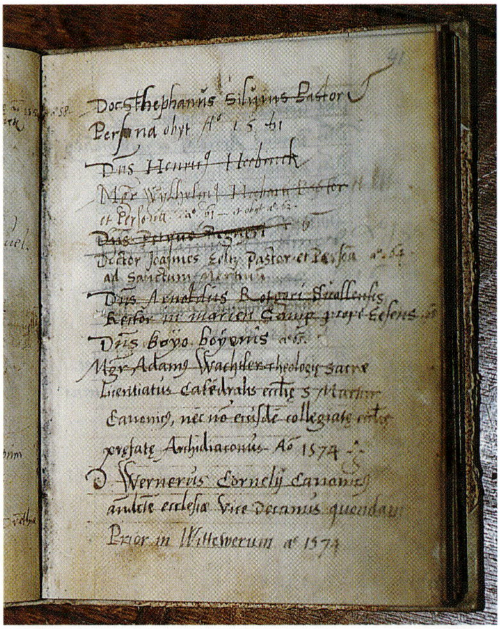

had been developed centuries earlier at the Greek town of Pergamum in Asia-Minor. Parchment is a non-oiled, smoothed animal skin.

The skin is thoroughly scraped before being treated with hydrated lime and

Title page of a book by Hugo de Groot of 1657, produced by the famous printer, Johannis Blaeu.

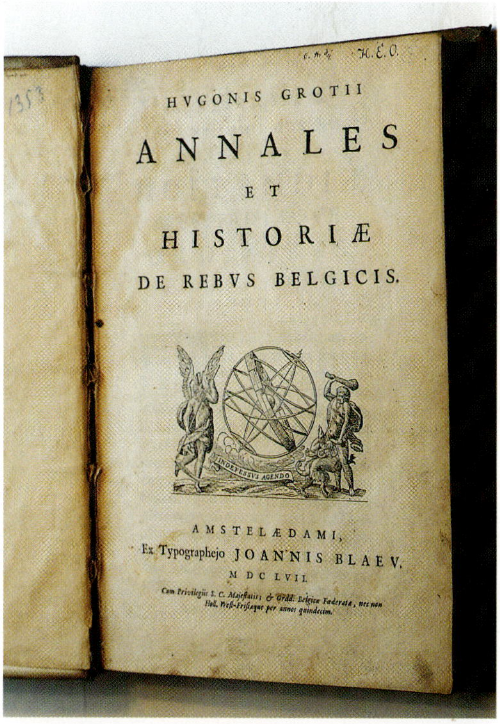

then dressed using a pumice stone before being cut to size. Parchment is yellow-white and somewhat translucent. Sheets of parchment are first folded double before being bound into a book. Four of these double-folded sheets form a quire. A numbers of quires were in turn brought together in a codex, derived from the Latin word caudex that referred to a pair of waxed forms joined together.

The Chinese invention of making paper from fibres found its way to Europe in the twelfth century. Parchment then went into slow decline. Books were once duplicated by slaves and professional scribes. This task was carried out by the monasteries in western Europe in the Middle Ages. The hand lettering and illumination of books was considered godly. Many superbly decorated books were created at this time. Because parchment was so costly it was not uncommon for

English Bible of 1777.

Dutch Authorized Bible printed in Dordrecht in 1777. The silver fittings show that as well as being read this belongs to a wealthy person.

old texts to be rubbed off so that the parchment could be re-used. Several lost texts have been discovered on these palimpsests.

Printing was invented in the Far East. The Chinese printed with blocks around 770 and soon after the start of the second millennium a system was developed to print using separate cast characters. At almost the same time in various places in Europe efforts were being made to develop a practical printing system. The first tangible results were achieved in Mainz in 1447 – probably by John Gutenberg – with the printing of an astronomical calendar for 1448. There are a number of potential candidates for the invention of the process including the Dutch man

Paper is not just for printing on. This loose-leafed album of poetry is from the early 19th century.

Laurens Janszoon Coster of Haarlem. Books printed before 1501 are known as incunabula. They are priceless and only to be found in libraries, museums, and in the collections of extremely wealthy persons. The art of printing spread quickly throughout Europe in the fifteenth century and it soon became possible to make large numbers of identical books. This also broke through the religious monopoly of literacy. This aspect in particular played an extremely significant role in Europe's history because it established a basis for the non religious.

With the establishment of letter cutters and founders in the sixteenth century a certain amount of specialisation occurred in printing but little else changed. The printer continued to be the bookseller, publisher, and printer for several centuries.

The first steam-driven press was installed at *The Times* in London in 1814 with printing only really developing more rapidly in the nineteenth century.

A major problem for the collector of written and printed material can be the paper and ink used. Certain inks were highly acidic so that in closely set text the ink has eaten through the paper. Much the same can be true of the glues used to bind books.

Not only do the bindings perish, they also damage the paper. Much paper made before 1800 used linen fibres which do not cause a problem but with the growing demand for paper wood pulp was used. This paper is of a lower quality.

A friendship album of 1787 with fine paintings.

An example is the newspaper left on a window sill. It becomes hard and brittle. This happens with other paper too that eventually will disintegrate. Neutralising the acids in books is extremely skilled work that can only be used for very special books.

American antiques

Those who decide to collect American antiques need to consider a number of points. Will they only collect pieces from the United States or does the interest include the rest of North America, including native American, Mexican, and Spanish objects. This chapter deals with antiques that originated in the United States and have a western cultural background.

These are objects from what is now the USA belonging to immigrants and their descendants of between 1620 and 1900. The objects must have been made after Christopher Columbus discovered America in 1492.
Canadian and imported antiques are not included and the same is true of pieces of native American origin. The majority of America styles bear a close affinity with English. Because most American antiques are more expensive than their English counterparts dealers try to sell English pieces as American.

With wooden objects an analysis of the wood will yield results. If the timber is not from the American east coast then the object is probably English but there are woods that can be found in both countries and not all antiques are made of wood. It is worth remembering that American style periods prior to 1830 ran about twenty to fifty years behind their English counterparts.
After this date the Americans were far more independent in their style choices and styles also spread more quickly because Americans used printed pattern books.

Prior to 1620 most furniture, household objects, and toys were brought to America from Europe and there is very little information available about them. After 1620 the colonists started to make these items for themselves. These objects are often extremely functional with virtually no ornamentation.
The pieces can be differentiated between those made by craftsmen and those made by other persons. The craftsmen in the towns generally produced finer pieces while the village carpenters turned out more simple items.
Household goods were purely functional. The craftsmen copied English styles but gradually over time they developed their own styles.

Two 19th century carpet bags. Carpet bags are central to American history. After the southern states had lost the Civil War countless 'carpetbagger" from the north got their hands on southern property by dishonest means.

Thomas Jefferson (1743–1826) was one of the Founding fathers of the United States and the country's third President.
In addition to his interest in politics he was also keenly interested in architecture and had a major influence in the adoption of Neo-Classicism. Jefferson encouraged his countrymen and women to direct their energies to establishing their country and not to the production of consumer goods that could be imported. This was fine for the rich of course but

the poor farmers could not afford the cost of shipping goods from Europe and so they quietly continued to make their own things. The effects of the Industrial Revolution became readily apparent after 1840.

Production of furniture was increasingly taken over by factories. Greater numbers of factory produced goods were to be found in the towns but local self-sufficiency continued in the country and particularly among religious communities such as the Amish and Shakers.
The Shakers and Amish people continue not to put their trust in machines. Factory made goods started to be bought by more country folk after 1900.

Sponge decorated American cup of circa 1880.

American styles

THE OAK AGE (1540-1660)

1500-1560	Elizabethan or Early Tudor
1560-1600	Late Tudor
1600-1650	Jacobean or Early Stuart
1650-1660	Commonwealth, known in America as the Puritan Period

THE WALNUT AGE (1660-1730)

1660-1690	Restoration; Carolean or Stuart; late Jacobean
1690-1700	William and Mary
1700-1730	Queen Anne; Early Georgian (incorporating Chippendale)

THE MAHOGANY AGE (1730- 1840)

1730-1810	Georgian or Colonial Style; Classical Revival (also known as Adam Style from the Adam brothers, who introduced an American version of the Classical revival), known in America as Sheraton Style; Directoire (1793–1804) with French influence; Federal Style
1780-1820; 1810-1830	Regency; Greek Revival; Empire. Regency is based on Greek Revival (with lots of Egyptian motifs).
1830-1860	Early Victorian; Gothic Revival

VICTORIAN AGE (1830- 1901)

1830-1860	Early Victorian. Mass production started to replace hand crafting in this era
1860-1880	Mid Victorian
1880-1901	Late Victorian. This style is a combination of Elizabethan, Gothic, and Romano-Greco, with Baroque accents.

Furniture

When the colonists arrived in America they found forests filled with useful timber. They were able to use the timber for all manner of purposes: building their houses, bridges, ships, wagons, spinning wheels, cradles, furniture, household objects, and even tools. In order to create land for a farm the ssettlers needed on

average to fell 6,000 trees. The excess timber was extremely useful for them.
The first settlers were unable to take much with them on the voyage and at first had no home. Until they had built a house or wagon they lived at first in hollows in the hills.
Because getting a roof over their head was the most pressing need for those first colonists there is no surviving American furniture from before 1640.

The political leaders encouraged the settlers to devote all their time and energy to cultivating the land and building their homes rather than to making consumer goods and furniture which could be imported from Europe.
The people had to have some items in their homes though and paintings and drawings from the time make it clear that the colonists quickly made their own furniture and other things they needed. These were used until they were totally worn out.
The homes of this period were sparsely furnished. People sat mostly on crude benches or stools without backs known as forms. Chairs were reserved for important people and honoured guests in the better off households. Most people had chests which served as storage space, seats, and tables. The white pine that grew in the north had few knots in its timber and was extremely durable. The first colonists found it extremely useful.

The oldest known piece of American furniture is assigned to Thomas Mulliner. It is certain that this joiner worked between 1639 and 1650 in the colony of New Haven. The trade of cabinet maker became more commonplace from 1680 onwards.
It is generally easy to ascertain if a wooden object from the seventeenth century was made in America or Europe because the Americans had different types of wood available to them.

Sheridan style 19th century American mirror.

There was a great deal of American oak in the colonies for example which produces an easily worked reddish timber.
Furniture makers in England at this time used the brownish-yellow English oak.
The ubiquitous maple (it is not surprising that the maple leaf is Canada's emblem) was often used for lesser pieces of furniture and soft cedarwood was ideal for the inner parts of furniture such as drawers.

Sturdy and lasting furniture was made with walnut and ash. The only timber that needed to be imported was mahogany that was extremely popular between 1730 and 1840 for the elegant Chippendale, Hepplewhite, Sheraton, and American Empire styles. Mahogany was imported from Haiti and Santo Domingo.
In addition to joiners and carpenters there were also wood turners who specialised in using lathes.

American apple basket, 19th century.

They made fine objects such as spheres, columns, rings, and even vases. By the end of the seventeenth century these craftsmen were mainly chair-makers although they also made objects such as plates, bowls, and handles for tools. What is striking about much early American furniture is that the turning is often of better quality than the rest of the piece. During the colonial era the American furniture makers followed the example of their English colleagues.

European styles arrived in America in three different ways: by the import of furniture, through tradesmen who emigrated to America, and through pattern books from Europe. The poor communications meant that most styles were twenty to fifty years behind England and the rest of Europe. Once more pattern books were printed in the eighteenth century the gap became smaller. The difference between Europe and the colonies meant that different styles overlapped more than they did in Europe. Pieces with elements of several different styles are known as transitional.
The creativity of the Americans also led to variations and even their own new styles. Despite this it can be difficult for the inexperienced person to determine whether a piece is of American origin.
The style eras in Europe and also in China and Japan often were synonymous with the reign of a particular ruler.
This was not the case in America. The furniture makers were dependent on the way in which styles were brought to America.
The Americans chose what they liked and found practical, making adaptations according to personal taste. There were many regional variations in style before 1830.

The introduction of machine production brought greater uniformity and reduced regional variations.
Regional styles were often determined by the type of timber available locally, the origins of the majority of the settlers, economic position, and the principal means of existence in the region. In general terms America had the following style periods in furniture.

Pilgrim (1640–1690)

Furniture of the Pilgrim era is generally characterised by proportions which give it a rather heavy appearance.

Three 18th century American Chippendale style chairs.

Most of the joints are held together with wooden pegs. Main ornamentation is carved relief. Most pieces are made of oak or pine. Authentic seventeenth century American furniture is extremely rare. Buyers need to make sure the piece is neither newer or imported from Europe. Many Pilgrim style pieces have been heavily restored, particularly the legs and table leaves. Ornaments and rungs have often been replaced.

William and Mary (1700–1730)

The dovetail joint was widely used in the William and Mary era. Wood carving is in high relief. The pieces of furniture are generously proportioned and contrasting surfaces. The use of lacquer, veneer, elaborate mouldings, and bun feet are characteristic. The main types of wood used are walnut, maple, and pine. A weak point is that heavy pieces often stand on very thin legs that have been turned several times. They are often therefore often replaced or restored. Many pieces sold as 'William and Mary' were not lacquered until the nineteenth century.

Queen Anne (1725–1755)

Queen Anne furniture is characterised by refined scrolled form. The lacquered furniture has cabriole legs and hooped seats. The most widely used types of wood were walnut, cherry, and mahogany. Many parts have also been replaced with Queen Anne furniture. Most American Queen Anne is reproduction and it is quite common to find the bottom of a tall chest of drawers reworked to make a dressing table. Genuine Queen Anne chests are extremely rare and to be found only in museums.

The highest prices are paid at auction for Queen Anne furniture from Boston, Newport, and Philadelphia but here too the buyer needs to be wary for the name of one of these cities can be assigned to increase the value of a piece.

Chippendale (1755–1790)

Chippendale style furniture is characterised by Chinese motifs, Gothic arches, 'C' and 'S' form scrolls, and claw and ball

American china cabinet with rounded glass front, filled with English strawberry pattern china.

American Hepplewhite style mahogany and veneer folding card table, circa 1770.

American Chippendale style late 18th century side chair.

American Chippendale style mahogany chair made in Philadelphia, circa 1780.

American Chippendale style table. Note the typical form of the table leaf.

feet. The centre part of chair backs are fretcut or 'woven'. Chippendale style furniture is almost exclusively mahogany and that from the southern states is often more highly ornamented. New England furniture makers made greater use of wood carving. The carvings have often been extensively altered to make the pieces more appealing. Some plain rims have been scalloped. Chippendale style is also a target for dubious pieces.

Federal Style (1790–1815)

After the American Revolution America changed from a colony into an independent federation of United States. The Federal Style borrowed much from European Neo-Classicism and since the French had supported the Revolution it was French styles that were used as a basis by American furniture makers. Three producers of pattern books – Alice and George Hepplewhite, and Thomas Sheraton – imprinted their stamp upon

the style and some experts consider that their influence was so important that they deserve to be regarded as styles in their own right.
The Federal Style is characterised by very refined rectilinear forms, geometric proportions, symmetry, mosaics, and con-

American Federal Style walnut dining set.

Late 18th century American Windsor chairs in original red lacquer made by A.F. Bullock.

American Hepplewhite style cabinet with 19th century hair combs.

American Hepplewhite style mahogany with inlay card table.

American Sheraton style bed, circa 1820.

trast of light and dark. Accents were often created by inlaid banding. The most widely used materials were mahogany with maple, ebony, and beech veneers. Both the mosaics and the veneers have often been replaced in the past and sometimes the surfaces have been too robustly cleaned or restored so that the contrast between light and dark tones has been lost.

The most popular pieces are those that remain closest to the original pattern books. Reprints of these books are available throughout the United States.

Empire (1815–1865)

American Empire style furniture is characterised by its heavy appearance. There is an emphasis on archaeological examples and ormolu (a mixture of copper and zinc used as imitation gold) is extensively used, together with gilding of parts, carv-

American mahogany chair made in Boston circa 1780.

ing, simple dark veneer, and legs resembling animal legs. American Empire pieces are chiefly made in mahogany and rosewood. Most of the decoration is ormolu and vert antique. The Empire style was not popular for long and there are few reproduction pieces being passed off because reproduction of Empire is extremely labour intensive. Gilded parts prove often to have been repaired and it is important to check if the piece has been re-veneered. A certain amount of restoration is acceptable but entirely new veneer is not. The Empire style is a good place for beginners to start collecting American antiques.

Pillar and Scroll or French Restoration (1830–1870)

After Napoleon was deposed people turned away from the excessively ornate Napoleonic architecture and furniture of the Empire style. Furniture from this period is characteristically simple, comfortable, and utilitarian. Sweeping curves are complemented with geometric shapes. The furniture has little ornamentation but does have large veneered surfaces.

The simpler designs made standardisation and therefore mechanised production possible in America. This caused regional style variations to start to disappear. Mahogany and rosewood were widely used. The large areas of veneer have a tendency to lift. The veneer may have been substantially repaired during the life of the piece.

Gothic and Elizabethan Revival (1830–1865)

The designs of the Gothic and Elizabethan Revival turn back to the Middle Ages and the reign of Queen Elizabeth I of England. The style incorporates pointed arches, banding, plaited columns, and spirals.
This style never became as popular in America as in England. American examples mainly result from architects incorporating them into buildings. Because this style was linked to churches in which men played the leading role, it was regarded as a masculine style and women often regarded the furniture as impractical. Generally only the library of large houses were furnished in this style, where the men sat to smoke. Although Gothic and Elizabethan Revival pieces regularly come on the market there is little interest in them. The excessive ornamentation is susceptible to damage and often restored. Many pieces are a combination of Gothic and Elizabethan.

Rococo Revival (1840–1870)

This style is characterised by 'C' and 'S' form scrolls. These were mixed in the

American 19th century dining table and chairs.

Revival with shells, leaves, and flowers (especially roses). This style is less a revival of Rococo than an exaggeration of major styles. Characteristics of the Rococo Revival include laminated wood and very precise and organic wood carving.

American Rococo Revival furniture was chiefly made of rosewood, mahogany, and walnut. Industrialised production had become commonplace by this time and many pieces are factory made. Craftsman made pieces are hard to find. Frequent temperature changes may have caused the laminated layers to separate.

Revival of Renaissance, neo-styles, Grecian and Egyptian (1850–1890)

These style revivals are all part of the Victorian style. Renaissance Revival is also known as Victorian Renaissance. The characteristics of these styles varied

American 19th century bonheur du jour.

American folding skating chair to push a lady over the ice. F. Ashley patented such chairs in 1861.

widely as a result of the freedom with which makers interpreted them. Generally it can be said that the proportions and details are exaggerated. At first the forms were rounded and organic but around 1870 furniture became more rectangular and lips and corners were frequently moulded.

Architectural styles were also imitated such as sphinxes, animal's feet, and exotic mosaics of Egyptian origin. Many American pieces from this era are often very confusing for newcomers to collecting. It is necessary to have seen many pieces before it is possible to differentiate these styles and their transitional forms. Initially most of these pieces were made from walnut or mahogany although rosewood and ebony were also popular. Pine was used for less expensive pieces. Restoration of the mosaics and carving of these pieces can be very expensive.

Innovative (1850–1900)

Styles constantly arose throughout the nineteenth century other than the current ones of the time. New materials were experimented with such as machine-produced papier mâché, metal, and natural materials such as stone and tree trunks. There were also attempts to equip furniture with all manner of gadgets. People were fascinated with portable, reversible, and fold-away furniture. The invention of the coil spring was one of the greatest innovations in the history of furniture. The most crazy items of furniture flooded the market.

The quality of these pieces varied enormously. The problem with this type of furniture is that the mechanical elements are often broken and the metal parts have been painted so frequently that the clean lines of the original design have been lost. Furniture made from papier mâché needs to be kept at a constant temperature and not be allowed to become damp.

Design Reform (1870–1915)

Design Reform was a counter to the unbridled ornamentation of the other styles that were fashionable at the time. Design Reform followed two parallel courses. One direction was inspired by Japanese art and the other by the Arts and Craft Movement which modernised Gothic. The magic word of Design reform was simplicity.

The Arts and Crafts Movement also wished to bring back hand made crafts and rejected machine production. Wooden dowels, pegs, and screws are widely used in making these pieces which helps to make them difficult to restore.

Shaker Style

A great deal was produced in this style between 1820 and 1870. Furniture is still being made in Shaker style. Although this style clearly left its mark on American furniture making many respected books on antiques such as Sotheby's Guide to American Furniture barely mention the Shakers, if at all. The Shaker Quakers are a strict religious sect that arrived in the New World under the leadership of Ann Lee in 1774. They started to make furniture for their own use in the late eighteenth century in the eighteen settlements that they had established since their arrival.

These were in Maine, Massachusetts, New Hampshire, Connecticut, New York, Ohio, and Kentucky. These were not experienced woodworkers. Before they could build their houses, barns, tools, and furniture, they first had to fell trees, learn the properties of the different types of timber, and dam streams in order to produce water power to drive their sawmills.

They quickly discovered that pine leant itself readily for use in making fitted furniture. For other types of furniture hardwoods were needed such as maple. Some Shakers also used timber from fruit trees such as cherry, pear, and apple wood Because of its wonderful and enduring sheen cherry was an extremely good choice for table leaves.

There are two types of Shaker furniture. The first type is fitted furniture that belongs in the house into which it was built and the second type is free-standing. The free-standing furniture can be further subdivided into church and home furniture. When people speak of Shaker furniture these days they usually mean tables, beds, benches, and above all chairs.

The Shaker Style reflects the beliefs of the designers. They believed that a frugal life style would help them to attain God's kingdom. Excessive ornamentation and comfort were therefore banished. Shaker furniture characteristically has strongly geometric lines with plain surfaces and functionality. Some people claim that the Shakers copied the style from the Pilgrims and are not themselves creative. This is certainly not true. Their talent lies in simplifying and refining. By removing all artifice and adornment the Shakers were able to design furniture that reflected the essential form and proportions.

The result is very commendable. Although individual achievements were subordinated to the interests of the group as a whole the germs of creativity were not stifled. The names of the extremely capable Shaker furniture makers were known far and wide. People like James Farnum, Gilbert Avery, John Lockwood, George Wickersham, Benjamin Youngs,

Amerikaanse Turner tall chair

Mid 18th century American slat back chair.

Thomas Fisher, and Robert Wagon were so imbued with the spirit of simplicity that they made very refined but unpretentious furniture.

Renowned furniture makers

The first furniture maker arrived in America on the Pilgrim ship The Mayflower. He shipped on board as ship's carpenter and cooper. He was one of the signatories to the agreement that the Pilgrims made before their landing on Plymouth Rock and was the first person to step ashore.
He was immortalised by the famous Longfellow poem that tells of his proposal of marriage on behalf of his friend Miles Standish to Priscilla Mullens. This carpenter's name is John Alden. Once ashore he was appointed magistrate and fulfilled this function for fifty years. John Alden combined his judicial role with his trade. Together with Kenlem Winslow, who also made coffins, he made the essentials for furnishing the homes. About twenty pieces of furniture attributed by experts to Alden and Winslow still exist.

Much of the furniture from the early colonial period was lost in the many fires that occurred through spontaneous combustion of hayricks and the use of naked flames in candles, torches, and open hearths. Ship's furniture has survived better and two dozen upholstered and richly decorated chairs were found on the ship of the infamous pirate Captain William Kidd that he has robbed from well appointed vessels. Pirate ships were a valuable place to search for a time for experts in American antiques. Many superb pieces of furniture were recaptured by these experts.

With the passage of time the country became richer and the houses grew larger. This led to an increased demand for furniture. Furniture makers no longer needed to earn their living with additional lines of work and were able to concentrate on their trade. Some of them made pieces for people further afield, outside their own local community but others had more than enough local work and left exports to others. John Cogswell, who worked in Boston around 1798, was one of these. He proudly labelled his furniture 'Made by John Cogswell in Middle Street, Boston'. Cogswell had good reason to be proud. he made the finest mahogany bombé (convex curving) furniture ever produced in America. Bending mahogany to a precise shape is not an easy process. The first coming together of furniture makers occurred in the wealthy town of Newport, Rhode Island. The rich pirateers and slave traders who lived there were prepared to pay good money for fine furniture made by the families Goddard and Townsend. These two families were related to each other through

marriage, business, and religion (they were Quakers). Thirteen Townsends and seven Goddards made superb furniture in the eighteenth and early nineteenth century in styles that were popular at the time. They introduced the block front and shell motifs.
At the same time Philadelphia was a busy trading centre. There were more than 100 furniture makers in the city in 1722. They made Chippendale style furniture of unparalleled craftsmanship and originality.

Despite the praise that many heaped on them, their lives were not always straightforward or easy. One of the leading furniture makers, Thomas Affleck, was banished to Virginia for seven months in 1797, because he was a Tory. Others were also kept from their work for long periods because of political or economic problems. While craftsmen in Philadelphia such as Jonathan Gostelowe, John Folwell, Thomas Tuft, James Gillingham, and William Savary specialised in well-made furniture decorated with very detailed carving, others concentrated on making items for poorer homes. These makers advertised in the newspapers, offered low prices, short-term credit, and even took furniture in part-exchange. They produced a lot of cane furniture and Windsor chairs that are inexpensive to make.

Many tradesmen lay down their tools and took up a rifle when the American War of Independence broke out. Others made tent poles, camp beds, and chairs for the army. Some furniture makers climbed to the heights in the American army. John Dunlap became a major, Stephen Badlam was an artillery captain and later a general in the Massachusetts' militia. Marius Willet, a renowned chair maker of New York, led the Sons of Liberty when they attacked a British supply column. Two years later he played an important role in the defeat of the British under General Van Burgoyne at Saratoga. The War of Independence made a major dent in the economic situation. Many furniture makers had great difficulty to get their businesses running again.

The War of Independence led to large numbers of European immigrants coming to America. These included the Fife family who scraped together the money in Scotland by hard work for their passage to America. They went to live in Albany, New York state and their son Duncan was apprenticed to a furniture maker. He soon proved to have a talent for the trade.
After his apprenticeship he opened his own workshop and became the most famous American furniture maker of the early nineteenth century. He is also the own American maker of whom there are pieces still in existence in each of the

A 19th century American ladderback rocking chair.

styles then existing. In order to attract more clients Duncan Fife moved to New York city and in 1794 found it necessary to change his name. In order to attract richer clients he now spelled his name as Phyfe.

He got married and could not find enough work to keep his new wife. Phyfe's financial worries ended though when he was commissioned to make furniture for the daughter of the wealthy merchant John Jacob Astor. The trading post of this wealthy merchant had been the cause of a border dispute with Britain that resulted in the United States successfully claiming Oregon. When the furniture was delivered, the Astors were so delighted that they recommended Phyfe to all their friends. Phyfe quickly discovered that he made 'elite furniture for elite people'.

He employed a number of craftsmen and companions. His workshop was too small for the employees and he moved to spacious and well lit premises. Now that he could afford it Phyfe bought pattern books and developed the designs in consultation with his clients. Because the French had supported the Americans in their struggle against the British, increasingly French styles came into vogue. The Directoire style in particular was liked by Americans.

Phyfe combined this with English styles, resulting in an individual style that can be recognised by the bronze lion claw feet. The front feet bend forwards and the rear ones bend backwards. Phyfe liked rounded forms. His chair arms were scrolled, sometimes with an urn-like form. His favourite wood was mahogany with a preference for reddish West Indian timber.

Phyfe was also a businessman through and through. When the Empire style came into vogue during the Napoleonic era, he responded immediately. His work though was more precisely executed than European pieces. Although he was lionised by New York's elite he took little part in the city's social life and was not given to courting publicity. His sons followed in their father's footsteps. In 1840 the style of furniture was not entirely to the Phyfe's liking but they felt forced to make this 'butcher's furniture' in order to survive. In 1847 Phyfe had had enough and stopped work. he still made a few pieces for family and friends while he managed his properties that had become worth $100,000. This highly respected and much copied furniture maker died in his house in Fulton Street, New York in 1854.

Hugo and John Finlay of Baltimore developed their own styles but made furniture to the designs of Benjamin Henry Lathrobe. Lathrobe was commissioned by President James Madison to rebuild the official home of the President after this had been put to the torch by the British in the war of 1812. Lathrobe created the name 'The White House' by covering much of the fire damage with white paint.

The Finlays made painted furniture which was very popular in New York city around 1795. This furniture was designed for use in the living rooms and music rooms of the wealthy citizens. The furniture was made by craftsmen. By 1825 though this furniture was to be found everywhere. Mass production had made them a great deal cheaper.

Lambert Hitchcock, born in Cheshire, Connecticut in 1795 was a major figure in the development of mass production. He set up a small factory in 1818 in Barkhamstead, Connecticut, where he made parts for chairs that were assembled by the people who bought them. There soon proved to be a major interest in his production. Hitchcock shipped his products through the country. In 1825 he stopped making parts and started to make complete, fine chairs. These chairs, that were painted with golden or silver flowers or fruit, were actually produced by a number of different people. In contrast with most other makers of his time though Hitchcock put a label on his furniture saying 'L. Hitchcock, Hitchcocksville, Connecticut, Warranted.' People therefore assumed that Hitchcock had designed the chairs himself and they therefore unjustly became known as Hitchcock chairs. Hitchcock was producing 15,000 chairs per year in 1828 but the competition was so fierce that he was bankrupt in 1829.

The receivers employed Hitchcock to manage the business. Within three years he had the business back on its feet and he got it back. Hitchcock entered into partnership with Arba Alford Jr. in 1830 and married his sister. Four years later he was elected to the state assembly but he continued to run his business. The partnership between Hitchcock and Alford terminated in 1843 when Hitchcock set up a new factory in Unionville, Connecticut. This attempt to start a new venture failed and Hitchcock died in Unionville in 1852.

Meanwhile the Alfords had closed the factory and sold the building. This was used for several purposes for a while and remained empty for a period before eventually being re-opened as a chair works to make chairs by the early nineteenth century methods. These chairs are labelled 'L. Hitchcock, Hitchcocksville, Connecticut, Warranted.'

Another furniture maker who needs to be named is John Henry Belter who originated from Germany. He established a major business in New York city together with his brothers-in-law. He brought over wood carvers from the Black Forest to staff his factory. Belter was also a first class wood carver who provided all his pieces with extremely complex patterns.

American Hitchcock chair with gold inlay, circa 1825.

Belter often gilded his carving so that it had the appearance of machined metal. He never repeated a design, not even when he made a set of 'matching' chairs. Each chair had a small variation. Belter's technique has never been matched. Although most of his designs are of luxurious appearance they were also very practical and comfortable. When he died in 1863 it transpired out that his debts were so high that there was little left for his heirs. He remains though one of America's finest makers of furniture.

After the Civil War manufacturers built factories where there was water available to drive the machinery but there were some people who wanted nothing to do with machine made furniture. Even Harriet Beecher Stowe, author of Uncle Tom's Cabin called on women to refuse to buy this machine made furniture. The designs of such furniture were not based on any given style. The manufacturers were not ashamed to mix all the style together. The 'furniture style' of 1870–1890 is merely a combination of all manner of styles from Grecian to Victorian.

At the end of the nineteenth century a new style eventually emerged. Art Nouveau, with its simplistic decoration that often used natural subjects fitted American tastes very well. With a few years there were a number of Americans such as David Walcott Randall, Thomas Hadley, George Pike, and Paul Frankl who created Art Nouveau furniture that was not inferior to the European examples.

Chairs

Chairs are often the most characteristic example of a given style era and therefore further space is devoted to them here than other pieces of furniture. Furthermore so many chairs have been made that more have survived than other antiques.

Few seats were made with backs before the middle of the seventeenth century. Most people sat on stools, benches, or chests. The few chairs with backs and armrests were much like a throne. Often these chairs had a raised knob on the end of the armrest which helped give the person seated in it additional authority and power. Only the head of the household and very important guests were allowed to sit in such a chair.

Of the three principal types of seventeenth century Pilgrim chair – the turned chair, panelled chair, and Cromwell chair – the most popular was the turned chair. These are now often called Carver or Brewster chairs by experts. These chairs have a double row of rails for the backrest and armrest and beneath the seat. A variant of these are the slatted back chairs brought to America from Holland and Germany.

Chairs with backs became the norm during the William and Mary style era. These high backs were often upholstered with fabric, leather, or cane. The Gaines family of Portsmouth introduced their own William and Mary style design of which the five flat rails are most characteristic. Those examples of the 'banister' chairs with four rails in the back are made by other people. The chairs got the name because the rails of the backrest resembled banister rails. Mahogany and walnut lent themselves best to the carving of minute ornamentation.

The earliest known lounging chair was made in New York around 1708. The chair has a straight backrest with a curved top which is flattened at the top. The rungs are turned and the legs are of Spanish style.

The best known and cheapest example of this type of seating is the 'Boston chair' with its slightly curving backrest that is sometimes known as 'crooked back'. Its frame is often painted red or black.
Towards the end of the William and Mary period the Boston chair got a more oval backrest. This characteristic was carried forward into Queen Anne.

During the Queen Anne period regional variations became apparent. Although everyone stuck to the new more rounded forms that are characteristic of the Queen Anne style, its application varied widely. Extensive ornamentation was used in the south and in Philadelphia but in Boston and Connecticut much more sober results were produced. The backrest was crested in Newport and New York, often with a shell form. The 'lost' space of the backrest universally had the form of a bird's head.

Generally Philadelphia chairs were the most robust because the joints were made with pegged double mortise and tenon. The Queen Anne style brought with it greater comfort. The severe furniture of the Pilgrims was put aside often to be replaced by upholstered seating with Queen Anne style backrests.

Chippendale style chairs, which became fashionable around 1755, introduced important changes in terms of both form and ornament. The seat was usually rectangular and well upholstered. The straight sides of the chair back contrasted with the arched form of the Queen Anne style. Regional variations were chiefly in the manner in which the central splat and the ball and claw feet were made. Central splats with 'owl's eyes' originated from Massachusetts.

The Connecticut makers continued to employ shells and scrolls. In the south there was a preference for graceful geometric forms and in Philadelphia they carved minute hairs on the claw feet. In New York the claws continued through the ball and with Newport chairs the fearsome long and sharp claws remained apparent. At this time lounging chairs were mainly bedroom furniture. Only the extensively sculpted feet related to the Chippendale style.

The 'lolling chair' or 'Martha Washington' chair from Massachusetts combined aspects of both Chippendale and Federal styles. This type of chair had a Chippendale style upholstered back with tapering turned legs in the Federal style. The straight back and thin wooden armrests do not make this such a comfortable lounging chair as its name suggests.

In the first decades of the Federal style dining room chairs had three types of back: the shield, rectangular, or oval back. Although Federal style furniture is generally of light construction American Federal style is finer than European examples.

The upholstered seat was stretched over a wooden frame and held in place by bronze tacks. In comparison with Chippendale style there were few regional variations. Except in New England hardly anyone continued to use foot rails that had featured in previous styles. The main form of decoration was mosaic. The 'scrollback' chair appeared in 1805. This was a forerunner of the revival by the Empire style of the ancient Greek *klismos* chair. The side rails of the chair back are decoratively scrolled towards the rear.

Duncan Phyfe was the leading maker of scrollback chairs. His workshop with its 100 employees made so many of them that they can still be widely found. The Empire style brought about further development and wider acceptance of the scrollback chair. These chairs had a continuous line from the top of the back to the bottom of the legs. In Boston these chairs were given a superbly carved garland and rolled top lath. Extensive carving was less popular in New York yet the central splat is often carved to form a lyre, harp, cornucopia, or an eagle. Instead of the rectangular legs that dominated elsewhere, Baltimore makers preferred rounded legs.

Many American notables such as Thomas Jefferson liked to sit in their 'sling seat' armchair or 'campeachy' chair. This type of chair rested on a cross-form base and was in existence in ancient Egypt. The Romans refined this type of seating by introducing curvilinear form. Campeachy chairs were mainly made in New York, between 1810 and 1820. During the French Restoration era dining room chairs were noticeably French gondola formed with amenable curved backs. Side rails that were curved forwards were intended as armrests.

The 'Voltaire' chair from this era is well-known. This is an easy chair with a sloping and curved back that was thickly upholstered. Many of these chairs were set on castors which is reminiscent of modern office chairs.

The Americans appear to have agreed with Voltaire that this was an excellent type of chair in which to sit and think. In any event they were widely sold. The emphasis shifted at this time to thick upholstery and this trend was to continue for a long time.

Rocking chairs

Americans are very proud that they invented one of the most popular forms of furniture – the rocking chair. It is no longer possible to ascertain who actually created the first rocking chair but the story that Benjamin Franklin was the first in 1787 to have had curved rails set under a chair is not true. An earlier bill from the furniture maker William Savery of 1774 bears the inscription: 'to putting rockers on a chair' for which the charge was one shilling and sixpence.

The rocking chair was brought back into fashion in the 1960s by President Kennedy but furniture makers had started putting curved rockers under existing chairs from the beginning of the eighteenth century to make them more comfortable.

American 19th century child's rocking potty chair.

These early rocking chairs were known as 'carpet cutters' because of the damage done to carpets by repeated rocking in the same place. Rocking chairs existed in whatever style was in vogue such as Windsor, slat back, and banister. Rockers were fixed by notching the legs of the chair which were then fixed to the rockers. This was used for attaching rockers to chairs that had not been made as rockers.

Soon chairs were being expressly designed and made as rocking chairs. These often had heavier duty legs which were jointed to the rockers themselves. These chairs were also often broader with some being up to three times as wide as the early 'carpet cutters'.
Rocking chairs are usually not upholstered and the seats are normally of wood or rush. In order to sit on a soft seat cushions were added.

Most rocking chairs had armrests but the Shakers – renowned for their frugal lifestyle – found this too much of a good thing. They made rocking chairs without armrests and relatively low chair backs. The Shakers were the first to widely use rocking chairs as bedroom chairs for elderly sisters and brethren of the sect, but soon every bedroom had a rocking chair. This led to disagreement with the Shaker Philemon Stewart asking why the Shaker's used so many rocking chairs, suggesting that generation might not be able to find God's way while it sought to make life so easy.

The Boston rocker is a popular form of rocking chair with the earliest known example of this Windsor style chair being made in 1830, probably in Connecticut. The rolled seat is characteristic of these chairs, with the front of the seat curved inwards and the rear curving upwards. Collectors and art historians are particularly interested in the decorations on the chair back and armrests that were often done in gold paint.

These decorations vary from the normal Windsor chairs that traditionally used baskets of fruit, floral motifs, or cornucopia. Instead Boston (known since the War of Independence for the many revolutionaries) stencilled images of important persons, landscapes, and houses on these chairs.
Sea captains who wanted to rock to-and-fro when on dry land took Boston rockers to every corner of globe.

Soon the grandmother knitting in her rocking chair or spinning a yarn became a familiar sight throughout the world. The best way to determine if a rocking chair is genuine or converted is to compare the history of paint on the chair with that of the rockers. If the rockers have fewer layers of paint than the chair then it is almost certain the rockers had been added later.

American cane-backed rocker, circa 1880.

Silver

Many European were drawn to America by tales of gold and silver mines. These mines were in South America and most immigrants who sought gold in North America were disappointed. Many gold and silversmiths made the journey to America in certainty that there would be a ready supply of their raw materials.

Silverware was popular in Europe because it offered better protection against theft than silver coins because the owner's name could be engraved on the piece which also bore the maker's mark. Because silversmiths received coins from their customers they took on a function similar to that of a bank and therefore needed the trust of their clients. Although there was less silver than anticipated in the New World, silversmiths were still able to establish lucrative businesses. Each piece of silver was made to order from the silver coins that the customer provided. On top of this of course the work input had to be paid for.

Just as was the case with other trades, Boston, New York, and Philadelphia were the first towns in which silversmiths flourished. Boston was the richest and most developed town of the colonies. Silversmith found ready customers. Because of the great demand for their wares and the trust they enjoyed, silversmiths enjoyed a higher social status than other trades.

The first colonial silverware was made in Boston. Nieuw Amsterdam (later to become New York) followed a generation later. Philadelphia followed fifteen years after New York. It was not until the eighteenth century that the depressed agricultural economies of North and South Carolina, Virginia, and Maryland saw silversmiths active.

The first silver of Nieuw Amsterdam followed Dutch styles characterised by sturdiness and practicality. The conservative silversmiths continued their Calvinistic Dutch style which proved acceptable to the British puritans. More forward-looking silversmiths combined the Dutch and richly decorated English styles.

Renowned New York (Nieuw Amsterdam) silversmiths were Jacob Boelen, Peter van Dijck, Cornelis Kierstede, Jesse Kip, and Adriaan Bancker. The Quakers made their influence felt in Philadelphia. This resulted in the simplest English forms of silverware. Prior to 1800 some 100 silversmiths were active in Philadelphia. There were three families in the city that had been silversmiths for three generations.

These were the Syngs, the Richardsons, and the Anthonys. Philadelphia had become the richest town in the colonies and capital of the new republic by the end of the eighteenth century. The town was known for its generous hospitality and could boast a number of the finest silver tea services.

There were also famous silversmiths in smaller places such as Hartford and New Haven in Connecticut, Albany in New York, Trenton, and Baltimore. Almost every American town had its own silversmith who might also be a farrier, clockmaker, or innkeeper. Silversmiths found life harder in the south because the rich plantation owners preferred to import English silver.

The Puritan's rejection of unnecessary frippery meant that silverware made between 1650 and 1750 in the New World was very functional. While silversmiths continued to melt down silver coins they started around 1750 to also make silverware using their own silver. The silver coins of the Spanish colonies of South America were extremely popular for this purpose. American silver mines only managed to meet local demands after 1852.

Because silver is a valuable metal and regarded as a sensible investment, many silver objects have survived. These are often family heirlooms that have been passed down through families for generations. A silver tea service is still a status symbol. The expression 'born with a silver spoon in the mouth' points to the advantages of being born into a wealthy family.

POST RENAISSANCE (1650–1690)

When the first silversmiths crossed the ocean around 1650 they took the style of the late Renaissance with them from Europe. People such as John Hull and Robert Sanderson were immigrants from England and started making in the English style until the Puritans stuck a spoke in the wheel. Silver destined for Protestant homes and churches needed to be simple and practical. A puritanical hybrid style arose that blended simplicity with post Renaissance that retained as much of the Renaissance as possible.

EARLY BAROQUE (1690–1720)

Early Baroque is a heavy style with large proportions, solid arched forms, with florid three dimensional details. The Dutchman Jurian Blanck of New York was one of the first to experiment with Baroque. Jeremiah Dummer of Boston also did ground-breaking work but the chief Baroque maker was John Coney of Boston. He produced the 'Monteith Bowl' with eight curved arches on its rim from which the head of a cherubim looked out at the world. The bowl is so richly decorated that the smooth areas on the underside appear like bars. Many followed Coney's lead.

THE HOGARTH ERA (1720–1750)

A reaction against the richly decorated Baroque was to be anticipated. William Hogarth of London led the way for a style that gave great emphasis to rounded contours, plain surfaces, and rhythmic curves. Decoration was left aside except for engraving. Hogarth published his book *Analysis of Beauty* in 1753 in which he set out his theory of style, based on the notion that every object should have the form of an 'S' at the central point of its design. He called this the 'line of beauty' or 'line of grace'. This line was not to be too exaggeratedly curved or too straight.

American Sterling silver butter dish by Crosby Morse of Boston, probably late 18th century.

Hogarth's philosophy was eagerly received in Puritan America. In the transition from the straight lines of Baroque and the elegant curves of Hogarth silversmiths often used octagonal forms. Important American exponents of the Hogarth style were Nathaniel Morse, Simeon Soumain, and Peter van Dijck.

EMBELLISHMENT OF ROCOCO (1755–1775)

Sufficient time had been given to experimenting with line and form to return to superficial decoration. Most of the Hogarth era designs continued but were now ornamented with flowers, leaves, and ruffs. The symmetrical ornamentation of Baroque gave way to asymmetric decoration.

Techniques such as *repoussé* or forging, chasing, and fret cutting became widespread. Benjamin Burt, Joseph Richardson, and Paul Revere made lots of items in this style.

American silver pap bowl, engraved 'C.A.B.B.' that belonged to Caroline Ann Buckminster Williams (1789–1825).

NEO-CLASSICISM (1775–1810)

Having had their fling during the Rococo era the silversmiths now turned back to order and regularity. Rococo had arrived from France but the Neo-Classicism had more to do with English influences. Neo-classical objects were characteristically simple, symmetrical, and well proportioned. The classical style was very popular with Americans. Richard Humphreys of Philidelphia was one of the leading exponents among the silversmiths.

Because this style arrived in America at the start of the War of Independence classical style objects only became available later. Other silversmiths who made in this style were Joseph Anthony and Paul Revere.

REINTRODUCTION OF ANTIQITY (1810–1840)

The forms of neo-classicism became bolder and more explicit. This created an interest among Americans for the classical forms and motifs of the ancient Egyptian, Greek, and Roman cultures. Not only were these forms larger but the silver itself was heavier. Horizontal forms were much emphasised. Rich households could be seen with amphora like objects and sphinx decorations. Leading silversmiths of this era were Anthony Rasch, Harvey Lewis, Thomas Whartenby, and Peter Bumm.

ROMANTIC (1840–1900)

Queen Victoria has hardly ascended to the throne before the effect was being felt in the arts.

For silversmiths this meant a return to the naturalism of Gothic and Rococo for decoration. Silversmith's techniques had improved to such an extent that they could now use handles made of fine wood and machines were increasingly being used to forge silver.

This made it possible to repeat motifs on objects that formed part of a set. The most important silversmiths in America

American 19th century silver candlestick.

Three -piece American silver tea set dated 1898, Van Berch, Rochester, NY.

during the Romantic era were Samuel Casey, Obadiah Rich, and Andrew Warner.

The work of the silversmith

Up to 1750 silversmiths made silverware by melting down silver coins. This was secure work. The clients brought the coins which were melted down and refined by removing other metals. Silversmiths then produced thin sheet silver with the thickness dependent on the objects that the silversmith was to make.

The sheet was then forged by beating with a variety of wooden hammers. If something needed to be hollow it was shaped over a form. This technique requires skill because silver has a tendency to spread in one direction. Hammering must neither be too hard or too soft and silver is also made brittle by being forged. The silversmith warms the silver to just below its melting point to prevent this and allows it to cool down slowly. Silver from this time is consequently softer and possesses a finer lustre than later pieces that were mechanically rolled in factories.

The process changed after 1750 when the silversmiths had their own supplies of silver. This silver came in the form of bars, that mainly originated from South America. These bars were rolled and then hammered to the right thickness. The sheet was then cut to shape with snips and then forged as described above. Handles and other projections were first cast in tin, lead, or sand moulds before being finished by hand with tools.

Ornamentation could be applied in three different ways: engraving, embossing, or the application of ornaments that had been cut out.

ENGRAVING

Designs were cut into the silver using a sharp stylus which removed a small amount of silver. This was the most popular method of decorating silver because it was easy to engrave names, initials, and family coats of arms.
The technique does required considerable artistry and skill. Many silversmiths also acted as book illustrators or signmakers. They were later hired to engrave the designs for bank notes. The sober New England silversmiths used engraving extensively, following English and European examples with Rococo elements such as acanthus scrolls and other motifs.

American Sterling silver toilet set, circa 1900.

APPLYING ORNAMENTATION

There are two ways in which a silversmith can add silver ornamentation to the surface of an item by either cutting them out from a sheet of thin silver or by casting silver in a mould. Cutting out requires a steady hand with various types of snip and if a mistake is made the silver will need to be melted down again and re-rolled.

The other technique is to make a wooden model of the decoration which is then pressed into sand or clay. The silversmith can then pour molten silver into the model and when cool remove the casting and clean it up with files as required. Finally the decoration can be added to the piece as intended.

American silver snuff boxes.

Renowned silversmiths

So far as is known, John Mansfield was the first silversmith to arrive from England in the colonies at Boston in 1634. It is unknown how he fared there. The most celebrated of the early silversmiths was John Hull (1624–1683) who started a silversmiths with Robert Sanderson (1608–1693).

Hull was the first to learn the trade in America. He kept a diary in which he comments that 'with God's help' he had learned the trade of goldsmith as a young boy and was thereby able to earn a living as an adult. John Hull was appointed master of the mint for the Massachusetts Bay Colony in 1652. Together with Sanderson he started minting the famous 'pine tree shillings' which are all dated 1652, even though some were minted later. Hull and Sanderson also made communion chalices, most of which now belong to churches around Boston. Later he also made silver cutlery and drinking vessels.

In 1659 Hull took on his first apprentice, Jeremiah Dummer. In his diary he hoped he would be fitted to the task the Lord had given him. Hull must have been a good teacher for Dummer and his colleague John Coney were excellent silversmiths. Coney even made the plates for the first American bank notes and the first seal of Harvard College. The apprentices Samuel Paddy and Timothy Dwight were also successful. All Hull's apprentices themselves subsequently took on apprentices who maintain the high standard of Massachusetts silversmiths. The trade was often passed from father to son.

PAUL REVERE

Paul Revere, who became famous through the American War of Independence, was the son of a French Huguenot, Apollos Rivoire who was apprenticed to John Coney. Once Apollos completed his apprenticeship he started his own business in Boston and anglicised his name to Paul Revere. His son Paul was born in 1735 and he was introduced to the silversmith's trade with the baby's feeding spoon.

When Paul Jr. was 19 in 1754 his father died, leaving the business to his son. At that time a silversmith, Revere also worked as a blacksmith, goldsmith, and engraver. Paul Revere's silver was of high quality but it was not just his craftsmanship that won approval. His elegant designs and extensive ornamentation made a big hole in the purse. His talent also expressed itself as an illustrator of books and magazines with copperplate engravings.

Revere was a member of the Sons of Liberty that wanted to see independence. He happily poked fun at the British in his satirical prints. His most famous print is of the Boston Massacre which was published in 1770. As a revolutionary, Revere also took part in the Boston tea party and acted as messenger for the Committee of Safety. It was for this group that he rode to towns such as Philadelphia and New York.

During the American War of Independence Revere closed down his business but he made ammunition and even cannons. During his famous ride to Concord in 1775 he warned people in the countryside that 'the British are coming.' His deeds were immortalised in poetry by Henry Wadsworth Longfellow, which

American silver plate spoon, circa 1900.

ensured that his name is engraved in American history.

Revere re-opened his business after the war and also had a flourishing jewellery and ironmongers shop and copper factory in Canton Massachusetts. Of his sixteen children, two of them (Joseph Warren Revere and Paul Revere III) also learned the silversmith's trade and continued the tradition after his death in 1818.

Revere made the most famous piece of American silver: the Liberty Bowl which is now in the Boston Museum of Fine Arts. This bowl was made to commemorate the House of Representatives of Massachusetts which protested against the laws that the British wished to impose on them.

Dating American silver

By contrast with their European compatriots, America silversmiths rarely date their work. European silver is hallmarked but only American wedding rings are dated.
Collectors of American silver therefore have to find other means of dating pieces.

NAME STAMPS

American silversmiths often stamp pieces with their name so if the date of birth and death of the silversmith is known and that he probably completed his apprenticeship when about 20 years old then an approximate idea can be gained of when a piece was made.
Account needs also to be taken that not every silversmith continued working until his death. Some retired and others changed profession.
Unfortunately deceit with name marks is not uncommon. Hence a teapot stamped 'Revere' or 'PR' is rarely made by the famous Paul Revere. The most recent examples fetched a mere $30,000 at auction (making it an expensive cup of tea despite his efforts at the Boston tea party).

DECORATIVE TECHNIQUES

Techniques change as new process are discovered and new types of objects become fashionable.
It is important for collectors of silver to know when different techniques were first used.

American silver plate salad servers, circa 1920.

Buying American silver

The decision whether to buy a piece of antique silver needs to be carefully considered because there are lots of reproductions on the market. The first decision that a collector has to make is if the piece appeals sufficiently to put the effort required into checking it out. In addition to this there are other factors to be considered.

AUTHENTICITY

Is the item truly what the seller claims it to be? Is the metal right, are the marks genuine or forged, is there provenance to establish the history of the piece, or can its authenticity be verified by other means?

If the potential buyer has doubts about any of these then the decision should be to turn one's back immediately on the item.

AESTHETIC QUALITY

If the piece passes the test of authenticity it must then be judged just as carefully for quality as with any other art form.

The craftmanship, correct proportions, beauty of the object, ornamentation, and functionality should all be carefully judged.

CONDITION

How does the present condition of the piece compare with its original condition? Is it badly tarnished, are there any dents, or if it is silver plate is the silver so worn that the copper is showing through?

With antique silver it is often reassuring to find signs of wear as additional signs of authenticity but if the item is badly worn it can severely depress its value.

PROVENANCE

Are there any marks on the object? Is the original bill for the item available? Are their anecdotes linking important persons or events to the object?

HOW RARE IS THE OBJECT?

If a silver object is unique, the best example of its type, or was made by a famous silversmith then it may become idolised so that it attracts astoundingly high prices.

This can only happen if all the other factors are right and there is certainty about the authenticity of the piece.

RELIABILITY OF INCRIPTIONS

A lot of trickery surrounds inscriptions and a sensible collector will commit the various changes in inscription techniques to memory.

IS THE STYLE RIGHT FOR THE PERIOD?

Many styles were revived in the nineteenth century making it extremely difficult for instance to ascertain whether an object originates from the colonial era or during the nineteenth century.

REPAIRS

Repairs are commonplace. Handles in particular have often been repaired.

Some handles and lids have even been taken from their original piece and married with later ones.

Lids and handles are the most susceptible parts to be broken through constant and careless use.

Honest silversmiths put their own mark on a replacement part. There should be some damage on a lid where the thumb presses down to lift it. If this is not the case or if there is wear in different places then the lid has been replaced.

Unfortunately areas of wear are less easily assessed the older an item is or if it was repaired a long time ago.

The spouts of tea and coffee pots are often later additions, replacements, or have been removed. This mars the overall lines of the object.

FORGERIES

The collector's greatest worry is to be deceived. This fear is not unreasonable for the inexperienced collector because there is a great deal of well made reproduction silver on the market that less scrupulous dealers sell for high prices.

Due regard needs to be paid with silver to areas of solder and unusual alterations. A popular fraud is the obliteration of later maker's marks. Traces of solder can usually be found in such places.

It is more difficult to detect forgeries in silver that is cast because silver cast ten years ago is difficult to differentiate from that cast in the seventeenth century.

The standards of craftsmanship and motifs used for engraving may provide the answer in such cases. Forged engraving is often poor in composition and technique. The motifs usually agree with the period that it is claimed the piece was made.

REPRODUCTIONS

There are honest and dishonest forgeries. With honest reproductions the modern maker imprints his mark alongside the maker of the original.

A forgery leaves the modern marks off. Companies like J.E. Caldwell in Philadelphia, Shreve, Crump & Low in Boston, and Gorham & Towle produce many fine and honest reproductions. These reproduction are sometimes of such craftsmanship that they are regarded as museum pieces.

Museums and experienced collectors get spectrographic analysis of the silver of objects which provides a detailed list of the content of the individual components of the silver. This makes it possible to discover if a lid, spout, or handle are original or were added later.

The considerable interest at the present time in American silver means that much more information is becoming available. Museum curators and collectors are becoming less easy to fool so that forgers are having to become even more ingenious. The silver collector therefore needs to constantly remain on his or her guard.

Clocks

Who the first person was in the New World that became fed up with the inaccuracy of sand timers and sundials and started to make clocks is entirely unknown.

Clocks were imported from both England and Holland. These were operated by

Hepplewhite style American clock in cherrywood with eight-day movement giving date and moon phases.

a spring mechanism. These were so expensive that only major settlements could afford them. Few people had a clock in their own house.
The first clock-makers were through and through craftsmen. They had to make every part themselves to the precise size. The tools available were often extremely rudimentary. The same person often had to make the clock case too.

Generally they sold too few clocks to make a living so that clock-makers were also locksmiths or gunsmiths.
This combination was particularly popular during the American War of Independence.

After this war there were still far too few people who could afford a grandfather clock and so the makers experimented with smaller clocks. Because a large number of original American clocks were introduced many homes soon had their own clock.

Clockmakers

The names are known of around 7,000 American clock-makers. Most of these made the usual types of clock but there are some of them that were so important in the introduction of major innovations that they have to be mentioned.

Abel Cottey arrived in America in 1682 on board the *Welcome* with William Penn (the Quaker leader whose name is given to the state of Pennsylvania).
He may well be the first clock-maker to establish a business in the colonies. In his workshop in Philadelphia he mainly made longcase clocks that became known as grandfather clocks.

These grandfather clocks later became very popular and can now be found through America. In common with other clock-makers, Cottey made the mechanism, the dial, the pendulum, and the weights himself but left the case to be made by a joiner. These joiners allowed their creativity to run free and many cases are superbly carved in minute detail. Philadelphia proved to be a good place for clock-makers to set themselves up.

American Gardiner-Parker clock (1772–1816). An 8-day clock driven by weights.

Great names such as Christopher Sower, four generations of the Gogas family, the Chandlee family, and Edward Duffiels ring out from Philadelphia. The last of these was a good friend of Benjamin Franklin.
Duffiels was interrupted so frequently by people asking the time that he made a clock with a face on both sides that he hung outside his workshop. The most convivial clock-makers was David Rittenhouse.

American banjo clock, circa 1900.

Of Dutch origin, he anglicised his name from Van Ritterhuysen. He started making longcase clocks and scientific instruments at the age of 19 in Norristown, Pennsylvania. His clocks were the most accurate of their time (circa 1756) in the colonies. Rittenhouse was so good a craftsman that he made an orrery (complete miniature planetarium) when he was 23 which he sold to Princeton University.

In addition to being a clock-maker he was also a leading physicist, mathematician, and surveyor. His surveys were the basis for the Mason-Dixon line that formed the border between the emancipated states and those where slavery still endured prior to the American Civil War. Rittenhouse was also chairman of the American Philosophical Society. When older he became director of the United States Mint from 1791 to his death in 1795. In addition to Pennsylvania, there were also famous clock-makers in Connecticut and Massachusetts. The Willard family of Grafton, Massachusetts, were born with a talent for clock-making.

Benjamin Willard (born 1743) learned the trade with Benjamin Cheney in Connecticut and passed his knowledge on to his brothers Simon, Ephraim, and Aaron when he returned to Grafton.
Benjamin started a clock-making business in Grafton and advertised in the *Massachusetts Spy* that he could supply clocks that played a different tune every day and a psalm on Sunday. His brothers travelled throughout Massachusetts to sell clocks to people. Simon Willard is the most famous clock-maker of the family.
He invented the bank clock. Aaron Willard developed a model of his own, the Massachusetts 'shelf clock'. Aaron's sons, Aaron Jr. and Henry did not want to be left behind by the rest of the family and developed the 'lyre clock'.

Eli Terry (born 1772) became known as the 'Henry Ford of clock-makers'. He built a small factory beside a stream in 1803 so that a water wheel could turn his machines and lathes. Terry also designed a machine to make cogs. This made production so much more efficient that he was able to accept an order in 1806 for 4,000 clocks.

The prices dropped so much through mass production that he was soon able to export them to Britain. The methods of production continually improved and became quicker and clocks were being made on a grand scale by 1860. Some clock-makers made as many as 100,000 clocks per year.

This was at the expense of the quality of the – mainly wooden – clock cases. Some were so poorly made that any right-minded furniture maker would have

Left: 19th century American banjo clock made by Simon Willard.
Right: American 8-day weight-driven banjo clock by Aaron Willard in mahogany.

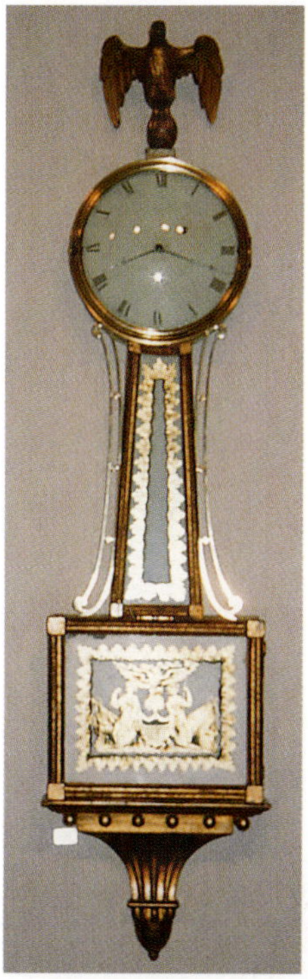

thrown them in the rubbish bin straight away. Around 1860, the Litchfield Manufacturing Company was even making cases of papier mâché, into which clock-makers then glued the mechanism.

Popular clocks of the United States

LONGCASE CLOCKS

The grandfather clock was the first clock for the home to be made in America. These stately clocks originally known as either tallcase or longcase clocks can thank their name to the children's song *My Grandfather's Clock*.
The first longcase clocks were made in England around 1600 and the earliest known American example originated in 1680. The long case was necessary to house the long pendulum. This case was often designed and made by a cabinet maker.
The mechanism of the longcase clock was made of bronze and wood. The clocks were mainly driven by weights but wind-up clocks came onto the market later. The dial was often made of bronze with engraved or etched Roman numerals and decoration.
The hands themselves often had fine tracery in order to catch the light. Grandmother clocks are a smaller version of the longcase clock and they were extremely popular in the early nineteenth century.
They were mainly made by a group of Boston clock-makers including the Willards, Samuel Mulliken, and Levi Hutchins. The grandmother clock was no taller than 1,200mm (48in).

SHELF CLOCKS

Shelf clocks came into fashion in the New World following the America War of Independence (1775–1783).
This was because their mechanism was driven by a spring. Such mechanisms were more complex and hence less accurate and these clocks were often more expensive. Because metal was in short supply during the war mechanisms were generally made of wood. The first American shelf clocks are so similar to comparable English clocks of the time that many collector has been confused.

The Massachusetts shelf clock (also known as box on box or half clocks) is no taller than 600mm (24in). The clock is set on a shelf instead of on the ground as is the case with longcase clocks.

The lighthouse clock (originally known as the 'Eddystone' clock) is one of the many innovations of Simon Willard who lodged a patent application for the design in 1822. The glass dome known throughout the British Empire was mounted on a rounded or octagonal base to give

Aaron Willard 8-day weight driven clock of 1825.

This American girandole clock has a Lemuel Curtis 8-day weight driven movement in a gilt pine case.

the overall appearance of a lighthouse. Because they were intended to be portable, lighthouse clocks had handles attached.

These clocks were fitted with an eight-day mechanism and also incorporated an alarm. The clock could be wound without removing the glass. This type of clock was not very popular and therefore few were made. This makes them now quite rare and therefore highly sought after.

The extremely eagerly sought OG clock first appeared around 1840. The simple rectangular case was completed with ogee moulding.

The wooden mechanism was replaced with bronze ones that were either weight or spring driven. The OG clock remained popular for almost a century. Chauncy Jerome developed a kind of conveyor belt (from an ideas of Joseph Ives) to mass produce bronze mechanisms for these clocks. His advertisements stated that these clocks were suitable for all manner of public places such as churches, banks, shops, ships, trains, saloons, corridors, and kitchens.

Jerome quickly dominated the American market and soon started to export his

clocks to Britain. Because they were so cheap the British Customs thought he was trying to avoid paying duty and they seized his first consignment. The Customs paid him his declared value plus ten per cent. Jerome was delighted and sent a second shipment to England. This too was 'purchased' by the British government but he sent a third consignment and by now the British finally accepted Jerome's valuation and allowed his clocks to be imported normally.
The style of his clocks follow furniture styles. The influence of Rococo is clearly apparent in the form of the clocks and their ornamentation in the Jerome & Co catalogue of 1852.

Clocks with pointed columns known as Gothic clocks first appeared around 1845 and originated from the imagination of Elias Ingraham (1805–1885). In common with the furniture style of the time these clocks had pointed columns on either side.

The mechanism incorporated innovations by Joseph Ives – the bronze eight-day movement was driven by an Ives spring. A closely related clock to the Gothic clock was the Beehive which mainly had cases made from mahogany and/or rosewood.

WALL CLOCKS

The 'wag-on-the-wall' clock is also derived from the longcase clock. This type of clock was mainly based on the ideas of Isaac Blaisdell for a clock for people for whom the longcase clock was too big. The pendulum is allowed to swing freely outside the case rather like a dog's tail wagging to and fro.
The banjo clock was originally named by its designer Simon Willard as an 'Improved Patent Timepiece'.

Despite the patent he was granted on this type of clock it was widely copied. There are some 4,000 genuine Willard banjo clocks. Willard introduced a number of improvements that enable his clock to run for eight days in spite of using lighter weights. The banjo clock was also more accurate than other clocks because the pendulum was suspended in front of the weights. The case was largely made of glass which was decorated with paintings of landscapes, flowers, and noteworthy buildings. This typical American clock is still very popular with the general public.
The 'girandole' was designed in 1816 by Lemuel Curtis of Concord, Massachusetts.
This clock is a variant of the banjo clock with a rounded case. The upper and lower parts of the case are decorated with small gilt spheres that are reminiscent of a mirror girandole mirror.
The rounded glass of the bottom section often has paintings of mythological or

Eli Terry 19th century pillar and scroll clock with wooden weight-driven 30 hours movement.

Wooden American mantel clock with broken glass front with original painting.

historical tableaux. Some described the girandole clock as the most beautiful American design of clock. The 'lyre' clock was designed by two nephews of Simon Willard: Aaron and Henry Willard.

The clock is clearly related to banjo and girandole clocks. With lyre clocks the dial is positioned on an elegant double scroll that is reminiscent of a lyre. The sides of lyre clocks are often decorated with leaf motifs.
The New Hampshire mirror clock is quite individual in style.

This clock has a mirror beneath the dial and is decorated in the style current when the clock was made. Most mirror

The name of Austin Chittendon of Lexington appears on the rear of this mantel clock.

American Art Deco clock, circa 1930.

clocks have movements that have to be wound once in eight days. The pillar or scroll clock was the first type of clock to be made by Eli Terry in large numbers. The most unusual aspect of this clock was that the pendulum was mounted slightly to the right rather than centrally.

American mahogany pillar an scroll clock in the Terry manner by Norris North of Torrington, Connecticut after 1825. The painting is original.

Seth Thomas (1785–1859) pillar and scroll clock from Plymouth, Connecticut with 30 hour weight-driven wooden movement.

This type of clock was very popular in the 1830s.
Around 1875 the Americans hit on the idea of using a clock mechanism to make figures move. The 'blinking eye clock' was often used as an alarm clock. The clock contained a miniature male figure that blinked its eyes when the alarm went off.

Watches

Watchmakers emigrated to America from Britain, Holland, France, Germany, and Switzerland quite early. They attempted to set up their own businesses but quickly discovered that so many watches were imported that they could not earn a living. Few watches were therefore produced in America before the mid 1800s. The first to try making watches in quantity as probably Luther Goddard (1762–1842) of Shrewsbury, Massachusetts.

He started to make watches in 1809 during a period that imports of watches were restricted by import regulations. He employed a number of other watchmakers but once the 'Jefferson Embargo' was lifted in 1815 the American market was once more flooded with foreign watches.

These were much cheaper than the American watches and so Goddard was forced to shut down in 1817. He then decided to become a clergyman instead of a watchmaker.

A second attempt to make watches in America was made in 1837 by Henry and J.F. Pitkin of East Hartford, Connecticut. They developed machines that made between 800 and 1,000 watches but this business also failed due to foreign competition. After the factory moved to New York in 1841 the Pitkins decided to abandon watchmaking. Finally Edward Howard and Aaron L. Dennison were the first to successfully mass produce watches.

In 1850, forty years after Terry started to mass produce clocks, affordable American watches finally came onto the market. The Waltham Watch Company, as their business was named, survived for a century.

The Elgin National Watch Company was set-up in Elgin, Illinois in 1864. Their first watch was not sold until 1867. At first their watches had to be wound up with a separate key but these keys were easily lost so that they are much prized by collectors.

The company began to make 'stem' watches in 1873 which had a small wheel on the side with which the watch could be wound. Although watches could now be made in greater quantities they remained expensive. The development of an accurate but cheap watch was a challenge to inventors.

Glass

The Native Americans had not made glass before the Spanish conquered Mexico and established a glassworks there. The ingredients of sand, lime, and soda were present in abundance. The native Americans did make arrow heads and amulets of quartz and obsidian.

Late 18th century engraved American Stiegel flip glass.

The first colonists discovered that the native people liked to use coloured glass beads for their wampum or necklaces. Wampum were made of beads, stones, and shells which were also used as a form of currency.

The first efforts to make glass in the colonies was therefore directed at making coloured glass beads. The first group of professional glassblowers consisted of eight Dutch and Polish settlers who were invited by the businessman John Smith to carry on their trade in Jamestown, Virginia and to teach their craft to others. The enterprise was not successful though and the group split up and spread throughout the colonies. The majority of wealthy citizens imported glass from Europe.
This was essential since the British had banned the establishment of factories in

the colonies. When someone finally took the risk in setting up a glass works the market proved to be too small but many attempts were made. Most failed within a year.
The first successful glassworks was established in 1739 by the German settler Caspar Wistar at Alloway, New Jersey. At first Wistar solely made bottles and green window glass but later he made household glassware.
After the American War of Independence the economy developed rapidly and the Americans no longer had to obey the English law so that industry grew too.

The census of 1810 counted a mere 22 glassworks, most of which went bankrupt in the war of 1812. In 1820 the number had grown to 40 healthy glassworks.
In that same year America started to put duty on imported glass so that American glass companies were better able to compete with European ones. About 90 new glassworks were established in the ten years up to 1830. The glass industry was concentrated in Pittsburgh, Ohio, and Virginia. These areas were ideal because there was ample coal and the rivers could be used for transport.

The glass industry in the east of the country at this time found times harder and harder. In this area wood was mainly used as fuel and this was becoming increasingly scarce. Many glassworks in that area disappeared. The original glassblowing techniques had been in use for centuries by Italian, German, Dutch, and Bohemian glass-makers.
Two new techniques were developed at the start of the nineteenth century that made glass much cheaper and within everyone's pocket. The first of these was the blowing of glass into moulds in the form and decoration of the finished product and the second was the introduction of the pressed glass machine. Craftsmen glassblowers opposed the introduction of these techniques because they were afraid of losing their livelihoods.
The authoritarian manager of the famous Sandwich glassworks where glass was first machine pressed was Deming Jarves. He was so threatened by the protesting glass workers that he remained shut up in his great house for six weeks to avoid coming to harm. The workers eventually gave in and other factories followed suit. For the modern collector it is now quite a challenge to assemble an entire service of glass from one of these works.

American cake or sandwich dish, circa 1835.

Most glass makers took little account of fashion and the style of furniture in use at a given time had virtually no influence on glass objects.

Renowned glass makers

There are many colourful and talented persons from the American glass industry. The legendary glass maker Henry William Stiegel originated from Germany. Stiegel arrived in Lancaster, Pennsylvania in 1750, when he was 21.

He quickly found work there in the ironworks of Jacob Huber.

He married his boss's daughter and in order not to be ungrateful he continued to work for his father-in-law for several more years. In 1863 he set up his first glassworks alongside the ironworks which in the meantime he now owned.
Within six years Stiegel had enough money through speculating in land to establish his own town in Pennsylvania. This town he called Mannheim.

In Mannheim he set up two glassworks. The inhabitants of Mannheim were expected to call him Baron Stiegel. Baron Stiegel wanted to conduct himself like an old fashioned German baron. He organised luxurious balls, dinners, concerts, and other festivities in his grand house on the market square of Mannheim. His house had a flat roof on which an orchestra would play. Guests could drink unlimited wine at his parties from superb Stiegel glasses.
The carafes were often made specially for the occasion. When he went on his travels he had a cannon fired to mark his home coming so that the inhabitants should know their beloved baron was back.

Stiegel spent far too much money and creditors pursued him but this did nor prevent him from building a school house for the children of Mannheim. In order to pay off his debts he started to produce bottles and window glass and was so successful that he was able to extend the works. He employed 150 people, most of whom he had arranged for them to emigrate from Europe. His accounts show that he produced 66,000 glass items in 1770. They also reveal that he had only sold 5,000 wine carafes, candleholders, dishes, bottles, and medical items.
The more the baron made the more he spent. His debts became so huge that he put everything on sale except his house and the glass works but there were no takers.

American 19th century vase of blue glass.

He then organised a lottery for a 'Manufactory of Public Advantage' but only $500 was raised. In 1773 his creditors took charge of the Charming Forge ironworks and six months later they got their hands on his Mannheim property.

The famous glassmaker was arrested and put into prison for debt at the end of 1874. When he was released he had nothing more for himself and his family than some clothes and bedding. Nothing more is known after this about this eccentric character. Even the year and place of his death is unknown. Ten years after the failure of Stiegel, his countryman Jon Frederick Amelung set up a glassworks in Maryland. Just like Stiegel he brought over craftsmen from Germany.

The output of this New Bremen Glass Manufactory was renowned for the superior quality of its engraving. The products were engraved with monograms, family coats of arms, inscriptions and such like. The copper wheel engraving was extremely refined and has become world famous.

In addition to window glass and bottles, the New Bremen works also started to make wine glasses and tableware. This glass is usually blue, green, or purple with a characteristic smoky tint. Little is known of Deming Jarves, mentioned earlier. Because he was born in a coach travelling through Europe he did not know where he was born in 1790 or 1791. At age 25, after he had had a number of jobs as salesman, he became agent for a number of glassworks. Together with friends, he bought a poorly performing glassworks in East Cambridge, Massachusetts.

This business was originally run by an English glass cutter, Richard Fisher. Fisher was smuggled aboard a ship in a barrel because the English law forbade glass cutters from leaving the country. Jarves reorganised his business significantly and changed the name to New England Glass Company.

The works quickly produced crown glass, which makes good quality window glass. In the following seven years Jarves tried out every aspect of the glass industry and introduced many innovations. Meanwhile he was also chosen for various political functions but was not successful in Cambridge.
He was not interested in discussing his plans with his colleagues, preferring to do everything himself. He withdrew from New England Glass and moved to Sandwich on Cape Cod in Massachusetts where he established the Boston & Sandwich Glass Company. This was to become the most famous American glassworks.

In order to transport his goods to the harbour Jarves had his own railway built which was the first private railway in the United States.

Jarves certainly liked to keep every aspect of business under his own control and when the factory was producing too much in 1848 to ship by the sailing vessels used until this time he contacted the director of the Cape Cod Railway and asked for a discount to ship glass. When this was turned down Jarves angrily informed him that he was going to have a steam ship built. The railway director

American 19th century Basset glass with Sterling silver decoration.

merely riposted "I think the acorn for the tree from which the timber for your ship will come is not even planted yet." A few months later Jarves launched his steamship named *Acorn*. This ship transported the glass to Boston until the railway gave in to his demands. Although Jarves was somewhat of a potentate it must be added that he was one of the first to consider the welfare of his workers.

The prices were kept low in the company shop and only low rents had to be paid for worker's houses. He also gave a pension to the widows of his former workers and he ensured that the boys who worked for him went to school for a few hours each day. The boys did not like this but Jarves made up for this by giving them fireworks for Independence Day.
Jarves worked in Sandwich for more than 30 years but he suddenly gave it all up on his 68th birthday.

No-one knows the reason but perhaps he had threatened once too often that if he did not get his own way he would give it all up. In no time at all he set up a new glass works at Sandwich which competed with the original one until his death. When Jarves died the spark went out of the new works and it was never rekindled.The old works eventually got into difficulty because more modern glassworks could produce glass more cheaply and in larger volume.

The Boston & Sandwich Glass Company could not cope with this and was closed on New Year's Day 1888.

This was not the only business that went under. William Leighton developed a process in West Virginia that used ordinary non-hydrated lime instead of red lead in order to make flint glass. Other glassmakers everywhere tried to reproduce the technique but this proved so difficult that it was not done until the patent on the process had elapsed. Competitors were forced to use a more expensive process for a longer period.

The glassworks in Pennsylvania and West Virginia also had the advantage of being close to the Appalachian mountains where there was coal. This significantly reduced their costs.

The one who survived these troublesome times was the famous glass maker Louis Comfort Tiffany, founder of the famous jewellers. Tiffany study art in Paris where he first wanted to paint. He became interested in stained glass through European cathedrals.

Tiffany did not lack self confidence and he soon believed he could create far more beautiful windows.

In order to prove this he established a studio in Corona on Long Island in 1893 where he managed to demonstrate that American windows are superior to the best windows of the Middle Ages.

Apart from being very creative, Tiffany was also a good businessman, for in order to make more profit from his already successful business he started to make decorative items from the scraps of glass left over from his other activities. He realised that he needed to better understand chemistry in order to bring about modernisation and indeed he brought together his creativity, craftsmanship, and chemistry in his Favrile iridescent glass that creates a play with light. Tiffany was also busy in the field of glazed copper, designing of jewellery, earthenware, textiles, landscape architecture, and mosaics. He continued to work until his death at 85 years of age.

Quilts

Patchwork is very old and has been done by women since they first discovered that textiles wear out. Although the quilt does not originate in America it has become an essential part of the American antiques scene. A few quilts will be found in almost every US antique shop.

The earliest illustration of a quilt dates to 3,400 BC. This is a sculpted figure of an Egyptian Pharaoh who is wearing clothing that is quilted but it is believed that quilting was carried out earlier than this in ancient China and India. The first oriental quilts found their way to Europe during the Crusades. The earliest known quilted bedspread was made in Sicily in the fourteenth century. When India formed part of the British Empire the British caught the rage for quilts.

They took the quilt to America where the technique was ideal for settlers who often needed to make do with very little. Many quilts travelled in the covered wagons that crossed the Appalachians as they headed westwards towards the Pacific. Although the quilt is popular in many European countries and was certainly not invented in America it is today regarded as if it was an original American manifestation.

Until the Industrial Revolution women spun their own thread with sheep's wool, flax, and cotton and then wove their own cloth, sewed their own clothes, and the household linen.
Girls learned to make quilts while quite young. Marion Nichol-Rawson (1878-1956) remembers that before she was three years old her mother taught her to make quilts, meaning patchwork. She was expected to carefully sew two patches together very carefully or otherwise the stitches were undone again. Between 1840 and the American Civil War (1861–1865) Americans moved house frequently. They moved to the cities or as pioneers to the west. The friendship or signature quilts reflected farewells to family and friends.

Those who died on the journey were often buried wrapped in a quilt. The pioneers had no regular supplies and had to be careful with what they had. Bits of old clothing were saved for use in quilts. In many cases these were their parents' and grandparents' clothes. They had remained behind in the east because the journey to the west was too arduous for them. 'Pull up the cotton kivvers, it's going to be a three dog night!'

As the family moved further west the quilts went with them. If it was a cold night the pioneers would call out: 'Pull up the cotton kivvers, it's going to be a three dog night.'

Nine patch American quilt by Mrs Arthur Perry, of unknown date.

This referred to the thickness of the quilt. Once the family settled somewhere the wife would join the local quilting bee. This is a group of women who make quilts together.

A major difference between quilts and most other forms of antique is that quilts are made by a group of people out of friendship and love.

When a quilt had to be made a pioneer woman would drum up support from the female members of her family, other women friends, and neighbours. An ordinary quilting bee would usually contain about eight participants but if they had a larger space available to them this might rise to twelve.

The women gossiped together as they sat around the quilting frame. They were often encircled by children playing, and pets. Quilting bees would last all day. When the men returned from the land there would be a festive meal of roast chicken or turkey after which everybody danced and sang. It was very important to make a contribution to a quilt.

So important in fact that people took offence to not being invited to take part in a quilting bee. Up to the beginning of the twentieth century virtually no quilts were sold. Young girls regarded the quilt as the most important part of their trousseau. The marriage quilt was usually made by the community in which the girl grew up. This quilt reminded her of the people who had always supported and encouraged her.

For many families the quilt was the only thing they did not lose in their travels. So many memories were associated of people they would often never see again. Today the quilt is considered a symbol of homeliness, family ties, and continuity. Because the log cabins were not very well insulated the quilts needed to be extra

American 'Wild Flower' quilt of 1887 by Mrs Samuel Hooper (born 1845), with flowers from her sister's garden.

Lois Hand wrote in the nineteenth century that when she was small they had very thick quilts. This she added was because the draughts were so bad in those cabins that you needed to be well covered in order to sleep. The slaves on the plantations were probably even more attached to their quilts than the white pioneers.

The self-made quilts from collections of fragments of material that were hard for them to acquire were all that most slaves had to keep them comfortable. Some slaves also had to make quilts for their master or mistress. When that quilt became worn it was sometimes given back to them. Early quilts were entirely hand made. When Elias Howe invented the sewing machine in 1846 many women were eager to acquire one for their community.

Godey's *Lady's Book* of 1860 reported that this invention made it possible for a woman to do her work in a comfortable manner, adding that tasks that would otherwise take to beyond midnight to do and even up to 20 hours to perform could now be achieved in two to three hours. Hand-made quilts were and remain the most admired though. Quilts are something of an oddity in the wide range of antiques because they were not influenced by the passing styles.

The quilts made during the era of William and Mary do not differ from those made during the period of the Federal style.

Documenting, keeping, and maintaining quilts

There has been a resurgence of interest in quilts since the United States Bicentennial. In certain states of the United States antique quilts even have to be registered. This interest has not only encouraged people to start making quilts once more but also to catalogue and document antique quilts.

When acquiring a quilt it is important to get as much information about the quilt as possible.

Some have fascinating stories behind them that the new owner would certainly not wish to miss out on. The Americans have also started to pay more attention to protecting quilts. The greatest danger for textiles is light.
A quilt must therefore be kept out of sunlight and it is also sensible to avoid great changes in temperature. Because it can stain, quilts should not be kept in paper, plastic, or in direct contact with wood.

The best way to keep an antique quilt is in a bag of a robust but not synthetic fabric. Another less suitable but practical solution is to hang the quilt on the wall of a dark room. This does have the advantage of being able to see the quilt. Antique quilts must not be washed and are therefore not suitable to be used.
Quilts can be used on wooden and metal objects such as beds but this absolutely out of the question for antique quilts. An antique quilt is solely an item to display.

Types of quilts

Friendship quilts

THE MARRIAGE QUILT

Marriage brought a very great change in the life of an eighteenth and nineteenth century woman. This not only marked the change fromgirlhood into womanhood and of becoming a mother but also meant a change of surroundings if she married outside her own community.
Furthermore she acquired a new role and status. Most of the quilting bees were very supportive during this transition.
The older women gave good advice to the wife to be and in order to give her something from her old surroundings the quilting bee made her a quilt for her marital bed.
The men often helped by providing the calligraphy on the back.
Members of the quilting bee who did not marry were also given a quilt on their 35th birthday. Since being unmarried was unusual in those days a spinster quilt would often be accompanied with certain wisecracks.

FRIENDSHIP, SIGNATURE, OR ALBUM QUILTS

Friendship quilts were popular around 1840. A friendship quilt was signed by the people who had made a financial contribution or who had worked on the making of a quilt. There was often also a poem or aphorism on the quilt. The person who initiated the quilt would make the design and establish the size of each square.

The centre of each square would have an area of white on which participants could write their names. All those taking part would make their contribution at home before the squares were sewn together. A special form of friendship quilt is the freedom quilt.

This was given to a young man when he had completed his apprenticeship and was free to decided about his future. During his apprenticeship a young man was answerable to his master and his rules. The freedom after the apprenticeship was a great relief for many. The historian Finley wrote: 'The parents or guardians could no longer force the young man to serve his apprenticeship, to carry out his duties, to make him do unpaid work at home, or judicially restrict all his movements. He was free.'

PRESENTATION QUILTS

Presentation quilts are much like a friendship quilts except more formal. They were usually intended for a respected or admired person such as a doctor, priest, schoolteacher, or others who held a special role in society who the community wish to honour with a quilt. The quilt would be given in the hope that the receiver would continue their good work. An anonymous writer wrote the following: 'Reverend Williams, the travelling Methodist preacher, was very important in our lives...Well now, Mrs Wilcox had thought of making a quilt for him. Something special...We exceeded ourselves with sewing on one square each. We asked the women from the other churches to take part.

The coachman collected all the pieces and put them in his saddlebag. We sorted them out and put them all together. That took lots of time. The Reverend said he had never seen anything so beautiful. It had priceless value to him.

COLLECTION QUILT

Making a quilt for a cause dear to the heart of women had been fashionable for a long time. Whether it was to help the poor or the sick or for maintaining the church or combating alcoholism, women who actually had very little spare time would get together to make a quilt. In order to be able to make part of the quilt the women would make a contribution of an amount agreed beforehand. They then made their bit with their name in the colour decided. People who did not work on the quilt could also have their names added by making a contribution. This was known as a subscription.

CONSCIENCE QUILT

Social reforms were often thought up by women who then initiated their menfolk into their plans. It is only a small step from a presentation of collection quilt to making one for a social or political purpose.

The needle expresses what society will judge. At the same time a conscience quilt also raised money. The suffragettes for instance made lots of quilts with the names of people who supported votes for women. Because these quilts remained hanging unlike a poster which would be

America Star of Bethlehem quilt, 19th century.

thrown away after a time these quilts certainly influenced public opinion.

A different form of conscience quilt is one that recalls a bad event, often with the intention of preventing it happening again. A very emotional example of this is the quilt that was made by former inmates of Dachau concentration camp. They used the rags worn by the inmates. Despite its simple design of 144 squares, this quilt is a lasting reminder of the holocaust. A modern example is the quilt produced about AIDS.

MOURNING QUILTS

Until the advances of medical science saved many peoples lives death was a constant companion for people. In pre-industrial America that had a population of just five million people the death of a person affected the entire local community. It was important to help those close to the deceased to bear their loss. A quilt was an ideal way in which a community could express its feelings.

Because women were regarded as greater believers, more sentimental, and more emotional they were expected to lead the way.

A young girl wrote in her diary that when she was four their neighbour's baby died and all the women were summoned to help. Her mother knew her task and had immediately taken some blue silk from her bridal chest. The girl remembered the silk because it was special and she had been allowed to carry it. When they got to the neighbours the men were busy making the coffin.
Her mother and three other women fixed up a frame and spent the entire day quilting. First they made the lining for the coffin and then they made a small quilt to wrap the baby in.

In times of great grief quilting was not an escape from reality but a means of making grief bearable. Quilts also served to formalise farewells. Men then made mourning quilts from the deceased person's clothes. Death among women was very high in those days with many dying during or after childbirth.

For this reason a quilt started by one woman might be finished by another. The second woman regarded the quilt as a memento of the dead woman.

QUILTS FOR USE

Special occasion quilts were hung on the wall or used with great care. Quilts were also made that were extensively used and regularly washed. These quilts were used as bedding, curtains, table cloths, room screens, and even as clothing.
In less well off homes quilts were made from cheap but hard wearing material. These quilts are often somewhat bleached and damaged from regular washing. Quilts that were used as table cloths or on children's beds came in fro rough treatment.

Double nine patchwork quilt by Mrs Harry Conser.

Quilting technique

Quilts are made up of three layers: the front with the main pattern, the centre with soft material known as batting and the underside with the lining.
The front and rear are made of wool, linen, silk, or cotton. The batting was once often made of wool or cotton but now is often of synthetic filling. There are two methods of quilting: *appliqué* in which a piece of fabric is sewn to another fabric or piecing in which the pieces of fabric are sewn together. The stitching often repeats the pattern of the quilt.

Quilt patterns

Quilt patterns have quite poetic names such as Album Patch, Bowtie, Brick Wall, Broken Dishes, Chinese Coins, Crosses and Losses, Diamond in the Square, Double Shoofy, Flower Garden, Monkey Wrench, Nine Patch, Ocean Wave, Paving Block, Railroad Crossing, Slave Chain (or Job's Tears), Star of Bethlehem, Sunshine and Shadow, Trip around the World, Tumbling Blocks, Windmill Blades, and Young Man's Fancy.

Some of these lovely names represent some extremely common patterns.

NINE PATCH

This pattern consisting of nine squares is the simplest to make. This makes it ideal for beginners. It was the custom for a young girl to learn to quilt as soon as she was able to control her hands. A girl of three or four years old would often practice her wavering stitches with 'nine patch'.

Her mother and the neighbours made most of the quilt of course but there is a good chance that a panel by a young girl was also included. Once she had mastered this she could move on to more complex patterns such as the 'reversed double nine patch'. Of course not every nine patch quilt contains work by young girls but work can be found in quilts by a less experienced seamstress.
Small girls liked to make small nine patch quilts for their dolls. There are countless variations of nine patch that can be recognised by the pattern of squares.

PRAIRIE STARS

Many variations of star motifs are found in quilts. Stars consist of triangles, squares, and other geometric shapes. The star of Bethlehem pattern can only be made by an extremely experienced quilt maker. On the other hand there is a simple star which was the most popular pattern for beginners after nine patch.

SIGNATURE QUILT PATTERNS

The most usual pattern used for quilts with names was the form of a white cross with two squares and a rectangle for the name. There are coloured rectangles and squares surrounding this. This relatively easy pattern enables even less experienced quilt makers to contribute.

This was particularly important with collection quilts where as many women as possible should be involved. There are countless patterns for quilts. Because quilting is regarded these days as an art form new patterns are constantly being added to the repertoire.

American 'crazy' quilt of 1907.

Oriental objects

The term oriental means 'eastern' and this has been equated for a long time with Asia, which starts at the Bosporus. The orient or Asia is the largest part of our world.
The continent is inhabited by diverse peoples with their own cultures and languages. The world's major religions and philosophies have their roots in Asia and their influence in the cultures of this part of the world: Confucianism, Taoism, Hinduism, Buddhism, Shinto, Judaism, Christian, and Islam. In addition to these major religions there is also widespread reverence for ethnic deities throughout Asia. This means that while the region can be defined geographically it cannot be so easily defined creatively.

The great cultures

Great cultural centres existed in Asia thousands of years ago. The most important of these were China, India, Mesopotamia, and Persia. In some of these areas, such as Mesopotamia, agriculture and cattle rearing were the prime means of existence from about 8,000 BC.
Between 3,000 and 2,000BC the oldest civilisations of the world came into being around these agricultural areas. These civilisations developed more or less independently of each other.
Their influence gradually spread itself throughout the rest of Asia.

Chinese art goes back to the late Stone Age. Cultural life in China had already reached a high level in China by 2,000BC and maintained this position almost continuously until the nineteenth century. External influences such as Buddhism played a major role in Chinese development. Chinese art exerted great influence on Japanese art around 500BC but Japanese art gradually developed its own direction. There was new artistic development in India around 300BC with the rise of Buddhism.

Polychrome 18th century chine de commande pot with lid on moulded base.

This religion took Buddhist art to much of Asia, including China and Japan. In India though Hindu art eventually dominated. Islamic art also pushed forward to the area in around 1,200AD.
Mesopotamian culture flourished under the Sumerians (from 3,000BC), the Assyrians, and the Babylonians (from 2,000BC).

The Persians outflanked the land of the two rivers several centuries before Christ. After the high point of the Persian Empire Hellenic influences were apparent in the western part of Asia. The Persian culture underwent a renaissance during Sassanian rule from sixth to third centuries before Christ.

Islam and Mongols

Following the death of the prophet Muhammad in 632 the Muhammadan sphere of influence extended to India and Indonesia. Buddhism continued to be the major religion in most parts of South-East Asia and therefore the most important artistic influence. This development resulted in the sharp contrast with the Hindu state of India and with Chinese civilisation.

Around 1200 the entire continent of Asia was in uproar. The Mongol hordes were spreading out from Central Asia under their leader Ghengis Khan. Khanates were established (areas under the rule of a Khan) in China, Central Asia, Persia, and Southern Russia. The Mongol expeditions introduced migration of peoples and caused important changes as far afield as South-East Asia and Japan. After the retreat of Mongol dominance came the rise of the Ottomans in South-West Asia.

The Ottoman or Turkish empire was to be the major political force there from the fifteenth until the twentieth century

Contacts between East and West

There was a mission from Caesar Augustus to the Chinese court around the time of Christ and traders from the Roman Empire dealt as far afield as the eastern coast of India. The Roman Empire and Chinese civilisation were also linked by the Silk Route – an overland trading route between Europe and China that was long used for the trade of silk from China.

A fine example of a chine de commande St Matthew plate in which both saint and house acquire Chinese characteristics.

Wool, gold, and silver were taken from the Roman Empire to Asia. The Silk Route was abandoned following the fall of the Roman Empire. In the thirteenth century people started to use the Silk Route once more.
Christianity spread by this means to the Far East when missionaries and explorers such as Marco Polo used the route. Buddhism from India also reached China by this means. There was little interest though in Medieval Europe for the Far East.
It was not until the sixteenth century that explorers once more restored close contact between Asia and Europe.
In the seventeenth but especially the eighteenth and nineteenth centuries the Dutch, Russians, French, and British established colonies in Asia. Only the strong Asian states such as the Ottomans, China, and Japan managed to prevent western colonisation.

Reciprocal influence

The arrival of westerns was not without consequences of course.

In the nineteenth century the influence of western art started to be felt in virtually all parts of Asia. In China and Japan special products were made for the European market and tastes.
This influence varied from adaptation of their own designs to the making of items that were completely European in style. One example of this is *chine de commande.* Western traders ordered porcelain products from the Chinese and this was decorated according to examples provided by the commissioning trader. Chine de commande was very popular and was shipped to the west in huge quantities.

The superficiality of the contacts between Asia and Europe really can be seen from the figures painted on *chine de commande* items. Their clothing and appearance are typically Chinese and the same is true of any buildings illustrated which frequently have Chinese style roofs. Despite the examples they were copying it seems as if the Chinese painters could not entirely free themselves from the work that surrounded them.

Chine de commande 18th century milk jug.

The Far East and Europe influence each other. Chinese and Japanese art were so popular in Europe that people started to make objects in the Chinese style. The chinoiserie of this Dutch Louis XVI style dresser is a good example.

Asia and Europe influenced each other. Legend has it that Marco Polo took Chinese noodles to Italy where they became spaghetti and macaroni.
Oriental art was directly copied in Europe but was also the inspiration for

new forms that led to *chinoiserie*. The quest for the means of producing porcelain that was once only made in China and Japan is another example of oriental influence on Europe.
After all the English word for this material remains china.

The attraction of the Orient

Oriental art has not always been admired in the west. The differences between the cultures caused more fear than praise. Voyages of discovery in the Middle Ages led to more being known about the rest of the world. Even then all that was known of the Far East was by word of mouth. Very few people had any direct contact with such strange cultures. The great fear of the unknown was receding though in this expanding world and people were now curious.

Westerners understood from stories that these far distant lands were very different and the import of artistic objects from this part of the world reinforced this impression.

The exotic form of these objects and the centuries of continuous civilisation were very interesting to westerners.

Chinese and Japanese culture

The enthusiasm for the written Chinese language has remained across the centuries. The Chinese who learned to write had to learn thousands of characters by heart and those who achieved this enjoyed high social status. The high regard for calligraphy has its origins in the administrative structure of the Chinese Empire.

The country was not governed by nobility but by officials who were selected by means of tough examinations.

A 80mm (31/8 in) Chinese bronze water buffalo of the 18th century.

CHINA

Artistic objects reflect the priorities of the Chinese elite. Many fine pieces were made for their desks: ink stones, water pots, paint brush pots, and seal boxes. These were normally provided with archaic ornamentation which reflects China's deep interest, even reverence for the past.
This interest extends to the language of form of antique objects. Chinese interest in antiques began in the tenth century when the well-to-do began to collect bronze objects. The language of form and decoration of these pieces was also adopted for objects then being made.

The educated elite connected this with Confucianism. Sculpture and other forms of art which evoked associations with Buddhism, which was distrusted by this elite, were avoided. Buddhism was so

Lacquered Chinese 19th century needlework case.

suspected by the authorities that it was evenly officially banned under certain dynasties.

JAPAN

The attitude of those in power towards Buddhism was different in Japan. During the endless disputes between the feudal overlords the Buddhist monasteries were sacrosanct. Japanese art is equally strongly influenced by Chinese art. The differences are mainly to be found in the emphases on particular aspects. The history of Japan is very different to that of China.

The Chinese 'Middle Kingdom' was a strongly centralised country that has been constantly invaded by barbarians from outside throughout its history. Japan on the other hand is an isolated archipelago. Unlike China it was not exposed to constant external influences. The absence of enemies caused divisions among its people with the local overlords constantly disputing with each other. Their courtly ways and feudal military preferences decisively influenced their culture. Typical Japanese objects include those decorated with golden lacquer that are associated with the tea ceremony and fine swords.

Except for religious objects most carved items were for personal used. These pieces were small and intended to impress others: paint brush pots, snuff bottles, and netsuke. Because of their practical nature, the usefulness of these objects was as important as their appearance. Japan only became peaceful under the Tokugawa Shogunate (1615–1867). Tokugawa rule forbade almost all contact with foreigners.

One of the few exceptions was the Dutch East India Company which established a factory on the island of Decima in Nagasaki bay. An urban culture developed in the 'land of the rising sun' with

Japanese 19th century dresser with lacquer and inlaid mother of pearl.

rich merchants. The decorative art reached high levels. The American navy ended this period of isolation in 1854.

Ceramics

Chinese ceramics

Many are of the opinion that China takes first place in the history of ceramics. The tradition of Chinese pottery starts long before our present Christian system of dates and was responsible for many important developments, innovation, and improvements. Formerly the more recent Chinese porcelain was much admired but in the twentieth century excavations uncovered exquisite earlier ceramics. The high point must certainly be the Sung Dynasty (960–1280).
The history of Chinese ceramics began much earlier though in about 2000BC,

still in the time of the Stone Age, when people in Honan and Kansu in northern China made fine earthenware that was painted with geometric patterns.
Expressive glazed tomb figures have been found from the Chou Dynasty (circa 600BC).

THE FIRST MAJOR PERIOD

During the Han Dynasty (206BC–220AD) the used of earthenware in the extensive burial rituals became even greater. Life sized sculpture replaced the traditional animal and human sacrifices. These figures accompanied the dead person to the after life.

A famous example of this is the recently discovered terracotta army of Ksiang. Techniques of painting and glazing also became more important, probably as a result of contact with Asia Minor. During the Tang Dynasty (618–907) the tomb figures were smaller.
During the Han Dynasty some green glazed pottery was made but during the Tang Dynasty they began to use three-coloured lead glaze, known as 'egg-with-spinach'. They also learned to paint earthenware with colour beneath the glaze and also introduced an early form of series production.

In addition repeated motifs such as the camel's heads, courtiers, limbs, horses, and bodies were printed on.

Kangxi egg and spinach, signed Lingzhi.

PORCELAIN

During the Tang Dynasty the slow process of refining stoneware took place. The use of kaolin or china clay resulted in a white opaque body that became known as porcelain or china. It would take another 1,000 years before people in Meissen could come close to this quality (see Meissen).

When the trade with the Far East began to increase Japanese and Chinese blue and white porcelain was one of the biggest influences on European ceramic production.

In the Sung Dynasty, that succeeded the Tang, pottery achieved a new standard of elegance. Through changes in the culture surrounding death, the tomb figures disappeared and interest grew in wares for tea. Thick walled bowls were often used for this purpose which conducted heat less quickly so that they could be held more easily. Coloured glazes too were developed at this time which were often used on this thick earthenware.

IMPERIAL WORKS

Just as in Europe, China also had Imperial pottery works that were set up by the rulers. During the Sung Dynasty these made a wide range of products during the period prior to 1127 when the Imperial works at Tsju-Loe-Hsiu were destroyed.

These were re-established south of Jangtsekiang. The move to central China was not just because it was safer there but with the increasing emphasis on porcelain the new works was in an area that was rich in kaolin.

The Loeng-Tsjuan-Jao earthenware of the Sung Dynasty with Celadon is famous. This thick-walled earthenware with a fatty, grey-green glaze was widely used throughout the Islamic world. Under the Mogul Yüan dynasty the organisation of Imperial works was improved and they were all centred around the Imperial works of Tsjing-Teh-Tsjen in Kiangsi province. It was at this time that it was discovered how to fire blue painted and glazed porcelain. This was to have special significance in the development of porcelain.

MING PORCELAIN

The Imperial works of Tsjing-Teh-Tsjen began to flourish during the Ming Dynasty (1368–1644). The old Sung works became of no significance and the Celadon works of Loeng-Tsjuan were moved to Tsju-Tsju on the coast. This was much more convenient for export. Ming Dynasty porcelain is extremely diverse.

The export of these ceramics grew in the sixteenth century. This led to mass production and to a readiness to meet the taste of the Europeans (and also East Indies) customers. Porcelain periods are named from the Imperial ruling dynasty of the time it was made. This was made easier by the Ming emperors requiring porcelain to bear a mark.

At first this mark consisted of four characters 'made during the reign of' followed by the emperor's name. After 1426 the dynasty mark appeared above this with the Chinese character for 'exalted'.

Unfortunately the early marks are often copied so that marks are not always a reliable indication of age and quality. It is therefore necessary when judging a piece to mainly rely on its style and present condition.

FURTHER DEVELOPMENTS DURING THE MING DYNASTY

The first period in which porcelain flourished during the Ming Dynasty was under Emperor Xuande (1426–1435) who added two additional characters to pieces. These pieces have fine blue and also red underglaze. Early Ming blue painting is softly greyish. Pieces sent to Persia often have a darker mixture. The second period of excellence was under Emperor Chenghua (1465–1487).

At this time fine cups and dishes were made with drawings of birds, flowers, and insects in enamel colours on a white background. A start was also made with a yellow ground at this time. After this time the influence of Islamic customers on the painted patterns increased.

Under Emperor Jiaqing (1522–1566), who was opposed to Buddhism, porcelain was often decorated with Taoist motifs and figures such as cranes, birch and pine trees, and tortoises. Large items of tableware and vases painted in dark blue typify this period. Under his successor this quickly became a paler blue.

EXPORT

Contacts with Europeans became more intensive around 1600.
The Dutch East India Company started to buy large quantities of – initially blue – porcelain. This preference has great bearing on the development of Dutch Delft pottery (see Delft).

This imitated the Chinese blue style and from the late seventeenth century also imitated Chinese coloured wares. The enormous growth in exports eventually caused a problem for Chinese production. Many items that came from private works were of poor quality.

The lower standards of the mass produced articles decorated with patterns supplied from Europe meant a great threat to the general level of quality. Production from the Imperial works continued alongside these mass produced items but almost none of this reached Europe before 1900.

A deep Chinese Qianlong dynasty famille rose *plate.*

A fine example of an 18th century Chinese famille rose *porcelain.*

TECHNICAL HIGH AND LOW POINTS (1662–1850)

A new highpoint was reached after a period of calm under the Manchu or Ch'ing Dynasty. The period of the rule of Emperor Kangxi (1662–1722) was particularly important in terms of the development of ceramics. Under his control the Imperial kilns at Tsjing-Teh-Tsjen achieved a high degree of refinement. The style name for these wares is derived from the dominant colour. These were the *famille* verte and much rarer *famille noire.* After this period the drawing was of lesser strength.

This was the time of *famille rose.* The Chinese also achieved the highest quality in the ground which they used. Some pieces are as thin as eggshells. They were decorated by Cantonese enamel painters and sometimes also had an underside of pink. The quality of porcelain slowly deteriorated during the course of the eighteenth century. The makers increasingly produced copies of earlier wares and this continued in the nineteenth century. Around 1850 Tsjing-Teh-Tsjen was destroyed. Although the Imperial kilns were rebuilt the high quality and artistic attainment did not return.

An 18th century Chinese Wanli plate.

Kangxi tea jar with moulded silver lid.

A fine import from China: 17th century drinking fountain with wooden partition.

OTHER PRODUCTS

In addition to the products from the Imperial kilns other wares were obviously also produced in China. From the

Large 18th century wine cooler in blue and white porcelain.

A fine 19th century polychrome Chinese vase 1500mm (60in) high.

A simple Chinese porcelain tea cup.

late sixteenth century *blanc de Chine* wares were made at Te-Hoan. The best known are the temple animals. This ceramic ware is of similar quality to porcelain from Tsjing-Teh-Tsjen. Older pieces from the seventeenth century can be recognised by their creamy glaze and the non glazed inside.

The quality gradually deteriorated until they ended up as mere bazaar goods. A lot of coarse porcelain was produced in

Chinese blue porcelain soup tureen circa 1800, made to European design.

Chine de commande 18th century mustard pot.

Two 18th century sauce boats and dish of Chinese blue and white porcelain.

the coastal region of Fu-Kian from the Ming Dynasty onwards. The composition of the body is not so refined as that used for fine porcelain and the glazing, painting, and firing is less carefully carried out. The main attraction of these pieces is that they are generally examples of folk art that portrays greater spontane-

Chinese 18th century porcelain covered dish.

Chinese 18th century rectangular blue and white porcelain salad bowl.

Chinese 18th century export ware cup and saucer.

Tiny lobed cup and saucer of Chinese blue and white porcelain.

ity and imagination. These objects were being sold to European settlements in the Far East from junks by traders by the seventeenth century. The East Indies archipelago and the Philippines were the main markets.

Japan

EARLY POTTERY

Early Japanese pottery has no individual character but is influenced by both China and Korea. Ceramics were imported into Japan from both these countries. Japan did not develop its own products until

A simple 18th century Japanese porcelain dish.

the thirteenth century. Through the increasing consumption of tea, a pottery was established in Seto by Toshiro where he copied Chinese wares. Elsewhere the potteries of Koreans, who had worked in Japan since the eight century, were extended.

Skilled Korean potters were also brought to Japan following the Japanese conquest of Korea in the fifteenth century. In some places several generations of famous Japanese potters lived. They made wares of high aesthetic quality. These items are often very simple and purposeful. They have a wonderful colour as a result of the thick glazes.

Small drinking bowls *(chawan)*, large drinking bowls *(temoku)*, and tea jars with lids *(chaire)* were made for tea ceremonies. The finest come from Seto, Kioto, Karatsu, and Satsuma. They are often dark, usually unpainted, but are sometimes decorated with simple drawings. These potteries produced such wares until the nineteenth century. Dating these pieces can be very difficult because the same family mark was often in use for centuries.

JAPANESE PORCELAIN

Porcelain was also produced in Japan. In common with their pottery, Japanese porcelain makers followed Chinese and Korean examples.

The Japanese only truly mastered the porcelain process at the beginning of the sixteenth century. The main centre for porcelain was Arita. Both the kaolin and

A set of Imari cups and saucers.

Japanese Imari dish.

Japanese Imari plate.

Imari bowl, 18th century.

Satsuma ware mantel set with clock, circa 1850 or earlier.

steatite used in China are found near Arita. After refinement these materials do not need to be mixed with any others. Arita produced white porcelain and the blue underglaze was more as less identical to Chinese practice.
The Japanese succeeded in producing superb enamelled wares. The potter Kakiemon was the first to perfect the technique. His fine coloured decoration were known by his name. They were extremely popular in Europe and imitated by Chelsea, Delft, Meissen. and St-Cloud (see also Ceramics).

Japanese Imari porcelain was extremely popular in Europe. This is named after the port from which it was shipped. Even the Chinese copied Imari wares, albeit in a darker blue. Imari is intensively decorated with at blue that is almost black, red, and gold.

Carving

Jade has been regarded as a very special precious stone in China since prehistoric times. Jade is rarely found in China but is bought from Khotan in Central Asia that

A fine large Imari dish.

is astride the trade route between Eastern Asia and the Middle East. Jade is harder than metal so it is worked with bamboo string operated drills together with a grinding medium such as quartz sand. The process takes a long time and is therefore very costly. Jade has been used as raw material throughout Chinese history. It was not exported until the nineteenth century when it began to be worked for foreign markets. The home market demand for Jade had dropped during the eighteenth century through the growing interest in carvings with other types of hard stone. Other materials that have been used for carving since early times are ivory and bone.

Ivory in particular became an important raw material for desk accessories for scientists after the seventeenth century. It was used for paint brush pots and boxes for sealing wax. *Okimono* is Japan ese carving that is purely decorative. Much of it was exported in the nineteenth century to Europe and America. *Okimono* can also be made from ivory.

Bronze

Bronze objects are among the earliest Chinese art. The process for making bronze objects became known in certain parts of Central Asia between 3000 and 2000BC and the knowledge then spread to China. All manner of objects have been made in bronze. Some of the oldest of them are weapons, agricultural implements, cooking utensils, and also ritual urns. Bronze casting was given a major impetus after the fifth century BC by Buddhism. This religion exercised a tremendous influence on the design of bronze objects.

Lacquered items

The basis for lacquer is the dried sap of the East Asian *Rhus vernicifera* that drips from this tree in summer and autumn. The lacquer made from this is extremely hard once it has dried. Because both time and experience are essential ingredients in the lacquering process,

Fine Japanese Imari antique vases.

lacquered objects have always been expensive. Even the drying can take weeks. In order to achieve the necessary thickness a number of layers of lacquer have to be applied.

The Portuguese, who were the first to trade in the Far East, took Japanese lacquer work back to Europe with them as well as porcelain. In the seventeenth century Japanese lacquered items were mainly decorated with landscapes and gardens. This type of work was copied in both China and Europe. Indeed the export of Japanese lacquer reduced in the eighteenth century because Canton in China had taken the lead in the market.

A fine 18th century Cantonese bowl.

Once the country opened its borders in 1854 though exports from Japan increased significantly.

Maintenance and restoration of antiques

Looking after antiques

Few collectors understand the influence the surroundings have on an antique. The climate of the surroundings in which the object is placed is the basis for all maintenance. The effects of sun and light, heat, and air humidity can be disastrous for antiques.

Creating the right circumstance is therefore the key to looking after antiques. Of course this is not always practicable and the ideal situation might not make a home pleasant to live in. Creating the right environment is therefore the result of a calculation that will be different for each collector. A house is after all a home. There are three rules of thumb for creating the right environment for antiques. Firstly it unwise to site them where there is a lot of sun.

This is especially true of textile and paper that are particularly sensitive to light. The ultraviolet light in sunlight harms these materials and hastens their decay. An extreme example is a newspaper left in the sun that will quickly become yellow and brittle. Textile and paper are better hung in a shaded place. Light them with spotlights temperature also has an effect on antiques. Too hot and too cold are best avoided. Keep the temperature preferably between 16–20°C (60–68°F). Beware of the heat radiated from lamps, heating, and equipment and the same is true of display cases, specially if they have their own lighting. Generally it is best to avoid sudden large changes in temperature.

The third matter which a collector needs to consider is the humidity of the air. It is worth buying a hygrometer in order check this regularly. The ideal relative humidity is in the range 50 to 60 percent. Here too sudden large shifts are best avoided. A critical time is autumn when central heating is switched back on. The relative humidity will then drop rapidly and it is sensible to use a humidifier at these times.

D-I-Y restoration

Most collectors do not have the space, experience, or skill to carry out major restoration work themselves. They can though perform many minor restoration tasks themselves. These only need a few tools and the antiques are not at risk of

Oak chiffoniere with 6 drawers, circa 1830.

damage from them. Collectors also enjoy cleaning and maintaining their pieces. Maintenance means looking after antiques constantly. It is therefore important to know which methods can be used and how they should be done. A collector who starts restoring an antique object him or herself should first consider whether it is better to use a professional restorer.

This consideration is closely connected with the value of the piece but the contents of the wallet or purse are also a consideration: will he or she be able to afford the restoration? There are many good tools, treatments, and materials available these days. There are also treatments which you can make yourself.

This is not the place to try to save a little money for the restoration may well be affected. But with care, particularly making sure not to spill any of the special treatments, costs can be kept within bounds.
Factors such as the complexity of the repair and capability of the person who is carrying it out also need to be entered into the decision making process.

A key factor is how much experience of restoration the collector already has. It is sensible when gaining experience not to start with a major repair, nor with a valuable or irreplaceable item. Collectors can assess their own abilities and need not underestimate themselves, without taking unnecessary risks.

Professional restoration is expensive and many things can be done yourself. It is important to think carefully about a repair beforehand.

What needs to be done? If a collector does not know all the answers then it is essential to get expert advice. A museum conservator may be a useful source. A dealer may be able to advise for smaller repairs but take care because not every dealer has the same amount of knowledge about restoration.

An early 19th century silver stopper and corkscrew.

Of course you may consult a professional restorer who may be prepared to tell you how to repair a piece without risk but do remember that restoration is their living. Patience is an essential quality when restoring antiques.

The final result of restoration is only visible in a late stage of the restoration and sometimes only at the final moment, yet all the preparation is extremely time intensive.

This can be so discouraging for some collectors that they give up. Others become convinced that the piece is ruined anyway and so they finish the repair off far too hastily. It is a golden rule always to remain patient and prepare the work well. This is equally true when a

An 18th century Southern German or Austrian commode.

collector has become more experienced. You will not improve if over confident and too hasty.

It is a good idea, where possible, to start with a test on a less obtrusive or unseen part of a piece. It is usually uncertain what will be found beneath layers of dirt or over- painting. A trial area can also provide information about the effects of the restoration that will be useful as the restoration proceeds.

Restoring and maintaining natural and artificial stone

Natural stone

Both hard and soft types of stone need to be regularly cleaned of moss and lichen. This is done by first hosing all dirt and growth off the stone. This process can take several days. If this is not possible the stone can be brushed with water using green household soap but the stone must be thoroughly rinsed afterwards.

Building suppliers, DIY shops, chemists, and ironmongers sell special products for removing stubborn dirt and moss.

Certain products seal stone with a layer of wax. Stubborn stains such as oil or grease will usually required expert treatment. These can rarely be removed with aggressive cleaning substances.

Cracks in natural stone can be repaired with epoxy resin. Both surfaces need to be thoroughly clean and grease free. The two pieces should be held firmly together while the adhesive sets.

With large repairs it is necessary to insert non porous metal rods into the stone. Drill holes for these into the stone and fill with epoxy resin which will also hold the rods in place.

Any filling can also be done with an epoxy based filler. The required colour can be achieved by adding pigment to the filler.

Ceramics

There are two types of ceramics: porous earthenware on the one hand and porcelain and glazed earthenware on the other. Porcelain originated from China and Japan.

Western potters sought the means to make porcelain for centuries. The German Böttcher finally succeeded in 1709. Important forms of earthenware (pottery) are stoneware (grès), majolica (maiolica)

A statue of a lion, pre 1782.

Wedgwood stoneware coffee service, circa 1900.

or faience, Delft, and terracotta. Stoneware bridges the gap between pottery and porcelain because it is non-porous. Majolica or faience is earthenware that is tinglazed. This glaze is opaque white, making it suitable for decoration. Delft is earthenware.

Terracotta is earthenware made with red clay that is not glazed. Valuable ceramic items should not be washed but merely brushed clean with a soft brush. Other ceramic objects can generally be washed in warm water with some washing up liquid.

It is best to avoid using brushes or nylon sponges and such like when cleaning these. Dry ceramic objects with a dry cloth to restore their lustre. Strongly discoloured items such as teapots can sometimes be cleaned with a solution of bleach. Use 20 per cent hydro-peroxide for this purpose. Steradent is useful for cleaning inside small vases and other inaccessible surfaces.

Most coloured pigments are not able to withstand the high temperatures needed to fire ceramic objects so they are often applied after firing. Cleaning decorated porcelain needs to be done with great care, especially if decorated with gold.

Tea contains tannic acid that causes the deposits on the inside of teapots. The acid sometimes penetrates through the pot to discolour the outside with a brown deposit. Teapots must therefore be cleaned regularly. Fill the pot with warm water and dissolve a desert spoon full of borax in the water.

Leave the solution to soak in for an hour before cleaning with a nylon sponge. The spout needs to be cleaned with a flexible bottle brush.

When repairing ceramics the surfaces to be glued must be clean and degreased. Broken ceramics can be repaired using epoxy resin adhesive, PVA adhesive or cyanoacrylate instant adhesives. As little adhesive as possible should be used. Adhesive that comes out of the joins must be cleaned off with a cloth using the appropriate solution (water for PVA glue, white spirit or paint thinners for epoxy resin.

Chinese porcelain plate, 18th century.

Dresden porcelain flower bearers.

An 18th century Chinese octagonal serving dish made to European designs.

German 17th century alabaster and ebony jewel case.

It is important while the adhesives set to hold the parts firmly together. It may sometimes be necessary to redo old repairs. These were often repaired in the past with a bone-based glue which can be dissolved by soaking in hot water.

Areas where small pieces are missing can be filled with an epoxy resin filler to which pigment may need to be added.

The filler should be applied slightly more thickly than the piece itself. When it has set this can be sanded down with a fine grade waterproof wet and dry emery paper. Retouching of any decoration is best done with acrylic paint. When the paint is dry it can be 'glazed' with a polyurethane varnish.

Alabaster

Alabaster is soft natural stone that is easy to work with. The marble like material is ideally suitable for making small objects. It can be found in a pure white form and also with veining from dirt. Colours vary from white through yellow and pink to brown. The veining is usually green or black but can be multicoloured. Both types can be polished.

There are two forms of alabaster: gypsum alabaster and chalk alabaster. Gypsum alabaster can be recognised from chalk alabaster because it is easy to scratch a mark in gypsum alabaster with a nail. The latter material is also characterised by the shine it takes on when washed with soap and water. The surface of alabaster can be protected with a little beeswax.

Alabaster used to be repaired with a mixture of gum and powdered alabaster or with white of egg and hydrated lime. Modern materials such as PVA or epoxy resin adhesives are also suitable though. Missing fragments can be remodelled with a mixture of epoxy resin and kaolin, chalk or titanium oxide.

Kaolin, chalk, and titanium oxide are naturally white. The removal of surface grime from alabaster is easily done with a clean cloth using turpentine. Stubborn dirt can be cleaned with distilled water (tap water contains acids that will harm the alabaster). A useful trick is to dissolve Steradent in luke warm distilled water. A cotton bud dipped in this solution will remove a lot of dirt. An even stronger option is to use a cleaning agent that is good for grease marks and old layers of wax. A last resort solution is to use paint stripper.

Amber

Amber is an organic material used as a gem stone that may be golden yellow (amber), brown, or white. The 'stone' is found along the German and Polish Baltic coast, on Sicily, in Romania, and Burma. Amber was created by the resin from a now extinct form of coniferous tree. Most amber is honey coloured, lending its name to the colour amber but some is dark brown.

Amber sometimes contains insects or parts of them or flower petals and leaves. Amber is often incorporated in jewellery. When rubbed it released a slightly musky scent. This is the way to recognise genuine amber from artificial copies. Artificial amber can look very real and even contain organic remains such as insects. One way of testing amber is to allow a drop of ether to fall on it. Artificial amber is soft and will mist over.

Amber's shine becomes even more intense when worn and used regularly. Cracks in amber can be repaired with a cyanoacrylate instant adhesive or epoxy resin. Amber is normally transparent but contact with water can make it dull. Amber must therefore never be cleaned with water. Amber can be wiped clean with chalk in a cotton cloth or chamois leather.

To get rid of any dullness caused by contact with water it is usually sufficient to place amber in a warm place (but not too hot, so not on top of a radiator). The haze will then normally disappear. If this does not help then hang the amber in the vapour from three parts of turpentine to one of spirits but take care for this mixture is flammable.

Cameos

Cameos are made with different coloured layers of precious stones – usually agate. Relief moulding is cut in the stone taking advantage of the natural colour nuances of the stone itself.

Shell cameo in silver mount, circa 1870.

Cameos cut from sea shells have an upper creamy white layer and red or pink ground. Semi-precious rock crystal and onyx are also used. Cameos can also be ceramic such as those by Wedgwood. Today there are also deceivingly real looking cameos for sale made of plastic. Cameos can be cleaned with warm soapy water and a nail brush. Any soap must be rinsed off thoroughly afterwards under a running tap. Broken slivers or cracks can be repaired with epoxy resin or cyanoacrylate instant adhesive.

Use sparingly and make sure no adhesive is left on the face of the cameo. The parts need to be held firmly together while the adhesive sets. Use a bed of modelling clay or Plasticine.

Plaster figures and ornaments

Plaster figures and ornaments were often treated in the past with hot wax or size that penetrated deep into the plaster. Examples include Victorian and later copies of classical works.

Plaster attracts dirt and can become very grimy. The layer can be so thick that it may not be certain if the substance is plaster underneath. This can best be checked by scratching off a little of the surface. Plaster is much softer than stone. Dirt can be removed with spirits but it is

Dutch brooch with jet, circa 1880.

sensible to protect the piece afterwards with soft white beeswax.
Repairs to plaster can be done with plaster of course but PVA adhesive is a good alternative. Missing parts can also be modelled. They must first set and dry thoroughly before being attached. Because plaster is extremely soft, repairs can be refined with a knife or sandpaper.

Jet

Jet is a form of fossilised wood that can be readily cut and polishes up to resemble a gemstone. Jet was widely used in late nineteenth century jewellery. Jet can be cleaned with a cloth dampened with water or methylated spirit.

Polish the surface afterwards with a soft dry cloth. Damage can be repaired with epoxy resin or an instant cyanoacrylate adhesive.

Marble

Marble can be easily worked and sawn. This sedimentary limestone has therefore been popular for thousands of years with sculptors and architects. Marble varies in colour from pure white to multicoloured. Marble breaks easily and must never be roughly handled.
Care in particular needs to be taken with large flat pieces such as table tops. Always carry these on their side and never flat for they can break under their own weight. White and light-coloured marble fades because fine dust collects in the porous surface. It is therefore wise to dust marble regularly. It should also be washed regularly with tepid soapy water. Polished marble indoors should always be thoroughly dried after washing. Very grimy marks can be cleaned with a degreasing agent.

It is best to start though with a solution that is half strength to that advised. The concentration can be increased if necessary. Paint stripper is a method of last resort. If used this must be done very slowly and carefully. Rinse the marble after using stripper with plenty of cold water. Once cleaned, marble can be protected with a thin layer of beeswax. White marble though can discolour this way.
It is therefore sensible to test it first on a small area, where it will not be seen.

French 19th century figurine of Joan of Arc on a red marble base.

An old recipe for gluing marble is 63 parts of carnauba wax and 37 parts of dammar resin melted together in a pan. The advantage of this glue is that it is also easily removed.

Onyx

Onyx is a form of agate. European onyx is generally green. This multicoloured stone is widely used for table tops and for lamp bases. Certain types of onyx are also used for cameos of which the upper white layer is cut away to reveal the colour beneath. Onyx should be washed with warm soapy water. It is a porous stone that absorbs grease and discolouring substances. Such patches can be cleaned with a cotton bud dipped in spirit.

To prevent the patch from spreading the stone needs to be thoroughly dried immediately after treatment. Small fissures in onyx can be filled with a paste of a suitable coloured filler made from kaolin and epoxy resin. In order to get the right colour a little pigment can be added to the mixture. Broken onyx can be glued using epoxy resin.

Restoring and maintaining glass

Glass is a fusion of silica – quartz, sand, or flint – with an alkali to add smelting. The alkali used is soda or potash. Soda can be derived from seaweed. Potash is wood ash steeped in lye. When glass was made in areas with forests it is green resulting from potash.

Glass from coastal areas, such as Venice, is colourless through the use of soda. The most common types of glass used for all manner of household objects are potash or soda glass.

Glass drinking horn or 'Sauhund' from Switzerland, post 1900.

Artificially produced crystal should not be confused with naturally occurring rock crystal. Rock crystal was used in very early cultures to make jewellery.
There are many other types of glass with variations occurring during the glass-making process by the means of additives. The addition of metal oxides can produce different coloured glass and the layering of coloured glasses over each other makes artistic effects possible.

Lead is added to crystal glass or lead glass in order to make the glass sparkle but this also makes the glass more brittle. The best crystal has a pure metal ring. This contains 24 percent lead and is known as lead crystal. When crystal is cut it reflects all the colours of a rainbow. Crystal is mainly used in chandeliers and drinking glasses. Glass can be worked in a number of ways. At normal temperatures it can be etched, polished, cut, and sandblasted. Glass can be pressed into shapes at high temperatures.

Originally glass was formed into shape by blowing. This is a laborious process. New methods for making glass objects were developed in the early nineteenth century and machine blown and later pressed glass were introduced. This made the production of glass much cheaper so that everyone could afford glass. Glass breaks easily therefore it must be handled carefully when being cleaned.

It is not a good idea to brush dirt off glass without washing because dust can contain abrasive particles which will scratch glass.

Washing in warm soapy water is usually sufficient but do not use hot water. Sudden changes in temperature can cause glass to crack or shatter. Glass first needs to drain then it can be dried thoroughly with a tea towel and polished with chamois leather. Hard water deposits of limescale can be removed with a dilute solution of hydrochloric acid. A simpler method of cleaning the insides of glass bottles and carafes is to use water with a denture cleaner such as Steradent.

There are first class modern adhesives available for repairing broken glass. These are the cyanoacrylate instant glues. Broken glass can be almost invisibly glued with these but it is sensible to first check how the pieces fit together. The broken edges need the be degreased with white spirit before the adhesive is applied to both surfaces to be joined and then held together for a short time.

Wineglass with white spiral stem. 18th century.

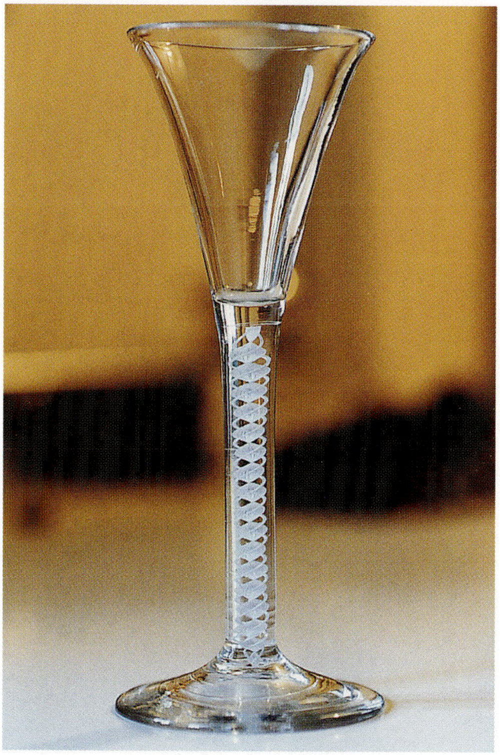

Excess glue can be removed with a cloth soaked in white spirit. If there are remains of the adhesive left on the surface after it has set these can be removed with a sharp craft knife or scalpel. Old glass can become chipped through use. These chips can be smoothed down using a very fine polishing paper. Coarser paper causes scratches that will make the glass opaque. Ground glass stoppers for carafes or decanters can become jammed if not used for some time. Try warming the neck of the decanter slightly in the first place.

This may allow it to expand sufficiently to release the stopper. If this fails make a solution of two parts white spirit to one part glycerine and add a few crystals of camphor to the solution.
Pour this around the stopper and leave for a few hours after which it should be possible to twist the stopper to remove it. A little petroleum jelly can be smeared around the stopper to prevent it jamming.

Chandeliers

Chandeliers are often made with glass crystal which is cut in such a way that it scatters the lights in every possible direction. Candles were formerly used as the light source in chandeliers but today these are usually replaced with candle shaped lamps.

The droppers, beads, and pearls of crystal are sometimes attached to a metal frame (usually copper or brass). Sometimes the entire chandelier is made of glass.

Louis XVI style Venetian crystal chandelier.

Because a chandelier hangs close to the ceiling it quickly becomes grimy with smoke and disturbed dust which makes it lose its sparkle. A chandelier therefore needs to be cleaned regularly. This can be done on a step ladder but it is far better done on the ground.

It is therefore sensible if the chandelier is attached to a pulley or other device which allows it to be lowered. Take care though for chandeliers are heavy with all that glass.

Chandeliers can be taken apart. They are held together with brass or other non ferrous metal. Once chandeliers were cleaned by rubbing them with a chamois leather glove but these days the parts are washed in warm water with a little washing up solution or ammonia. Dry each part with a piece of chamois leather or a soft cloth.

The metal in the chandelier has to cope with all the movement during cleaning. As the years progress this may suffer metal fatigue. The wire threads should be replaced as required. This is not difficult because each crystal element has one or two holes in it but do not use steel or iron wire because it can rust and discolour the crystal elements. It can take a great deal of time to locate replacement parts for chandeliers in antique or lighting shops

Mirrors

The first Venetian mirrors were made in the early sixteenth century. Mirrors were made in England from 1615 by Sir Robert Mansell.

Glass for these was blown into a cylinder which was then cut open. The glass was then polished on a stone and finally the back was silvered with mercury or tin foil.

French 19th century hall mirror with raised frame.

The size of these mirrors was restricted for a considerable time. Larger mirrors were made using more than one piece of mirror glass. The technique of silvering mirrors with silver was greatly improved in the seventeenth century. Everyone has seen a distressed mirror at some time and this is the most common problem with mirrors.

Damp quickly distresses old mirrors so they should not be cleaned with water or at least water should be used sparingly. It is better to clean them with a soft cloth and some methylated spirits. To get the glass to shine, polish it with old newspaper.
If you want to use an old mirror frame store the original mirror glass in a special case or frame and put a replacement mirror in the frame. For the new glass do not choose one that looks too harsh.

Old mirror glass needs very careful handling because it is very thin and brittle. Resilvering a mirror or replacement of the mirror is work for a specialist.

Restoration and maintenance of metal

Aluminium

Aluminium is a material with a relatively short history of use. Aluminium did not start to be used in any volume much before 1855.

Once new techniques were developed for the production of aluminium in 1886 it use became more widespread. Aluminium is very susceptible to corrosive substances so the first rule for keeping aluminium objects is to prevent then coming into contact with such substances. Oxidisation of aluminium can be recognised as a white hard deposit on the surface. Such matt areas should be polished clean with very fine wire wool and then protected with wax. Many aluminium objects are anodised to prevent oxidisation which can give the surface a coloured finish.

Increasing use was made of modern materials in the twentieth century. This Art Deco radiator in copper also uses some aluminium parts.Thin metal painted tobacco box, post 1600.

Because aluminium is a very soft material the anodised surface should not be cleaned with any abrasive cleaners which will irreparably harm them. Shiny and anodised surfaces of aluminium should be cleaned with a soft damp cloth.

Stubborn grime on aluminium can be removed with a solution of borax. Dissolve one dessertspoon of borax in 300 ml of water (10 fl oz).

Take great care with this method for this solution may damage the surface. A last ditch solution is to polish the surface with chalk, jeweller's rouge, or powdered pumice.

Thin metal painted tobacco box, post 1600.

Tin

Collecting old kitchen things of tinplate is fashionable. These objects often need some restoration. In many instances this is because of rust as a result of the protective tin layer wearing through. Tin was widely used in the past for food containers because it protected food from decay, oxidisation, and was also tasteless. Wash tinplate first in hot water with soda. Clean bare and rusted patches with a fine abrasive cleaner.
The art is in removing the rust without damaging the remaining protective are of tin. Dry the object thoroughly in an oven or with a hair dryer. To protect the item from further rust it can be coated with a thin layer of wax. Painted decoration can be restored using acrylic paint. Wait until the paint is thoroughly dry and then rub down carefully until smooth. If required the tinplate can be coated with a gloss varnish.

Toys were also made of tinplate. An unusual good's wagon for acid from Märklin of 1929, catalogue no. 1990.

Bronze

Bronze is an alloy of copper and tin. Bronze was the first hard metal widely used by humankind after the Stone Age for making tools and implements. Bronze is formed into shape by casting or forging. It is an expensive metal due to the scarcity of raw materials. It was used for axes, knives, probably for ploughs, religious objects, dishes, jewellery, and swords.

The Bronze Age started in the third millennium BC around the Aegean Sea and nearby parts of Asia. This occurred around 2000 BC in central and western parts of Europe. There was no Bronze Age in Africa. Although its use continued longer in some areas, the Bronze Age continued until about 800 BC. The constituency of bronze alloy depends on the use for which the metal is being made.

Cannons for instance were made with 90 percent copper and 10 percent tin. For bells, that is slightly above 75 percent copper and just below 25 percent tin. An entirely different composition is used for bronze statues, normally using copper, tin, and lead. In the twentieth century many pieces of sculpture were also cast in plastic.
In the nineteenth century many were made with spelter.

These busts or statues are then given a bronze finish. Some of these imitation bronzes are so real looking that they are sold as such. It is therefore sensible to check that an item truly is bronze. Plastic betrays itself by the sound when tapped and is also much lighter than bronze, although this can be deceptively overcome by placing weight inside. Spelter can be detected by its silvery colour in places where the bronze has worn away.
Bronze should be cleaned with care to avoid harming its patina. The patina is the layer which forms on bronze, copper, and pewter through contact with the air and climate.

A patina can also be artificially applied using etching substances. New bronzes can therefore acquire a patina and many old bronzes had this done immediately after they were made. Genuine patina is a sign of age and has a direct bearing on the value and quality of the piece.

Artificial patina may be of a different colour to genuine patina. Restoration of damaged patina is work for an expert. A bronze that has not been cleaned for a long time needs first to be washed with luke warm soapy water. Never use any cleaning substance or steel wool to clean bronze which can damage the patina.

A good way to protect bronze is with beeswax to which five percent carnauba wax has been added. Bubbles or green places on bronze is caused by chlorine in the air which attacks the copper in the alloy. Smaller areas of damage can be treated with a 10 percent solution of acetic acid (available from chemists). Dab the solution on the affected place and keep it moist so that the acid can work into the damaged area.

Scrub the area afterwards with a soft brush (a hard one will damage the patina). In the event of serious damage seek help from a professional restorer.

The French term for bronze fittings is *or moulu* (anglicised as ormolu). It is widely used for furniture and is gilded after casting and chasing.
The term ormolu is also used for all sorts of fittings on clocks, furniture, and other objects. Before ormolu is cleaned it always needs to be separated from the surface on which it is mounted.

This can usually be done by undoing a few screws or a couple of nails. Care needs to be taken in removing nails to prevent damaging the surface beneath. Often it helps to prise the ormolu item slightly with a chisel or filler knife before the nails are removed.

Gilt on ormolu is often damaged and it is usually best to leave this as it is. Old furniture often looks better with a little bronze showing through beneath the gilt. The bronze can of course be electrolytically replated but the result can appear very new and harsh. It is always a fault to renovate one part of an object – in this case the ormolu. This upsets the harmony of the whole and merely highlights any defects in the rest of the piece.

Ormolu should be cleaned with water to which a squirt of ammonia has been added. A nail brush and sometimes also a toothbrush are useful tools. Because the ammonia will mark ormolu it must be rinsed immediately with plenty of water after cleaning. Ammonia marks cannot be removed. Special cleaning agents are sold such as dips for semi-precious and precious metals but your own cleaning agent can be made with one litre of water (33 fl oz) and 75 grams (2_ oz) tartrate of sodium and potassium.

Ormolu can be carefully revived with a solution of two percent saltpetre in water. This must be rinsed off immediately and care needs to be taken in carrying out this treatment because even a weak solution is extremely aggressive.

A Southern Dutch 17th century bronze candle stand.

Ormolus is sometimes covered with lacquer. This can be removed with amyl acetate or acetone. This can be a long process. Both substances have health risks attached so it is essential to work in a well ventilated area.

Copper and brass

Copper is a pure metal, brass is an alloy of copper and zinc. Brass is fairly resistant to corrosion and is therefore widely used for small utensils and objects and for equipment. Both copper and brass can be polished with ordinary brass polish and then waxed.

Wax forms a thin layer which protects against oxidisation. Wax is far better than the best metal lacquers because they are not entirely invisible. Sometimes copper or brass has long been neglected and is both grimy and oxidised. The metal discolours to green or black or somewhere between the two.

Many copper or brass objects in the past were expressly given a layer of patina so it is worth considering if this patina should be removed. In some cases this can significantly lower the value.
If the layer of corrosion is too thick then cleaning it will have to be carried out by a professional restorer. The best way to remove corrosion yourself is to rub the surface with half a lemon sprinkled with salt.

Small objects can be soaked in 500 ml (1 pint) of water with a cup of vinegar and a dessertspoon full of salt. This treatment removes even the most stubborn corrosion. A means of last resort is to use a paint stripper. After this has been applied by brush it should be left for several minutes to work and then be rinsed off. A solution of 5 cc oxalic acid and a dessertspoon of salt in 500 ml (1 pint) of water also works well.

Oxalic acid is very strong so work with rubber gloves and make sure there is plenty of ventilation. Rinse the object well afterwards with water. It can then be polished with Brasso or a mild polishing agent.

Woodwork is easily damaged when cleaning brass fittings on furniture so it is best to remove them before cleaning. This only applies of course to fittings and not to inlaid brass. Fittings are sometimes attached with bolts right through the timber but they can also be held in place with nails or screws. Inlaid brass should be cleaned with an electric polisher using a specialist cutting polish, with fine wire wool (grade 000 or 0000), copper polish, or a polishing cream.
Working too hastily is out of the question. It is essential to ensure what is the

Copper bedpan of the early 19th century.

best manner of proceeding. Steel wool should always be used with the grain of the wood to avoid leaving visible scratches.

The wood surrounding the brass will suffer from the treatment but when the brass is in poor condition the wood usually also requires maintenance. Long-term restoration of brass furniture fittings that still have to be used is possible with the help of silver or hard solder. This is work for an expert. Broken brass that no longer needs to be used should first be cleaned with spirit before being glued.

The surface of the break can be lightly rubbed down if necessary. The broken pieces can be stuck together with epoxy resin adhesive. Gaps in brass can be filled with epoxy resin only when the brass fitting is no longer used.
This is done by mixing metal powder of the right colour with the resin. Make a thick mixture to fill the gap.

An 18th century brass mortar and pestle.

If the gap is right through the piece then some support will needed to be given at the back. Some adhesive tape will suffice with smaller gaps.

More sturdy support is needed for larger gaps. Once the resin has set it can be rubbed down and varnished. Metal powder can be found in shops selling artist's materials.

Replacement antique brass handles and grips are almost impossible to find. If they are badly damaged or lost then they will have to be replaced with a modern copy.

Lead

Lead is a soft metal with a very low melting point. It lends itself well to both casting and forging. Newly poured lead is silvery in colour but it quickly becomes grey and dull. Lead can be cleaned with turpentine.

Polish it until the colour is as you desire but take care for lead misshapes easily.

Once the turpentine has evaporated and the lead is dry the lead can be protected by coating with wax.
The wax can be polished with a soft brush or cloth. Tears and gaps in lead need to be repaired by a plumber. If the rear of a lead object is accessible dents can be knocked out with a rubber hammer. Do not use a metal or wooden hammer because that will mark the lead.

Nickel

The silver coloured metal nickel is used for many different purposes. This ranges from electroplating of cutlery to minting of coins. Many nickel alloys have been used in the past.
An alloy of copper, zinc, and nickel was used for nickel plate or nickel silver which is also the basis for electroplated nickel silver or EPNS.
Another alloy with nickel mainly uses copper. It is chiefly used for things like doorknobs. Nickel silver can be cleaned in the same way as real silver.

Nickel was widely used in the past for things for which chrome is used today. Although it shines and reflects in much the same way, nickel is much more like silver than chrome.

The metal does not corrode and can be polished. Polishes can remove superficial scratches. Nickel can be cleaned with a silver polish or cleaner.

Copper pipe-smoker's bowls from the mid 19th century.

A 19th century brass candleholder.

Pinchbeck

Pinchbeck is also known as 'poor man's gold'. This alloy is named after the watchmaker Christopher Pinchbeck who first made it. It is a yellow coloured alloy of one part zinc to five parts copper. Those who do not look carefully may be fooled into thinking this is gold. The material darkens with age and does not bear any gold hallmarks. Pinchbeck was used around 1900 to make baubles. Pinchbeck can be cleaned with a cleaning agent for jewellery.

Pewter (and tin soldiers)

Antique pewter consists of 85 percent tin with the rest of the alloy comprising antimony, copper, and lead. Harder types of pewter contain no lead. In common with silver, pewter is often marked. The absence of marks though has no bearing on the price of antique pewter. In the past owners have also had their own marks put on pewter.

Pewter inkpot with 'pewter plague'. When this is found on an object it must be removed from other pieces to avoid it spreading.

When it is carefully handled and polished, pewter acquires a fine patina over time. Pewter can be polished up to be almost as shiny as silver but it can also be left to become dark.

Pewter used to be polished with pumice mixed with animal fat or vegetable oil but this method is too severe for antique pewter pieces. Ordinary metal polish is suitable for pewter, allowing it to shine without losing its patina.

An intense lustre can be achieved by using jeweller's rouge with salad oil. Wire wool must never be used because it always leaves scratches. Grimy pieces can be cleaned in a bath of paraffin. Depending on the extent of the dirt the piece can be soaked for a few hours or a couple of days. Afterwards it must be thoroughly dried with old newspapers and washed in soap suds.

Badly tarnished pewter reacts well to aggressive solutions such as soda and ammonia but care needs to be taken to avoid losing the patina. After cleaning pewter should be protected with a layer of beeswax. This keeps the pewter looking fine for longer.

The removal of dents is work for a jeweller or silversmith and solder repairs should also be carried out by a specialist. Small repairs can be carried out with epoxy resin adhesive. Small holes can be filled with a paste of epoxy resin, filler, and pigment.

Some pewter mugs have glass bottoms. If the glass is broken a new piece of glass will need to be cut to fit. With valuable old pieces glass should not be replaced because it will reduce its value. Because they have been played with a great deal, much of the paint is usually knocked off tin soldiers.

Before deciding to repaint them it should be born in mind that the value of newly painted soldiers is lower than those with chipped or flaking paint.

Pewter chestnut pot, 19th century.

Breadbasket forged from a single sheet of Indonesian silver, made between 1780 and 1820 in the Dutch East Indies for sale in Europe.

Silver

Both silver and silver plate will become tarnished in time. Polishing imparts a deep bluish patina with age. Anyone comparing antique silver with modern pieces will see the difference immediately.

Old silver looks far more attractive than modern silver with its high gloss. Repairs to silver items should be entrusted to a jeweller or silversmith. The purity of silver, except for English, can be tested with nitrous acid.

A small scratch is made through the plate for this purpose and a little nitrous acid is dripped into the scratch. Less pure silver will turn dark grey and pure silver light grey. When there is a hissing sound and the metal turns green then the metal is not silver. The metal must be thoroughly rinsed in water following this test.

Silver plate/Sheffield plate

Sheffield plate was made between 1750 and 1850 by rolling silver onto copper sheet until it was very thin. Items made of Sheffield plate do not have silver edges. The inside of Sheffield plate pots and pans are usually tinned.

It is therefore sensible to ask the question whether a piece of Sheffield plate should be replated. Later silver plating was made by electrolysis or electroplating whereby silver adhered to a metal object. In addition to copper, other alloys are also used as a basis for silver plate.

Examples include British plate. Repairs to silver plate should be carried out by a jeweller or silversmith. Silver plate becomes dark and unattractive when it is exposed to smoke from a fire or other polluted air.

It is therefore sensible to keep silver plate in an airtight display case or to pack it in acid free paper. The best way to look after silver plate is to keep it in a tailor made case of impregnated cotton. Every time silver plate is cleaned a thin layer of silver is removed. Eventually the piece will need to be replated. Modern polishes keep wear to a minimum. Home made silver polish can be made by creating a thin paste from a mixture of ammonia and spirits with chalk.

To prevent scratches it is better to use cotton wool than a fine cloth.

English silver plate pedicure set, circa 1900.

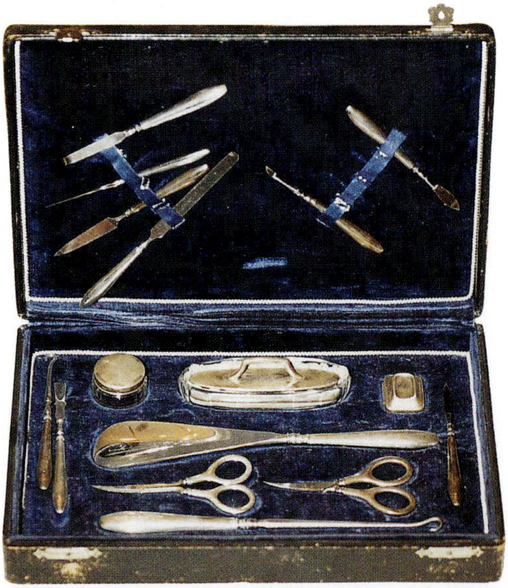

Classical revival silver candlesticks between 1890 and 1900.

British plate

British plate is an alloy of copper, lead, tin, and antimony that looks like pewter but is lighter and harder. This alloy was used in the late eighteenth century for cutlery, drinking tankards, and teapots.

British plate also forms a good ground for silver plate but has a tendency to break if roughly handled. British plate should be cleaned in the same way as other silver plate. When it has not been cleaned for a long time it becomes dull grey.

In order to remove this oxidisation it is best cleaned with a fine silver polish such as Silvo. Because the layer of plate is thin it should be done with care. Repairs to British plate are much more difficult than other metals and soldering is best left to an expert. Re-plating is best done by a specialist company.

Iron

There are two forms of iron objects: cast iron and forged iron. Cast iron is brittle and breaks easily. cast iron stoves and fireplaces. cooking pots, and other utensils were traditionally cleaned with pot black.
For maintenance, pots can be polished with graphite. Iron will soon rust in damp situations so it needs protection from the atmosphere. Rust on iron can be removed with a wire brush or larger areas chipped away with a screwdriver or chisel. This can then be coated with a rust proofing primer which turns the metal surface into iron phosphate which prevents further rusting. Objects that are indoors also need to be protected.

A thin coat of machine oil is sufficient. The problem is that this has to be repeated frequently. Beeswax or varnish can also be used to protect the outside of antique cast iron.

Broken cast iron can be welded by a blacksmith. Small cracks can be repaired by joining them together with epoxy resin.

Enamel

Enamel is a hard, glassy layer applied to metal to decorate it. The raw material for enamel is colourless ground glass to which metal oxides have been added.
The oxides give the enamel its colour. The glass and the oxides are applied to the metal and the piece is then heated in

Late 19th century agricultural worker's cookpot with iron tripod.

a kiln. The technique of enamelling was already known to the early Egyptians and Greeks. From the Middle Ages the centre of enamel production was Limoges in France.

In the *champlevé* technique grooves are cut in the metal underground which are then filled with various oxides. *Cloisonné* is the technique in which enamel colours are separated with thin metal wires placed between them. This is mainly used on vases and other ornaments.

Check first to see if a damaged piece is restored. If this is the case make sure that the repair is waterproof.

The safest way to clean enamel is with suds of green household soap in water. If this is not possible because it cannot be separated from the rest of the piece then the enamel will have to be cleaned with acetone or dry cleaning fluid (tetrachloroethylene).
Sometimes discolorationpersists in fissures and seams after cleaning. This can be bleached with hydrogen peroxide. Metal objects do not break when dropped but enamel on an object does. For this reason there is plenty of damaged enamel. Missing areas of enamel should only be replaced with paint because enamel cannot be reheated.

Acrylic paint is suitable for this purpose. After retouching cover the restoration with a thin layer of gloss varnish with a sable haired brush. An excess of varnish on the original enamel can be wiped off when the varnish is semi dry. Use a wad of cotton wool soaked in a mixture of one part cellulose thinners to three parts turpentine for this purpose.

Enamelled ring decorated with open bible and text from Philippians, circa 1600.

Jewellery

Jewellery collects grease from the skin which in turn catches dirt and dust. There are good jewellery cleaners on the market in which jewellery can be soaked. Jewellery also acquires a fine lustre by wiping it with household ammonia. Diamonds should always be kept separately from other jewellery because they are so hard that they can easily scratch other jewellery and gem stones. Because pearls acquire an improving lustre from the oils in the skin over the years they should not be washed.

Emeralds are extremely brittle and chip easily so handle them with care. Turquoise, opals and other opaque stones are porous so they must not get wet. These can be cleaned by wiping with a piece of chamois leather. Repair of valuable jewellery is best left to a jeweller. Other pieces can be self repaired. A jeweller's eye glass, that can be worn to leave the hand's free, is useful when gluing.

Two strings of cornelians with a gold clasp, circa 1880.

Metal can be stuck using epoxy resin or cyanoacrylate (instant glue). Stones can be glued with cyanoacrylate or PVA adhesives. Glass and paste should be glued with cyanoacrylate

Coins

Cleaning coins reduces their value so ask yourself first if you really wish to do so. Golden coins are in principle never affected by corrosion. They can be washed in warm water and then dried with a piece of chamois eather. For cleaning silver coins see the section on cleaning silver.

Antique copper coins can be cleaned by dipping them for a few seconds in a bath of 5–10 percent nitrous acid but working with this is very dangerous. Poisonous gases are released when coins are dipped that are very aggressive. The area of work needs to be well ventilated and protective impermeable gloves must be worn.
Cleaning coins that have lain in the soil for a long time is specialist work. Seek advice from a museum or restaurateur. Coins can be protected with beeswax or a special varnish.

Cash table with marble top, 17th century. By letting a coin drop onto the table could be heard if its silver content was good or not by its ring.

Heavy 17th century treasury chest with iron fittings. Chests for keeping money in have solid and complex locks.

Locks

Almost all eighteenth and nineteenth century furniture is fitted with locks. Keys easily become lost, especially when furniture changes hands. A good locksmith can make new keys for old locks. In most cases all the drawers in a chest of drawers use the same key which makes things easier (but the flaps on bureaux usually have a different key). Locks need to be removed from the furniture before they are cleaned. With cheaper locks the cover plate is usually riveted fast. In this case the head of the rivet will have to be filed off. High quality locks are held together with bolts.

After removing dust and fluff the lock should be soaked in a bath of penetrating oil and before refitting the lock lubricate it with machine oil. If it is necessary to take the lock apart it is sensible to place the parts in sequence to make it easier to reassemble. This is only necessary if individual parts need to be cleaned.

Screws and bolts

Screws can sometimes seem to be stuck fast. Try dripping a few drops of penetrating oil or paraffin into the edge of the screw head. This simple method can be very effective.

Some bolts and screws are rusted in to wood or iron. These need to be freed by heating them by means of a piece of iron, such as a file, that is heated until white hot. By heating, the screw or bolt expands and as it shrinks it can free itself. Another method is to turn the screw anti-clockwise while also tapping on the screwdriver with a hammer. It is essential to use the right size and shape of screwdriver to avoid damaging the slot in the screw.

If none of these methods work then a stud remover will need to be used. These can be bought from specialist tool shops and ironmongers.

First a hole has to be bored in the head of the screw and then the stud remover is screwed anti-clockwise into the screw. Once the stud remover is firmly in place it will then unscrew the bolt or screw. Bolts and screws with broken heads can also be removed with a stud remover.

Late 19th century metal tool chest with wooden base.

Restoring and maintaining organic materials

Textiles

There are four important points to consider when cleaning textiles. The first is to determine whether the colours will run in water. Each colour needs to be checked separately. This can be done by making a corner of the textile wet where it is unlikely to be seen and then immediately pressing it between two sheets of tissue paper.
If the tissue paper becomes coloured then the textile must not be washed. It is also important to determine whether the colour is painted or printed for this makes the textile more vulnerable. Painted textiles can easily be damaged by dry cleaning.

In the second place you need to find out if the textile has been dressed with any chemical treatment that will be undone by contact with water. Mercerised cotton for example is treated under pressure in a solution of sodium or potassium hydroxide which gives it its lustre and the pattern of moiré silk is created by pressing silk between rollers. Such fabrics have to be treated with great care. In the third place one needs to ascertain how delicate the textile is. All organic substances gradually decay with age.

Dry cleaning of an item of clothing can hasten this process. Almost all modern detergents contain chemicals that can damage old delicate fabrics. These textiles need to be protected with a supporting layer of nylon or their increased weight (as they absorb water) will cause them to tear when they are removed from the wash.

In fourth place one needs to find out what sort of dirt is affecting the textile. Ingrained dirt can be removed by soaking but this does not apply to oil and grease. Each stain caused by a chemical reaction – such as contact with rust – requires its own solution. If in doubt consult an expert. Superficial dirt and dust can be removed with a vacuum cleaner. To prevent damaging the fabric the suction needs to be set as low as possible.

Place a piece of gauze over the nozzle to prevent buttons or pieces of cloth being sucked into the cleaner. Distilled water in the bath is a useful way of washing antique clothes. The item of clothing should be kept as flat as possible and there needs to be sufficient distilled water to just immerse the clothing.

The water must to be agitated from time to time but do not touch the fabric. This process can take several hours. After the final rinse the clothing should be placed on a thick layer of tissue paper.

Many stains that cannot be removed in distilled water will yield to a bath of 50 g (1¾ oz) soap spirit per litre (33 fl oz) of water.

The water must not be hotter than hand hot. Sometimes antique clothing cannot be washed but may be cleaned with a solvent.
All these substances are very flammable so there must be no smoking in the area which must also be well ventilated. Carbon tetrachloride is not flammable but its vapours are very harmful if someone smokes while cleaning. Anyone working with tetrachloride needs to wear protective gloves. If trichloroethylene is used the same measures apply. Tri (for short) can also be used in a solution of 10 g (5½ drams) of soap spirit per 500 ml (17 fl oz) of this solvent.

Signs of age in white fabrics can be removed by immersing them in a bath of chloramine.
After using chloramine the textile must be neutralised in a bath of 2 percent sodium sulphite. The textile must then be thoroughly rinsed with distilled water. Patches of rust can be removed with a special agent such as Blankit F from BASF. Following the instructions on the packet very carefully.
If white textiles such as linen and cotton need to be bleached – and that is not always the case for textiles do not all have to be sparkling white – this can be done with a home-made solution. Add 5 g (2¾ drams) sodium carbonate, 5 g (2¾ drams) sodium hydroxide (caustic soda), 20 g (11¼ drams) sodium metasilicate , and 50 cc hydrogen peroxide to each litre (33 fl oz) of water.
The water needs to be warm to dissolve all these substances. Only add the hydrogen peroxide once the other substances are fully dissolved and stir the mixture well. Place the textile in the solution for five minutes. Afterwards place the textile on an old towel covered with several layers of tissue paper to remove any excess liquid while leaving the cleaning agents to continue to work.

Place the item in a plastic bag to prevent it from drying out. Depending on the extent of yellowing the bleaching agent needs to be left to work for one to three hours. Afterwards the treated fabric will

A cast iron flat iron from the late 19th century. Flat irons were previously used to press clothes.

need to be rinsed, first in ordinary water but the last two rinses should be with distilled water with a dash of vinegar added. The vinegar prevents chalky deposits on the fabric.

Appliqué

An *appliqué* item is where other fabrics are sewn onto a base fabric to form decoration. This is one of the earliest means of creating decorative textiles. Cleaning of *appliqué* items is troublesome because of the delicate nature of the piece, the irregularity of the base material, the risk of colours running, and the material used as filling.

A vacuum cleaner with a special nozzle can remove a great deal of dust and dirt but make sure the cleaner is not set on too high a suction.

Textiles with *appliqués* can be washed but detergents are out of the question. Before washing it is essential to test that the every colour in each different piece of fabric will not run. Do this by making a small part of each sample slightly wet. Press the top and bottom of the item onto a piece of thick tissue paper. The paper will reveal if any of the colours in the *appliqué* will run when washed. The item cannot be washed if any of the colours runs. Because of the acidity of tap water only distilled water should be used for washing cotton and linen items.

Long term soaking of several hours in several changes of water is usually sufficient to remove most of the dirt. During soaking the fragile parts of the piece will need to be supported and the item should be lifted by the support rather than the fabric when it is taken out of the water. This prevents delicate fabric from tearing under the weight of the water it has absorbed. Grease and oil patches can be removed with carbon tetrachloride or trichloroethylene. Because both substances are extremely toxic the use of them requires plenty of ventilation to the space where the work is done. Carbon tetrachloride is heavier than air so the floor area also needs to be ventilated when this is used. Before large areas are cleaned a test first needs to be made to ensure the various dyes can withstand these solvents.

Detail from an American 'crazy' quilt of 1907.

If possible the textile should be soaked in the solvent for a fifteen minutes. Otherwise the fabric can be dabbed with a wad of cotton wool with the solvent. Make sure the dirt is removed and not pushed to the edge of the area treated for this can cause dark rings.

Embroidery

Embroidery is the technique in which clothes or fabrics are decorated by sewing a pattern with different styles of stitch and different coloured threads.
Expert advice is required before cleaning a valuable old example of embroidered fabric. Because textile can easily shrink or stretch it is best to set textiles on a frame before washing. This is particularly necessary if all the embroidered stitches follow the same direction.

With chairs with embroidered upholstery there is great risk of shrinking. The fabric can also be cleaned with solvents such as carbon tetrachloride or trichloroethylene. Stubborn patches can be carefully removed with a little carpet shampoo.

Lace

Lace was formerly used as decorative edging for clothing and other textiles. Good lace is made of linen but there is also plenty of cotton lace. Silk lace is quite exceptional.
The restoration of old lace needs to be done by an expert.
Antique lace is usually so delicate that it will damage easily. Lace is often yellowed with age or discoloured. In order to wash lace a piece of previously washed bleached cotton needs to be sewn fast around a large bottle. The lace is then wound around this so that it is wound between the cotton with each turn. This prevents the lace from shrinking or otherwise becoming damaged during washing.

First wash the lace in tepid soapy water using a gentle detergent for wool. Afterwards rinse three times with ordinary water and then finally rinse with distilled water to which a dash of vinegar has been added.
The lace must be dried by laying it between thick layers of tissue paper.

Three 18th century painted Friesian lace boxes.

Shrinking can be prevented by fastening the lace with stainless steel pins. Lace should never be ironed.

SAMPLERS

Many samplers are framed. In order to clean them they need to be removed carefully from the frame. Start to clean at first carefully with a lens cleaning brush with a rubber bellows attached. Both sides of the sampler need to be cleaned.

It is not wise to dry clean samplers and washing can also be harmful, especially if the sampler contains wool which might shrink. It is also possible that the colour in the threads might run.
Before washing is considered the colours need to be tested to ensure they do not run. Clip little bits of thread from the back and lay these on wet filter paper. Place a sheet of glass on top of them.
You will be able to see after several hours whether any of the colours runs. If even one colour runs then the sampler cannot be washed.

For washing use a mild detergent without bleach and whitener. First soak the sampler in water and then in a soapy solution for 20 minutes. Press the sampler gently and sprinkle with soapy water. Do not wring the sampler out. Rinse the first three or four times with tap water and then twice with distilled water.
The final rinse should have a dash of vinegar added. Dry the sample face upwards on a layer of white felt. Pin the sampler to the felt with stainless steel pins (to prevent rust).

The best way to frame a sampler is to support it on a firm background. First cover a strong piece of acid free cardboard with a length of unbleached cotton. Stick the cotton to the cardboard with double-sided adhesive tape.
Place the sampler on the base and sew it to the background with small stitches

Folding Hindeloper table. The many special pleats in the local traditional costume could be ironed with the help of the many sides to the table.

around the edge. When it is framed the sampler must not touch the glass because condensation from the glass could make the sampler damp, which could causes stains or mould

TAPESTRIES

Loosely hung tapestries are suspended by their upper edge from a wall. Old tapestries must not be hung or stretched too tight.

Care needs to be taken that the tapestry's own weight is not borne in just a couple of places but is spread evenly throughout its length. A wide strip of Velcro can be sewn to the top of the tapestry for this purpose. The other half of the Velcro needs to be attached to a trip of wood that is then fixed to the wall. The wall on which a tapestry hangs must always be dry and the tapestry must never be hung in the sun.

Valuable tapestries are best given a rear lining of sturdy textile. Cleaning of tapestries is work for experts.

Bone

Quite precious objects have been made with bone. Examples of these vary from lace boxes and salt scoops to model ships. Bone is usually the colour of ivory and the difference between bone and ivory is not always readily apparent. Bone though is softer than ivory and it therefore lends itself to very detailed carving.

The substance is more likely to have irregularities and be cracked than ivory and it does not polish up as well. Bone was also widely used for inlay in small objects and furniture.

Bone can be cleaned with a paste of hydrogen peroxide and chalk. The paste must be as thick as toothpaste. Apply the paste thickly and leave it to dry. Later carefully remove the dry paste with a brush or soft cloth. Damaged bone carving is best soaked for five minutes in a bath of molten candle wax. Immediately remove excess wax and rub the

Like tapestries, antique textiles need careful handling. A Persian Beloudj camel bag, circa 1910.

Bone skates, 18th century.

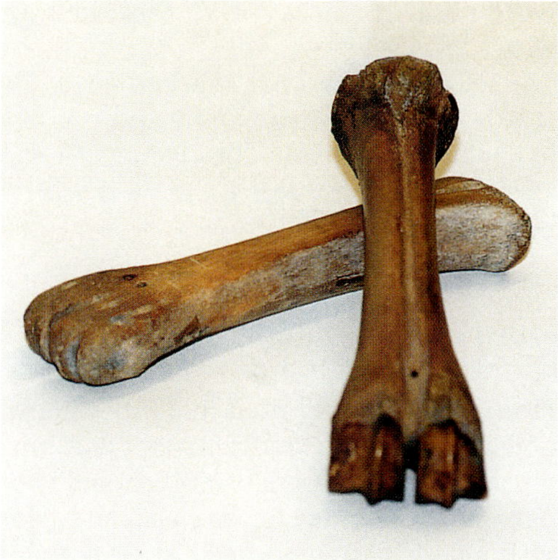

object until the wax hardens. Lost parts of bone or ivory inlay are best trimmed with a fret saw. Glue new parts with PVA adhesive. Broken bone objects can be stuck together with epoxy resin or acrylic glue.

Damaged areas can be filled by adding magnesium silicate to either of the adhesives.

Ivory

The difference between bone and ivory is not readily apparent. Ivory relates solely to the tusks of elephants but the teeth of whales and tusks of walruses is also treated as ivory.

Once worked it is difficult to ascertain which animal the ivory originated from. There is a great deal of imitation ivory that is sold as genuine. Some of it is so good that it has fooled experts. Before plastic, countless objects were fitted or made from ivory.

It was widely used in furniture for inlay and provided an excellent material for miniaturists. Ivory is very susceptible to drying out and will turn yellow through

Gilt 19th century sewing kit in ivory box.

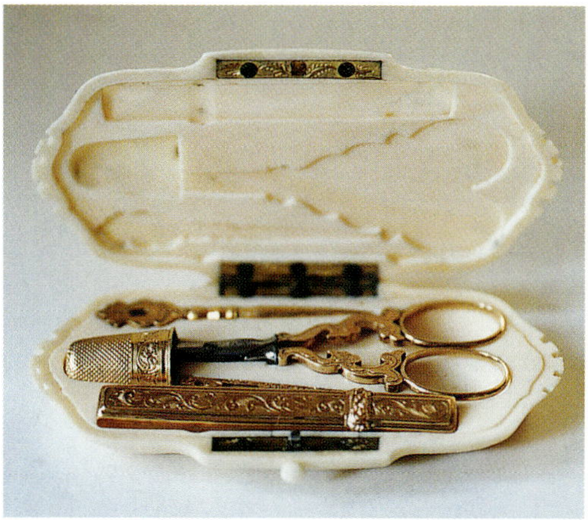

exposure to sunlight. Yellowed ivory will become white again if left for a long time in a darkened room. Before starting to clean ivory objects it is best to consult an expert.
Ivory can be cleaned with ethanol or acetone to which a drop of ammonia has been added. This mixture should be applied with a soft cloth.

Oriental carving is sometimes coloured to accentuate detail. These areas should not be cleaned.

Ivory can be polished to a shine with Champagne chalk. Protect ivory by wiping it with almond oil.

Surfaces with many fissures or cracks need to be impregnated with PVA glue thinned to the consistency of water. Ivory

Silver 19th century tea strainer with ivory handle.

generally has fine sharp fracture lines. These can usually be invisibly repaired with epoxy resin or PVA glue.

Tortoiseshell

Tortoiseshell is a translucent material that comes from the horny carapace of a tortoise. It is often therefore mounted on a colour underground – often red – or inlaid with gold or silver thread.

The texture and colour nuances of the material are extremely important. Heated tortoiseshell can easily be formed into various shapes.

Like other natural materials, tortoiseshell becomes more beautiful with use. In a time before plastic, tortoiseshell was widely used for small objects such as combs and powder compacts. Tortoiseshell must not be exposed to sunlight as it will lose its appearance if left for one day in the sun. This creates chemical changes in the shell that can affect the whole of the material. Polishing will not overcome this problem. Tortoiseshell can be cleaned with soapy suds.

Matt tortoiseshell can be given a lustre by wiping it with jeweller's rouge and olive oil. To protect it either olive oil or beeswax can be used. These not only make the tortoiseshell shine but nourish the material.

Dirty patches can be removed by vigorously polishing with a cotton cloth and Champagne chalk or talcum powder. Deep scratches need the attention of a restorer.

Breaks in tortoiseshell can be glued with Canadian balsam. The shell needs to be coated with the balsam and then held together for at least 24 hours. Once the balsam is set surplus balsam can be removed with a blunt knife. Missing pieces of tortoiseshell can be replaced with another piece of tortoiseshell or with hard wax stopping.
For this purpose heat the end of a file that is inserted into a handle and use this to melt the wax into the damaged area. Once set the wax can be formed with a chisel.

Horn

Horn was formerly used in all manner of objects such as snuff boxes, lanterns, musical instruments, and items for personal grooming. It was also used for making drinking vessels and powder horns. Some items of horn are finely decorated with silver or mounted in silver.
Horn can be cleaned with soap suds in luke warm water, using green household soap.

Make sure the water is not hot. Many types of horn become soft if soaked in warm water so for this reason bone must be dried quickly because the risk of deforming is real.

Dull horn can be polished with Silvo or other fine polish but make sure not to damage colouring of any engraving. If this does happen it can be restored with lightly pigmented wax.

This wax catches in the engraved areas. It is best not to clean valuable horn objects but to polish them with white wax which provides a good protective layer for the horn. Old horn can break and splinter. Repair it with epoxy resin.

Badly affected items can be treated with acrylic varnish that is used by artists, which gives protection from further deterioration. Antlers are usually mounted on walls but because they are out of reach they seldom if ever get cleaned and collect a lot of dust.

The antlers of stuffed deer also need to be protected.

Stuffed animals are susceptible to being eaten by insects and need to be protected against them.

Most of the dirt can be removed carefully with a vacuum cleaner. The rest can then be cleaned off with a cloth dipped in white spirit.
To protect the antlers they can be coated with wax. If the antlers are mounted on the head of a deer or part of the skull with skin attached the skin needs protection too. This can be done by spraying or sprinkling with insecticide.

Stuffed animals

Generally only small animals kept behind glass avoid this problem. The insect problem can lead to hair falling out and the skin itself being affected. When treating stuffed animals the skin must not be loosened or removed because it is extremely difficult to get things back as they previously were.

The best solution is to clean the skin and to treat against insects.

First clean the surface of the skin with a stiff brush. Do this carefully to avoid pulling out hairs or feathers. To get rid of stubborn dirt you need to use fuller's earth.

This is sprinkled over the skin and then brushed in the direction of the hairs. Deal with insects with an insecticide powder or solution dissolved in alcohol. This latter substance leaves no traces as the alcohol evaporates.

Mites can be difficult to get rid of. One certain way to get rid of all insects is to have the entire stuffed animal treated with gas. Animals kept under glass can be protected with mothballs or pieces of flea collar inside the glass cover. The display case, bracket, or plinth on which the animal is mounted also needs to be looked after.

These need to be kept clean to prevent them becoming prey to insects and it is worth spending time dealing with the look of the area in which the animal or animals are kept.

The best way is to use acrylic paint. Water based paints can cause damp and mould. A natural looking base can be made with plaster or filler. Before the plaster or filler has set scatter sand or stones on it. The bottom can later be painted.

Dried grass can then also be placed on the bottom. This is available from handicraft shops. New glass bell jars can be bought from several different types of shop such as clock makers.
A glass case can be made from glass plate with linen backed adhesive tape. Beaks, noses, paws, and such parts are best touched up with an acrylic paint of the right colour.

Leather

Leather has been used much more widely than for shoes and clothes over the centuries. It has been used for cases and trunks, and many other purposes. Leather slowly perishes and can be seriously troubled by rot. Except for suede, all types of leather can be cleaned.

Leather is best kept supple by 'feeding' with saddle soap. Suede is better cleaned with one of the special products available for this purpose.
Crumbling and brittle leather can no longer be treated with saddle soap. Instead treat with a brush with a solution of one part French polish and one part ethanol. Antique leather can be extremely thin and sensitive.
This needs to be cleaned with leather dressing which is done with a brush or soft cloth and left to dry for one or two days.

Then the dressing is carefully polished. If necessary the leather can then be coated with a thin layer of shoe cream. Worn leather surfaces can also be treated with shoe cream but make sure they do not end up looking like new. A useful middle course is to use neutral shoe cream.

If leather is suffering from 'red rot' it cannot be treated. Store the item as safely as possible. Red rot can be recognised by the dull red powdery texture of the leather. It is a process of decay due to sulphur dioxide in the air. When leather becomes damp this hastens the process. Torn leather needs to be restored by sticking a new piece to it.

Leather with a porous grain should be used because glue adheres best to this. It may be advisable to trim the edge of the new leather so that its edge is as thin as possible. This is done with a special leather worker's plane.

Gluing the leather should be done with PVA glue or one of the specialist leather adhesives. Sewn repairs with leather requires use of shoemaker's thread.

The thread first needs to be wiped twice past a candle or with wax before being sewn.

Leather chair of the 19th century.

Parchment

Parchment was discovered in ancient times in Pergamum in Greece. It is made by stripping animal hides, liming them, and stretching them. Originally parchment was made from sheep's hides. Sheets of 'parchment' made from skins of pigs, goats, and other animals is called vellum.

Although vellum is of better quality than parchment they are all known as parchment in common parlance. Before paper was made in Europe, parchment was the only material on which people could write.
When parchment is stored in dry conditions it has an amazingly long life. For this reason it was used until the start of the twentieth century for important legal documents.

Legal documents though are often folded and making parchment flat again once it has been folded is exceptionally difficult. Parchment must never be moistened because this causes it to distort and to blister. Restoration of parchment is work for a specialist and must be left to someone specialising in restoration of leather and paper.

One can try to flatten out less precious parchment documents. First one needs to check with a moist cotton bud if the ink is waterproof. If the ink does not run then the parchment can be softened by placing it between two layers of moistened tissue paper or by hanging it in the steam of a boiling kettle. The parchment is then laid on a sheet of glass sprinkled with grease free chalk.

The parchment is covered with a couple of sheets of tissue paper and then covered with a straight plank or second sheet of glass.
The upper side should then be weighted down with bricks or books. The weight should be evenly spread. The parchment should be left to dry for at least a day

Hand written and illuminated 15th century Zeeland breviary on parchment.

Coral

Coral originates from the sea. The finest coral originates from the Mediterranean. The material is of animal origin and consists of small particles of chalk held together by protein. Jewellery has been made from coral for centuries. Delicately carved pieces of coral can be surprisingly valuable. The restoration of expensive pieces is best left to a specialist restorer or jeweller.
Coral should be cleaned in warm soapy water.

Inaccessible parts can be cleaned with a toothbrush. Coral can lose its wonderful lustre through contact with acidic or alkaline substances. The exterior can be restred by polishing with jeweller's rouge. Because coral is porous nothing should be used that is oily or greasy because this will mar its appearance.

Broken or damaged coral can be glued with epoxy resin or cyanoacrylate instant glue. It is best to use tweezers for sticking small parts together because you can see better what is happening and there is less risk of adhesive on your fingers.

Leave the parts to set thoroughly before handling again.

Spindle-back chairs with rush seats, late 19th century.

Rush mats and chairs

Rush mats can be cleaned with detergent in warm water. If woven rush seats of chairs are worn they need to be replaced. Repair is not possible. Specialists can be found in directories who can weave new rush seating for you but rush weaving is not that difficult. If possible watch someone who knows the art first.

Rush can be bought from handicraft shops. Rush should first be soaked in water for 24 hours to make it more supple. First study the seat to be replaced and if possible keep an example to hand. Continuously twist two or three rushes together. To create a continuous 'twine' new rush has to be constantly added on the underside. The art is to twist the rushes together that they are of uniform thickness throughout.

Basket work

Basket work should not be confused with rush weaving. Basket work is made of plaited willow osiers, rush is used for matting and chair seats. Basket work can be cleaned of dust and dirt by brushing it firmly with soapy water using green household soap. Rinse it thoroughly afterwards with a garden hose. When basket work is badly discoloured it can be bleached. It is best to start with a solution of 200 cc bleach per litre (2 pints) of water. If required the strength of the solution can be increased. Hydrogen peroxide is a good alternative.

When basket work in antique furniture is completely worn out it is best replaced by an experienced upholsterer or weaver. Old basket work becomes fragile and dry so that the osiers break easily. Broken parts can be glued with acrylic or PVA adhesive.

Missing osiers can be replaced with willow or hazel. The dry osiers first need to be soaked in luke warm water. Once it is dry and the basket work is restored it can be coated with varnish once it has thoroughly dried. New basket work on furniture can be brought to the desired colour with wood stain or darker furniture wax.

Woven reed

Woven reed has been widely used in areas with a ready supply for mats and

Two French country chairs circa 1900. Woven reed was popular in the 17th century but has always been used for country pieces.

French country chair, circa 1910.

the seats and backs of chairs such as those of the Dutch Seven Provinces in the seventeenth century. At that time many chair seats and backs were made of woven reed.
The popularity of this material ended around 1700 but returned again in the late eighteenth century. All manner of dirt and grime collects between the woven reed. The surface dirt can be cleaned by bushing with warm soapy water but for stubborn dirt the reed needs to be thoroughly wetted with warm water.

Then brush in baking powder with a paint brush. The reed should now be allowed to dry thoroughly and then brushed once more. Finally the reed should be rinsed with cold water and then dried in the sun.
Broken reed can be repaired by sticking new reed to the back with a quick-drying acrylic adhesive. Reed can be found in handicraft shops.
Reed increasingly darkens and turns brown with age. This means that a new reed seat or chair back is always too light but it can be stained with aniline dye, thinned with ethanol. For the right effect the dye should be wiped off again just after it has been applied. Sometimes woven reed has been protected with varnish which gradually darkens and flakes off.

The first approach is to see if it is possible to remove the old varnish with wire wool. If this does not work then a varnish stripping solution will need to be used. It is important to make sure that none of this comes into contact with the rest of the chair.

To prevent this mask off the rest of the chair with masking tape. Wire wool will still have to be used to remove the varnish after applying the stripper. This is dirty work for which protective gloves are essential

Paper

Paper that has been kept in a damp environment can exhibit brown marks which can be bleached out. If there are just a couple of marks they can be treated with chloramine (available from chemists).
The paper must be placed on a layer of filter paper during this process. The marks are dabbed with a brush or cotton bud. Marks can only be dabbed again when the paper has dried fully.

After treatment the chloramine has to be neutralised. This is done by dabbing the treated areas with a two percent solution of sodium thiosulphate in water. Finally the areas are dabbed with distilled water. Before starting this treatment you first need to check whether the ink is water-proof or not. This is usually the case. Check also any signature on the paper because this is often in a different type of ink.

Paper antiques take many forms: a box filled with prints of Napoleon's battles.

Opening the box reveals a surprise.

Water colours and coloured engravings must never be subjected to water and the same is often the case with stamped ink markings. When there are a lot of marks on the paper then it will need to soak for half an hour in a bath of chloramine. This process needs a very careful approach because wet paper has much less strength than dry paper. It is a good idea to place the paper in the bath on a sheet of glass so that this can be lifted out with the paper on it.

After the soaking treatment the paper has to be neutralised in sodium thiosulphate. In order to remove this bleaching agent the paper is finally rinsed in distilled water. Wet sheets of paper are dried between filter paper which must be pressed down until most of the water has been removed. Then the paper is place between new sheets of filter paper to dry for at least 24 hours.

The base on which they dry must be flat and a heavy glass plate should be placed on the upper sheet of filter paper. Never use an iron on dry paper.

Gum should never ever be used to clean dirty paper. A good method is to rub day old bread crumbs over the paper. If the result is a disappointment then the paper can be placed in a bath of distilled water. Yellowed paper can be bleached in chloramine or a solution of two percent bleach that does not contain thickening agent.
The treatment is as previously indicated. Bleach too must be neutralised with sodium thiosulphate. Ink stains, with the exception of ball-point pens, can be removed with a teaspoon of oxalic acid in 500 ml (33 fl oz) water.

After treatment the paper must be rinsed with distilled water and dried as described. The use of oxalic acid is not without its risks. The acid also affects most printing inks. Grease or oil stains require localised treatment. First use ethanol but if this is not sufficient then try ether or carbon tetrachloride.
This is applied with a brush. The oil or grease dissolved in the solvent must be removed immediately with filter paper.

The battles of Napoleon box contains a veritable paper treasure.

This treatment should be repeated until the stain had been removed. These substances are toxic and the task must be done in a well ventilated space. The paper must be dried as described.

Crumples or folds in paper can be removed by moistening paper with a plant sprayer and then drying the paper as described earlier between filter paper. In the past damaged paper was often repaired with adhesive tape. This gradually bubbles up, becomes brittle, and lifts. Adhesive tape that is still in place can be removed by heating with a hairdryer.

If this does not work you can try moistening the paper with ethanol, and if this fails stronger means such as acetone, amyl acetate, or ether will have to be used.
These substances are very flammable so the area must be well ventilated. The brown marks left by adhesive tape can be removed by using solvent on a cotton bud.

Tears and holes in paper need to be repaired by sticking a thin layer of Japanese paper on the back with starch paste. The edges of Japanese paper are less apparent if torn rather than cut.

Papier Mâché

Objects and even furniture have been made from papier mâché since the eighteenth century. Papier mâché is produced by softening paper with water and binding it with a filler such as kaolin. The mixture is then pressed into shape.
It is very easy during this to inlay the item with mother-of-pearl and papier mâché forms a good surface for painting or gilding.

Papier mâché production reached its heights in the second half of the nineteenth century.

Ballhead van was-over-papier-maché, leren lijf, ongemerkt, circa 1870

Papier mâché objects usually have a black ground, often feature mother of pearl inlay, and tend to be highly decorated with fruit or flowers. Papier mâché objects resemble enamel work but can easily be differentiated. Papier mâché objects can become extremely grimy through both wax and dirt. Most people think the surface will be easily damaged by cleaning but a good clean freshens the pieces up.

Removing old wax with a wad of cotton wool soaked in turpentine is unlikely to harm the surface but of course one needs to take care with painted decoration. Old layers of varnish can severely reduce the sheen of mother of pearl. This can be removed by carefully rubbing with 000 gauge wire wool and turpentine.

The cleaning process can leave the surface looking dull. This needs coating with acrylic varnish or polishing. Protect papier mâché with a coating of wax. Replacements for missing pieces of mother of pearl will need to be cut to fit and then stuck in place with epoxy resin, having first checked the piece for fit. Mother-of-pearl that is too thick can be thinned down by sanding the reverse side (see Mother-of-pearl).
Holes and cracks in papier mâché can be filled with a cellulose filler. Once the filler is set it is sanded to shape and retouched with mat paint. It is a good idea to test the colour first on several strips of paper. The paint needs to be completely dry before comparing it with the original colour on the object to be restored. Mixing the precise shade of black can be quite a difficult task. The lustre can be restored by coating the repair with varnish.

Mother-of-pearl

Mother-of-pearl is the inside of a sea shell. The iridescent colours of this material were widely used in the nineteenth century to decorate papier mâché furniture. Mother-of-pearl is a soft material that is easily cut or engraved.
Mother-of-pearl can be cleaned with Silvo or turpentine. Replacements for missing pieces should be cut to size with a fret saw. The new piece can be made to fit precisely with a file. Mother-of-pearl is stuck using epoxy resin.

Mother-of-pearl decorated tea caddy and teaspoon case, circa 1890.

Brass, leather, and tortoiseshell 17th century writing case.

Tortoiseshell and Boulle work

Boulle or Buhl work gets it name from André Charle Boulle (1642–1732), cabinet maker to the French court (member of the marquetry specialist's guild), architect, and painter who worked during the Louis XIV period. Although he did not invent.

Boulle work he refined the process sufficiently for it to be named after him. Boulle work is inlay and marquetry with tortoiseshell (with French pieces) or either rosewood or mahogany (with English pieces) and brass glued together before having a pattern cut in them.

The two materials are then separated and the gap is replaced with a further pattern created from brass and tortoiseshell. If brass dominates then this is termed *seconde partie* in French but if tortoiseshell dominates it is termed *première partie.* Although it is not always readily apparent, the brass often comes loose. Before repair all dirt, dust, and glue remnants need to be removed. Only then can the brass be replaced. Sometimes it is necessary to remove the entire piece but it may be that only part of the brass is loose.
Flatten the brass carefully, if necessary using a fine file. Glue the brass in place

Part of a late 18th century 'Strawberry' tea set made in UK for export to USA. Tea stains are easy to remove from tea sets.

with epoxy resin. The traditional method is the rub the brass with garlic and then to use glue rendered from animal bones. The garlic is necessary for old traditional bone based glues to stick.
Cleaning of boulle work needs great care and patience because it is difficult to clean the brass without damaging the tortoiseshell(orrosewood/mahogany).
The best means is to use powdered pumice mixed with acid free petroleum jelly. The petroleum jelly also nourishes the tortoiseshell. If the shine has gone from the tortoiseshell this can be brought back by wiping with a wet soapy cloth. Rinse the tortoiseshell afterwards with clean water and dry it. Then finally polish with a piece of chamois leather and glycerine.
Extensive treatment of the tortoiseshell is pointless if the tortoiseshell has been damaged by exposure to sunlight.
Loose pieces of tortoiseshell can be fixed with epoxy resin or a bone based glue. Missing pieces can be filled in with wax stopping. Larger pieces can use imitation tortoiseshell which can be made with different coloured wax stopping being heated on a filler knife. Allow the mixture to run into the area to be filled. Once the wax sets cut the wax to remove any surplus.

Restoration and maintenance of wooden objects

Maintenance and care for antique furniture

Fear of maintaining antique furniture just because it is antique is unfounded. On the contrary, good maintenance is their salvation. With all maintenance and restoration it is extremely important to retain the authenticity of the piece as far as possible.
It is quite easy to replace affected parts but this significantly reduces the value while good restoration will increase value. Up to 1600 furniture was made of timbers native to the area in which the furniture was produced.

Oak is the most durable of these. Beeswax is mainly used to give a sheen to wooden furniture. When antique furniture has been regularly polished for years and years it acquires a wonderful and very intense lustre. Another method of maintaining wood is to use linseed oil.
After 1700 walnut became so much all the rage that it became hard to find any more European walnut trees from about 1720 on.

After this period a great deal of walnut was imported from Honduras and Cuba. Furniture making saw heady days in the eighteenth century with names such as Sheraton, Chippendale, Hepplewhite, but also Weisweiler, Riesener, and Roentgen.

French polish was introduced at the end of the eighteenth century. This is the application of an invisible thin layer of shellac based lacquer to protect and enhance the wood that made polishing with wax unnecessary. In more recent times people liked to see their furniture shining as new.

Our parents and grandparents even went so far as to have their antique furniture dyed almost dark purple with the new aniline dye wood stains before having them French polished to give the same finish as a piano. Since the start of the twentieth century all manner of synthetic materials have been incorporated in paint, varnish, and lacquer.

A simple and non damaging means of cleaning the surface of antique furniture is to wipe it with a cloth soaked in warm water with a little vinegar. This should be followed by wiping down with a piece of chamois leather.

It is also possible to make your own cleaning solution for furniture using four parts vinegar, one part ethanol, four parts raw linseed oil, and four parts turpentine. These must be mixed together well. Until more experience is gained it is sensible to go carefully with this substance at first, especially with French polished surfaces. It should be very sparingly used. Sometimes it is necessary to remove the old finish from a dull surface in order to restore its lustre.

Start by wiping the surface with a cloth soaked in turpentine. If this does not achieve the desired result then ethanol can be used but check first that the piece is not French polished because this dissolves in ethanol.

The old finish can be removed using 000 or 0000 grade wire wool and turpentine. Rub the wire wool always with the grain.
Rings and other marks can occur in wax treated furniture from water, alcohol, or hot objects.
The way in which they are removed depends on how they were made. The treatment consists of a combination of a smearing a substance onto the surface and the heat of the rubbing action. A mild burnishing polish can also be used if necessary.

The first action is to rub a cork with wax on its end over the affected area. The cork needs to move as rapidly as possible over the wood in order to make it hot. If the cork becomes harder to move then it must have more wax added. It is best to limit the area treated. Twenty square centimetres (3 sq in) is about the maximum.
Another way of getting rid of rings and marks is to rub them with pumice and linseed or olive oil. Brasso or Silvo can also be used in place of pumice but do not use these methods on French polished surfaces because it will harm them. It is most sensible with a table top with lots of damp patches, rings, and patches to completely remove the French polish or lacquer.

This is less time consuming than dealing with each of the individual places. It may also be necessary to take this course of action with stubborn marks. This is best done with special stripping substances available from ironmongers or chemists.

Alternatively you can make your own with two dessertspoons of oxalic acid mixed with a litre (33 fl oz) of water. Because this would leave a lighter patch if just one area was treated the whole surface needs to be dealt with.

Pour a little of the mixture on the surface and rub well with wire wool. Once most of the mark has been removed it must be left for about ten minutes for the oxalic acid to penetrate and the wood must not be allowed to dry out. Rinse the wood afterwards with ample water and allow it to dry for at least 24 hours. In most cases the mark will be gone or invisible after a new finish has been put on the piece.

The removal of French polish, paint, and varnish from furniture is work that has to be done carefully. There is no point in applying paint or varnish stripper thinly and evenly as with paint.

English Victorian French polished ebony table.

This will not work effectively and more layers will be required. It is better to apply the stripper as thickly as possible. This must then be left until the French polish, varnish, or paint has bubbled up and split. An old layer of French polish though can be removed with white spirit or ethanol. because of the fire risk of these substances some prefer the other method.

Old layers of varnish and certain types of paint can also be removed with acetone or turpentine. This can be a more convenient way for small areas, otherwise a varnish stripper will have to be used.
The French polish, paint, or varnish first has to be completely and carefully removed with a scraper. Take care to avoid damaging the wood. In many cases additional layers of stripper will need to be used before all the old finish is removed.
Only then can the wood be prepared. Use coarse wire wool to remove the final two layers of old finish.

This retains a patina in the wood. The wire wool must only be rubbed with the grain to prevent scratches. Difficult to access corners and mouldings are dealt with pieces of wire wool and scraps of wood cut to shape. After cleaning the wood it must be finally wiped down with vinegar.

This neutralises any remnants of the stripping fluid. The moist surface from this treatment gives an impression of how it will look once it has been treated with wax or French polish. Casein based lacquer was also used on furniture in the nineteenth century and it cannot be removed with paint or varnish stripper.
It is difficult to see if a finish is casein based but since the way to strip it is to use ammonia it makes sense to first test a piece with ammonia to find out.
Ammonia is rubbed into the casein lacquer with wire wool and then allowed to soak in for a time. Make sure the wire wool is used with the grain of the wood to prevent damage. The old finish can then be washed off. An remaining lacquer is removed with wire wool. Acrylic can be used to replace the old layer. Coatings of wax are probably the finest protection for old furniture. Maintaining that layer is very important. It is a good idea to also coat any metal parts of the furniture with wax for it protects them against corrosion.

Not every type of wax on sale is of equal value. Spray cans of wax may be easy to use but they are very expensive. The greatest part of their contents is the propellant which does nothing to enhance the furniture. The best wax is one containing a high percentage of beeswax. Antique waxes can be bought in a range of different colours. Use of these darkens the furniture. Furniture cream is not suitable for antique furniture. It is solely intended for cleaning modern furniture.
The best results are achieved by preparing your own wax polish.

For this 500 grams (1lb 1½ oz) of pure beeswax is grated into a pot. Then sufficient turpentine is poured over the wax until it is covered. The pot of wax is then heated using a bain-marie. It is best to do this on an electric hot plate because turpentine is flammable. Those who want that little bit of extra sparkle should add five to ten percent carnauba wax while the wax is being heated. The mixture must be well stirred and then allowed to cool.
If the cooled wax appears to be too hard to remove from the pot then it needs to be reheated in the bain-marie and have a little more turpentine added. Allow to cool once more after stirring. Antique furniture is best polished with wax two to three times each year. The best results are achieved by letting the wax soak in overnight before rubbing down. It is a good idea to use a brush to reached difficult corners. A soft cloth that does not lint needs to be used for polishing off. This should only be done with the grain. Once the wood starts to shine change to a clean cloth.

In between the furniture solely needs a regular wipe over with a soft cloth. Scratches in wood are dealt with by using the right colour of shoe cream. Even dealers use this most effective method. Furniture makers in England and Europe started to French polish their furniture around 1820. Today this technique is less popular. The difference between French polish and beeswax is not obvious to the eye but the difference is important for wax cannot soak in to furniture that has been French polished.

When French polish is coated with wax it always leaves a fatty deposit. French polishing is a very hard work. The procedure consists of four phases. A uniform foundation is established with the French polish base coat.
This is then lightly sanded and after a day the furniture is then coated until it is completely smooth. Once the French polish has hardened the surface is then polished up. French polish is a clear spirit in which shellac has been dissolved. It is available from specialist suppliers. The area in which it is applied must be dust and draught free and the temperature must not be colder than 20°C (68°F). The furniture must be made absolutely free of dust and grease. Nothing must remain of the old French polish surface.

To make a French polishing tool roll up a length of cotton that has been doubled folded. This is then placed in a second cotton cloth that does not lint and fastened. The tool is filled with the polish by pouring some over it followed by adding some spirit. Polish is released by hitting it with the free hand or by squeezing. Polishing is done by working in a circular motion.
The polishing cloth or tool must never stop for this will cause a dull patch that is difficult or impossible to remove. It is important that the corners gets just as much polish as the large surface areas. At least twelve layers are needed. There is a pause of five minutes between each layer of polish.

The following day the surface is sanded lightly with very fine grade sandpaper. When the next layer of polish is applied the tool is not just moved in circles but also with the grain. The process is continued until all the polish in the tool is used up. Less polish is used at this stage and only a little polish is added to the cloth for each layer.
The process is continued until the grain of the wood is entirely filled and the surface is entirely smooth. Several days must elapse for the polish to harden before the final polishing off. Sometimes the polish sinks into the grain so that further coats are required. In the final stage of polishing off mainly spirit with very little polish is used.

French polish can flake or become unsightly as it ages through badly done French polishing or exposure to sunlight or heat. A yellowing damaged layer of French polish is no longer firmly in contact with the wood and will need to be entirely removed. With other types of damage to French polish it is worth trying to see if the layer can be re-coated.
Renovation of French polish is done with a mixture of two parts linseed oil, five parts spirits, and two of turpentine. This solution must be rubbed over the furniture with a cotton cloth in a circular manner. This softens the uppermost layers of French polish and reduces flaking and scratches. There are also substances sold for renovating superficial damage to French polish.

Damaged beading on drawers can be repaired yourself. Damaged pearl or egg and tongue moulding as here is work for a specialist.writing case.

The surface of old furniture should radiate a warm glow. Although there are exceptions, this is generally best achieved by regular maintenance with coats of wax. Sometimes the wood is very discoloured. In such cases the wood may require a timber dye or stain.
Each type of timber has its own specific colour. Oak varies from reddish brown to almost black, a lot of mahogany is a soft red and walnut a soft mid brown colour.
When wood is too dark it needs to be bleached.
Good means of doing this include oxalic acid or a 30 percent solution of hydrogen peroxide. Wear protective gloves and old clothes when doing this work. These solutions are applied with a brush of vegetable fibre (other materials will perish immediately). The wood will need to be rinsed with water after treatment.
Once the wood is dry the raised grain of the wood will need to be sanded. Careful sanding is very important because this is the basis for further finishing. Wood can be coloured with wood stain or dye. There are both spirit and water based forms.
Water based stain has been used since long ago and gives good light resistant colours. One disadvantage of this type is that it takes longer to dry. After using water-based stain the wood will need to be sanded. Modern spirit-based stains are normally aniline based and reasonably light resistant. The stain must not contain any varnish or other binding agent so take great care when choosing. The stain is applied with a soft cloth or brush.

As little stain as possible should be used. There must never be so much stain on the wood that it forms drips or runs. Build the colour up in thin coats. One or two thick coats never provide satisfactory results. A highly thinned stain may even require many coats. Anyone who has never applied wood stain should not start with their finest piece of furniture. Staining is very much a technique one has to become accustomed to. Practice makes perfect. Certain types of hardwood such as palmwood and holly, which are widely used for edges of inlay, absorb virtually no stain so do not worry that the stain does not work on these materials.

If you are determined to colour them then a concentrated water-based stain with a little ammonia added or concentrated spirit based stain will have to be used. Woodworm is a different problem.
Woodworms emerge in Spring and gnaws

their way into wood. This can be seen by small heaps of sawdust. Oak, mahogany, and teak are rarely affected by woodworm. Beech and softwoods such as deal and pine are favourites with woodworm. Many different types of wood are used though in some furniture. Therefore you should check regularly for woodworm even with furniture that has been treated. To check if woodworm are still active tap on the wood. If woodworm are still living in the wood then sawdust will fall from the holes. There are special treatments for woodworm but petrol works extremely well.

All these treatments are sprayed into the holes with an injector but they are toxic so gloves must be worn and used injectors thrown away. For bad infestations of large areas you can use a specialist company who will gas the woodworm in a chamber. Woodworm holes in furniture can befilled with shoe polish.

Nineteenth century Hamburg pine cabinet on bun feet

Restoration of antique furniture

Some repairs to antique furniture need not be carried out in a specialist workshop. More major and or complex repairs though need to be left to a craft specialist.

In addition to a bench, wood lathe, and bench vice with wooden jaws the following list of tools is needed as a minimum for repairing antique furniture: chisels of 6, 10, 16, 18, and 26 mm or _, 3/8, 5/8, _, and 1 in, small plane, metal smoothing plane, wooden plane, electric drill, combination pliers, punch, fret saw, gouges, 200 g and 300 g (7 and 10_ oz) hammers, hand drill, hand saw, tenon saw, mortise gauge, band saw, various sizes of clamps, pincers, compasses, bradawl, rat's tail file, steel scraper, coping saw, range of different screwdrivers, steel rule, set square, callipers, cork sanding block, cramps, keyhole saw, key files, grinding wheel, router plane, spokeshave, Stanley knife, hacksaw, mitre box, mitre gauge, whetstone, and a half-round smooth file.

Some furniture has moulding attached to cover joints or for decoration. The edges of table tops and leaves sometimes have fine inlaid edges. Corners, edges, and mouldings are easily damaged even if it is just a matter of a duster getting caught in them. It is worth sticky small bits of broken moulding back in place with adhesive tape until they can be properly repaired.

Broken mouldings will in most case have to be made yourself. They cannot be bought off the shelf. Fortunately it is usually just a question of small piece. Firstly the edges of where the broken piece comes from need to be made square and cleaned thoroughly. The old glue should be removed and the area where the replacement moulding is to be fitted must be made square and flat. With broken moulding cut the broken end to form a mitre with a tenon saw for corners.

Where the break is in the middle of a moulding make 45 degree cuts in a wedge shape on either side of the broken area. The replacement for the moulding is cut in the matching wedge shape. The replacement must be of the same type of timber as the original moulding. It can be carefully adjusted until it fits perfectly. Cutting the appropriate profile is best done when the replacement piece of wood is glued in position. Many can be trimmed to shape with a plane and sandpaper but for more involved forms gouges and files will be required.

Drawers with beaded edges, which are commonly found on eighteenth century furniture, are often damaged. A decision first needs to be made whether the entire edge needs to be renewed or just part of the beading. Beading which is damaged in more than one place is better replaced. New beading can be made from thin strips of the right sort of wood. They are often made of walnut. A good alternative is ramin (a tropical hardwood from Indonesia). The beading should be carved to shape when the strips of wood have been glued in place.

Dents in wood need first to be completely cleaned of any wax or French polish. Then cover the dent for 24–36 hours with a soaking wet cloth. The cloth must remain wet.

Solid timber furniture gradually exhibits shakes (splits) in time. Where these are visible such as in a table leaf or somewhere the light catches it is worth having a professional restorer tackle the problem. If you are able to do the work yourself then the method of restoration depends on the size of the split. The split must first be thoroughly cleaned. Larger splits can best be filled with a made-to-measure wedge. This must be glued in place and then held in position until the glue has set. Afterwards the wood can be planed and cut to the required finish. Most splits can be closed up with a cramp. In places where the split is not immediately apparent it could be filled with wax stopping or 'liquid wood,. Liquid wood is available in a range of colours.

Antique furniture is often jointed with mortise and tenon joints. Cupboard doors, chairs, and tables may have become wobbly because the joints are damaged or loose. Joints held together with wooden pegs must not be glued. Mortise and tenon joints without a peg can be glued with a rendered bone glue or PVA adhesive.

Repairs can sometimes be avoided by driving a wooden wedge beside the peg. If a repair is necessary then in the case of a chair the peg will first have to be removed with a hammer and a rounded piece of wood. (Pegs are driven into joints to hold the joined parts firmly together). The damaged part of the joint will then have to be repaired with glue. Where necessary this may mean insetting a new piece of wood. The peg is often badly damaged and since it is crucial to the joint it must be solid and fit perfectly.

If part of the peg is broken it can be repaired with a new piece of wood of the same type. Drill the hole into which the peg is driven 1mm (1/32 in) closer to the top of the rail.
The rail will now be more firmly held when the peg is driven home. It is a good idea to drive a steel conical pin into the hole before refitting the wooden peg and to then remove it. This makes it easier to insert the wooden peg which should be driven home with firm blows but not so hard that the peg is broken. It is a matter of feeling.

A completely broken peg will have to be renewed. Such pegs cannot be bought so a new one will have to be made. It is possible to buy 8mm ($^{5}/_{16}$ in) beech or hardwood dowel in specialist shops supplying wood crafts. This can be fashioned in the manner described below. Where possible the same type of wood should be used for the pin as the rest of the chair. Cut a length of wood 80 mm ($3^{1}/_{8}$ in) long.
This is then worked with a chisel to 8 x 8 mm ($^{5}/_{16}$ x $^{5}/_{16}$ in). It is best to measure the actual size of the peg before starting since some are slightly smaller.

Once the peg has been made with as straight an edge as possible it is then cut, leaving the one end at 8 x 8 mm ($^{5}/_{16}$ x $^{5}/_{16}$ in) while the opposite end is gradually cut down to 6 x 6mm (¼ x ¼in). The peg is then cut octagonally until one end terminates in a point that makes it easier to hammer home.

The feet of furniture often suffer more than other parts. This is because they are more readily affected by damp that rises from the floor. This can result in fungal growth and woodworm. Complex damage to legs of valuable chairs through woodworm, fungus, and damp are best repaired by a professional restorer.

In many cases it is sufficient to strengthen and re-glue the foot. Some types of foot such as console feet can be reinforced by gluing a wooden block against the back or inside of the feet. The ends of some chair legs can be strengthened by drilling a hole in the centre of the 'foot' to take the appropriate size of dowel. If a leg is worn then the dowel can protrude slightly to compensate. The leg needs to be quite dry before the repair begins.

Feet or legs should only be replaced when absolutely essential. Make sure when a foot or leg is replaced that they all remain the same length. Nothing is more unpleasant than a wobbly chair, table, or cabinet. Uneven legs must not be cut down. It is better to fit a piece of protruding dowel or a screw or glue a block of hardwood underneath.

Clean breaks in chair legs are best glued with a good quality woodworking glue. It is essential the two parts are firmly held while the glue hardens. For rounded legs this may mean acquiring a special clamp. Glue joints can be reinforced by fixing a dowel in the centre of the chair leg through the break so that the dowel will absorb most of the forces exerted. If the chair leg is rather fragile then the broken parts should first be glued together. Then the leg is sawn in two 20 mm (_ in) above the joint. These parts are then joined together with a dowel by drilling matching holes.

Dagobert chair with relief carved leaf and lion's head motifs, 19th century.

A common problem with chest of drawers is the wear of the running plates of drawers.
These wear more rapidly at the front than the back causing the drawers to sag. All drawers slide over a pair of rails or plates fastened to the side panels. Although the speed at which it occurs depends on the weight of articles kept in the drawer, the undersides of drawers always wear deep grooves in the running plates.

This problem can be relieved by reducing the wear. This can be achieved by rubbing the running plates once per year with paraffin or rubbing a candle over them. A further advantage is that the drawer opens and closes more easily. The problem can often be solved by adding a second lath with PVA or hot glue to each side of the bottom of the drawer, provided the running plate is wide enough. This prevents the drawer from running in the worn grooves in the running plate.

To prevent the drawer coming too far forward some of them are fitted with stops. These stops suffer a great deal with use and eventually often become damaged. To repair or replace one it is essential to know the precise location.

Hinges can come loose. With repeated use the screw holes can become enlarged and if this is not tackled in time the wood will split and new screws will not solve the problem. Where wood has split the split needs to be opened up slightly with a chisel so that PVA or hot glue can be added to repair the split. The wood will need to be clamped while the glue sets. In the most serious case the wood cannot be repaired and a new piece strong enough to carry the weight of the door will have to be inserted.

Where the screw holes have become too big the hinges will first have to be removed. The holes can then be plugged with conical pieces of softwood that are glued with PVA adhesive. Once the glue is set the projecting part of the plugs are cut off with a chisel and the hinges can be re-fixed with the screws. The correct size of screw must be used. Too small a screw will become loose again after time and too large a screw will force the wood and also cause the hinge out of its correct alignment. The head of the screw must fit precisely in the countersink in the hinge plates.

Normandy cupboard in cherry, circa 1820.

A key that has been lost can cause much annoyance, particularly if a drawer is locked. It is sensible to first try every key you possess on the lock and also worth trying to open the lock with a bent hairpin or paper clip. Locksmiths can usually open an old lock without too much difficulty but this costs money of course. If even this fails then one needs to weigh up whether it is acceptable to damage the wood by forcing the lock.

Restored Spanish 'commode chest' from Burgos, in chestnut, 1820–1830.

The shoot of the lock is often so short that the drawer or door can be forced open merely by prising slightly with a broad chisel. This needs to be done carefully. Another method is to cut through the lock's shoot with a hacksaw but the wood needs to be protected with a thin strip of card or veneer.

The lock can often be accessed from behind or by removing a drawer. It may even be necessary to remove the back panel of the piece of furniture. In certain cases it is then possible to remove the entire lock. In extreme cases wood can be cut out with a keyhole saw from above (or to the side) of the keyhole where the lock connects.

Although used as early as the seventeenth century, the use of castors only became widespread in the nineteenth century. Since then they have also sometimes been added to older furniture. It is a consideration then whether to remove them or not. The connections between the castors and the legs often suffer through use and become loose. The connection can be restored by strengthening the underside of the leg with metal filler. The stud of the castor is located in the filler before it sets and once the filler hardens the castor should be firmly held. The hardened filler can then be coloured to suit with acrylic paint.

Restoration and maintenance of furniture: other materials

VENEER

The technique of making and applying veneer began in the seventeenth century and quickly become commonplace. Veneer is the technique of gluing thin layers of more durable and often expensive types of wood onto a piece of furniture so that it can be made for less money. Formerly all veneer was sawn from trunks or occasionally branches. Today veneer is stripped from the trunks so modern veneers are much thinner than their antique counterparts.

The shortage of walnut was the reason that cabinet makers started to use walnut veneer. The carcass behind was often made of oak. This shortage led English furniture makers to switch to mahogany in the eighteenth century. Veneer provides the opportunity to make attractive designs using for example the root stock of walnut which has wonderful figuring.

When the finish on veneer is removed with paint or varnish stripper this does not remove the glue but care does need to be taken with any areas where the veneer has come away from the substrate. Such places need to be stuck down first.

Veneer moves in the opposite direction to the wood beneath. Through shrinkage and expansion it is possible that the veneer will eventually work loose. By tapping on the veneer it is possible to hear if it is loose or not. If loose the sound is more muffled and echoes. Loose pieces of veneer can sometimes be stuck down by using heat and moisture. Place a damp cloth first on the veneer and then press down with a hot (household) iron. Veneer can be so warped and deformed that it cannot be re-glued. In this case cut through the raised bubble of the veneer. Now one piece of veneer will cover the other when pressed flat. When old veneer will not stick down, first cut a slit in the veneer and then with a palette knife or thin strip of wood introduce glue to the back of the veneer.

Acrylic adhesive used in combination with a smoothing iron is quite effective. This adhesive sets in about one minute under a hot iron. It is important to retain pieces of veneer that come away. They cannot be replaced by the modern thinner veneers. When a piece of veneer is lost it is difficult to find a replacement. In order to match the texture and grain of the wood, most professional restorers saw their own veneer so one can try such a source first. If this does not succeed then you may have success with a merchant in finetimber.

When replacing old thick veneer it can happen that a number of layers of veneer have to be used. The new piece of veneer should protrude above the surrounding area.

It can be finished smooth later. The edges of irregular broken or splintered pieces of veneer need to be cut with a sharp thin knife into straight or flowing lines. Follow the grain of the veneer as much as possible. Make the ends rounded rather than clean and square. If a square end is essential this should still be cut with a curve which will be less noticeable.

Old glue and dirt can be removed by scraping with a chisel but stubborn glue residues may need soaking in water. They can then be rubbed off.

To make a template for the veneer first place a piece of paper over the gap to be veneered and mark this by rubbing with a pencil held at a slant so that the edge of the gap is imprinted.

This template can then be cut out and checked for fit. Subsequently the tem-

Veneered French bedroom chest, circa 1900.

plate is stuck to a piece of veneer and the veneer cut around the template with a sharp knife. The knife should be held at an inward facing angle as the cut is made so that the veneer slightly overlaps the gap.

When the veneer has been cut it must be checked for fit. It can be adjusted if needed with sandpaper tightly stretched around a cork sanding block or with a file.

The veneer can then be stuck in place with acrylic or PVA adhesive. The inset piece must be firmly held in place with a clamp. A piece of softwood or cork sanding block must be placed between the clamp and the veneer to prevent damage.Parts of border inlay may be missing. Guitar builders can find ready made sections of inlay for their purposes. If what you seek is not available then the edge can be inlaid with maple or pear. This can later be retouched to the correct style with a pen. When the repair is to be covered with French polish this little trick is virtually impossible to see.

BAMBOO

Bamboo is a hard, hollow form of tropical grass with a creamy ridged stem. The famous British cabinetmaker Thomas Sheraton wrote his famous *The cabinet maker's and upholsterer's drawing book* (four volumes, 1791–1794) in the late eighteenth century.

Spanish cupboard in poplar from around Salamanca of 1850–1850. Woodworm emerge each spring and bore their way in to old timber so it must be checked.

Colonial cabinet of teak, circa 1900. Even tropical hardwood should be checked for woodworm.

He was inspired by the French Louis XVI style and turned to light in style furniture, particularly using tropical hardwood.

In his later book *Cabinet Dictionary* (1803) he pointed to bamboo as a material for making chairs. In the late eighteenth century furniture makers also turned and painted beech to imitate bamboo. Imitation bamboo can be hard to recognise.

Bamboo can be cleaned with a nail brush and warm soapy water.

Bamboo can then be protected by waxing it but this can only be done when the bamboo is dry.

Another way of giving bamboo a protective layer is with polyurethane varnish. This protects the surface of bamboo from splitting and splintering for some considerable time. The disadvantage of this varnish is that it darkens the bamboo and reduces the authenticity of bamboo furniture. If bamboo breaks it splinters. It is best glued using a hardwood dowel in the centre hollow. If required, drill out the bamboo core for the dowel.

Check in advance how broken pieces fit together. Smear the dowel and any splintered fragments of bamboo thinly with glue and press them together.
Provided no bits are missing and they fit perfectly together then glue with hot glue or PVA adhesive.

If there are missing bits then fill with a good quality wood adhesive.
If it is necessary to cut through bamboo use a fret saw for the purpose, preferably at one of the thickened parts where there is less risk of the bamboo splitting.

LACQUER WORK

Lacquer work originally came from the Far East and was most widely used in that part of the world. It consists of several layers of hard resin from *Rhus vernicifera,* which are then decorated and inlaid with different materials.

Chinese lacquer was first imported into Europe around 1600. The demand was so great that it was imitated. The 'oriental' scenes of some European lacquer work are laughable and the quality is not as high either.

Japanning is the early eighteenth century technique used by European craftsmen to imitate oriental style painting on cream, yellow, green, red, or black grounds. Gold leaf was also widely used with lacquer work. The technique can be found on bureaux, cabinets, chests, longcase clocks, and chairs. Grime and dust on lacquer work must be removed with a soft cloth and a little turpentine.

The turpentine does not affect the finish but does remove the wax but care needs to be taken that the turpentine does not damage the painted decoration. If the results are not as you wish then it will be necessary for the item to be cleaned by a professional restorer. European lacquer work is often based on a gesso ground.

This can crack or loosen. Restoration in this case is a task for the professional. Small bits can be repaired with a cellulose filler or with plaster.

Lacquered 19th century Chinese tea caddy.

When the filler is dry it must be sanded to the appropriate level. Any retouching is best done with acrylic paint which dries quickly and can also be applied thickly. Dull lacquer can be polished up with wax which is then polished off.

MARQUETRY

Marquetry is decorative inlay used in furniture. Various materials, such as wood, tortoiseshell, or pewter are arranged in a design and glued together.

The whole is then sawn to provide inlay (see also Tortoiseshell and Boulle work). There are two types of marquetry: cut and sawn. Furniture decorated with marquetry is cleaned in the same way as other furniture. Surfaces that have been wetted with water or solvent must be dried as quickly as possible. Bits which come loose are best removed completely. If the part does not come away easily then it is best to glue it back in place. Apply glue with a spatula and press the piece firmly home (see also Veneer).

Missing bits of marquetry can be copied. Choose veneer of the same type of wood, paying particular attention to the wood's grain.

The colour can be adjusted with stain. A template is first made as described under 'Veneer'. The newly cut piece is then checked for fit to see if any adjustment is needed. Only then is it glued.

Accents or details can then be added in with a lining pen as the glue sets.

Restoration and maintenance of combined objects and materials

Tools

Old tools and implements used by craftsmen have become very popular. The manner in which these should be cleaned and restored is described in the sections relevant to the materials used, such as wood and iron.

The wooden parts of old tools were formerly often treated with linseed oil. When this has not been done for a long time and the wood has dried out then copious amounts of oil need to be applied.

Dutch Louis XVI style commode with very fine marquetry.

Inset cameo from the commode (see left).

Once the oil has soaked in the surface can be wiped with a soft cloth.

Metal parts need to have rust or other corrosion carefully removed and then be polished. Metal can be protected against corrosion with a coating of wax.

Two 19th century planes.

Cameras

The collecting of antique photographic equipment is currently very popular. Old cameras need to be cleaned with some thought. They are a combination of the work of instrument makers, leather workers, and cabinet makers. In many cases the wood and brass are varnished.

Because they have generally been handled with care the varnish is normally intact and antique cameras usually only suffer from dust.

This can be removed with a soft brush or blown off with a bellows lens brush. The lenses themselves should be cleaned with a lens cleaner.

Scratches on the wood can be removed with fresh French polish (see Restoration and maintenance of wood). For the treatment of leather see Restoration and maintenance of organic materials.

An Exakta camera by Ihagee. The Ihagee camera works of Dresden developed the world's first single lens reflex camera before World War II. This camera was made until long after the war and are still use to take photographs, Exaktas are highly collectable.

Photographs

The earliest type of photograph was the Daguerrotype. The process was invented by the Frenchman Louis-Jacques Mandé Daguerre who patented it in 1837. The picture was captured on a silver plate treated with iodine.

The exposed plate was developed with mercury and then fixed. This photographic technique was in general use until about 1855. Following this photographs were printed out on to paper. Daguerrotypes can only be restored by specialists. The surface of the plate must not be touched.

Prints were formerly made on paper that developed very much more slowly than our present day photographic papers. In some cases the fixing process was insufficient. When the picture is exposed to sunlight the image fades.

In principal the image can be developed once more but the restoration of photographs is work for a specialist.

In some old photographs the fixing process was insufficient. The image can be developed once more but restoration is work for a specialist.

A late 19th century miniature book as souvenir of Dutch royalty. Inside are photographs of Queen Emma and King Willem III.

Negatives must not be touched with the fingers, regardless of whether they are on glass or celluloid. The acid in a finger print will quickly make a visible imprint. Care needs to be taken with celluloid which is extremely flammable. Restoration of negatives if work for a specialist restorer.

Scientific instruments

Old scientific instruments are very valuable. Restoration of these needs therefore to be done by professional restorers. Most of these instruments stem from the eighteenth nineteenth century

Carpenter's level of the late 19th century.

Mercury barometer of 1821 with English and Rhineland scales.

and are made of mahogany and brass with other mateSome medical instruments are made of pewter, others of steel and they are often kept in special mahogany cases. (For the maintenance and cleaning of the various materials see the relevant sections of this book).

Some lenses used in scientific instruments have special protective coatings and must therefore be handled with care. A non expert should limit themselves to dusting with a brush. The breaking down of these instruments into their different parts is much more complex than it appears to be.

Clocks

The maintenance of the clock case is described in the section on furniture.
The cleaning and repair of the movement depends on the experience of the

collector and the value of the clock. Antique clocks have two types of driving mechanism: those with a spring that is wound up and those driven by a weight. Both types have mechanisms to regulate the passage of time such as a pendulum. To prevent them from being damaged by being knocked over, longcase clocks can be fixed against a wall.

A clock should always be level and some indeed will not work if they are not. When a clock is set going it is possible to hear from the sound of the pendulum if the clock is standing straight. Pendulum clocks are adjusted with a regulation nut on the pendulum which enables the weight to be adjusted up or down.

Moving the nut upwards makes the pendulum swing more rapidly and the clock to go faster. Adjusting downwards causes the clock to slow down. Smaller clocks are generally provided with a screw to fix the pendulum when the clock is being moved. It is sensible when a clock is being transported to remove the weight and the pendulum. The pendulum is attached to the mechanism by a flat spring with a bit of metal at its other end. The pendulum moves to and fro in a long slot and sways backwards and forwards between the end of the anchor fork which controls the escapement. The pendulum must be carefully removed because a pendulum spring is easily damaged.

Once the pendulum and the weight are removed the entire movement can be safely removed from the case. Damp, which can cause corrosion, is the clock's great enemy. Most damage to clocks though is caused by dust. When dust combines with lubricants on the moving parts it forms a sort of grinding paste that damage the teeth and bearings.

The cover for the mechanism is intended to protect it from dust. Dust is most easily removed from clock mechanisms with a pipe attached to the outlet end of a vacuum cleaner. A hair dryer can also be used. A clock should be cleaned and oiled at least once every five years. This needs to be carried out by someone who understands what they are doing. Someone determined to do this themselves should use the special types of oil for this purpose.

The mechanism of this Comtoise clock should be cleaned and lubricated once in five years. This is work for a specialist.

Never use ordinary lubricating oil. Only lubricate the bearings and never the cogs or wheels. Many longcase clocks from the eighteenth and nineteenth century have pendulums.
This type of clock is mechanically very reliable and simple. They run for between one and eight days between each winding. There are one or two weights in longcase clocks. One drives the hands mechanism and the other drives the beat of the pendulum. The mechanism cover

can usually be removed to gain access to the mechanism. With older clock the entire upper part of the case needs to be lifted off. With newer ones the top can usually be slid forward with its glass door.

One of the nice things about clocks is that they have to be wound up. Clocks run better if they are wound regularly.
To prevent unnecessary wear, the weight of a 'thirty hour' clock should be lifted with the hand and supported while it is being wound up.

Winding of a clock with a key should occur at regular intervals. It is not good for the spring to wind it as tightly as possible. It can happen that the striking mechanism gets out of phase with the hands.

Some clocks have a catch that allows the striking mechanism to run on. This allows the right number of strikes to match the hands to be restored. Other clocks require a certain amount of fiddling and patience. Some clocks have a large disc with slots which can be overrun.

In this case the catch which drops into the relevant slot needs to be released. This can usually be done by lifting it slightly which makes the clock strike. Repeat this procedure until the number of strikes matches the time on the dial.

Dolls houses

Antique dolls houses were originally made for children but one needs to think carefully before letting children play with them. Dolls houses in good condition sometimes have extremely high values. Remember that children really have no understanding that they must not change things in a dolls house.

Toy shop, circa 1890. restoration of dolls houses and toy shops can be a lot of work.

It is 'just a toy' to them and they will not be specially careful.

The interiors of dolls houses are a great passion for some people into which they devote a great deal of time and money. To restore the interior of a dolls house one must remember that the materials will react in the same way as their larger counterparts. The patina, for example, equally needs to be cared for and protected. Every repair should be carefully considered. For the sake of authenticity it is important to leave things just as they are so cleaning is often a better choice than renewal. Dolls houses have often been stored in attics where they were prey to grime and dust.

Particularly when plywood has been used there is a chance of woodworm. This can be treated in the same way as with furniture (see there). Surface dust should be removed with water an a cleaning solution. Paper stuck to walls as 'tiles' and wallpaper should not be made wet or it will become loose. The house should be cleaned a little at a time and each part dried before moving on to the next.

Toy shop, circa 1900.

Missing bits should of course be replaced in the same style and sphere as the rest of the doll's house.
Damaged bits must be restored and old repairs made invisible. Old glued joints that have become loose should be re-glued with PVA or acrylic adhesive. Old paintwork often has wonderful shades of colour that will be difficult to recreate. It is best to leave this intact so far as possible and to clean with great care. For touching up or additional painting use acrylic or poster paints. Because differences easily catch the eye the colours need to be mixed with great care. The opaque paint will cover tears and scratches but should not be applied too thickly, making sure the paint is worked off with a flat brush.

Acrylic and poster paints can be made glossy by coating them with a layer of varnish but if a high gloss is wanted then it is better to use enamel paints. When refurnishing a dolls house it is important to keep an eye on scale.
There should not be a great difference either in the extent to which the different parts of the interior are restored. Interior fitting out and decorating is a matter of imagination and skill. There are museums where people can get ideas for different styles and antique books and books about different styles of interior decoration can also be of help.

Dolls

Dolls were made in the past from all manner of materials and often of several different materials in one doll. The head, arms, and leg are often of ceramic while the body is fabric.
Ceramic dolls are mainly made from glazed earthenware or porcelain. Sometimes unglazed porcelain or biscuit is used, also known as parian ware. This unglazed white ceramic material resembles marble. The heads of porcelain dolls are usually made in one piece with the shoulders. These have holes with which to attach the body.

Glazed porcelain heads are easily cleaned. Glue residues are removed by first making them wet and then brushing them off. Stubborn glue dissolves with a solution of one dessertspoon of ammonia in 500 ml (1 pint) of water. The rest of the porcelain can be cleaned with warm soapy water. The dark hair on nineteenth century dolls is often painted on but they sometimes have real hair which must not be allowed to get wet. (For treatment of the hair see further on).

If the doll is very dirty it may be sensible to remove the hair if at all possible. Splits in the porcelain should be carefully glued and any seam camouflaged as well as possible. A break can sometimes be hidden by rearranging the hair style. Use either PVA or cyanoacrilate adhesives. When a larger piece is broken it is a good idea to prepare a supporting layer first of linen or strong card. Coat this with PVA glue. The missing piece can then be covered with filler.

Marbleised and biscuit dolls are not glazed so the surface absorbs dirt more readily and they are more difficult to clean.

Furthermore the paint can flake off with this type of doll. Carry out a test first therefore somewhere not too noticeable. A biscuit or marbleised doll can be brushed with a toothbrush and a solution of washing up liquid with a little ammonia in warm water. Stubborn patches can be removed with care using powdered pumice. The ceramic can be retouched with water-colour paints. Once the ceramic surface is dry coat it with a thin layer of wax.

In the past dolls were also made of composition and papier mâché. Composition resembles papier mâché but instead of paper consists of cellulose residues and wood fibre. Rye flour was often used as a binding agent. Papier mâché dolls are made of pressed paper pulp, glue, and a filler such as china clay. Both types of doll are painted so cleaning needs to be done with care. First clean with a cotton bud dipped in turpentine. This is repeated with cotton buds dipped in soapy water. Work with great care and stop immediately if the paint comes away. Missing paint can be retouched with acrylic paint.

For flesh tints mix cadmium yellow, yellow ochre, and a little black. It is wise to experiment first and the right colour is rarely achieved the first time. It should be borne in mind that the paint darkens as it dries.

Because acrylic paint dried to a mat finish it will need to be coated with a quick drying varnish if a shiny finish is desired. The final layer will need to be coated over the entire doll.

Wooden dolls are often coarsely carved. Some of them are very old and have acquired a wonderful patina that would be harmed by thorough cleaning. The surface dirt though has nothing to do with the patina. The doll can be happily cleaned with a cloth or a soft brush. If necessary a second cleaning can be done with a soft cloth with some turpentine. To create a sheen wax can be used.

Damage to a wooden doll is repaired as for other wooden objects. Arm and leg joints are often held with metal pins which can break. If the joint is not intended to move then the pieces can be glued together.

Wax dolls are often very old and extremely valuable. Because wax distorts at relatively low temperatures wax dolls damage easily. The surface dirt can be cleaned with a cotton bud with cosmetic cleansing cream.

More ingrained dirt needs to be treated with a cotton bud dipped in turpentine. This has to be done with extreme care because turpentine will dissolve the wax. Celluloid was first used to make dolls around 1880.

The material is extremely flammable and therefore not really suitable as a raw material for toys for small children. Because celluloid is quite thin it dents easily. The dents can sometimes be removed by placing the doll in hot water and then sucking the dent out. When this fails a pin can be pushed through the celluloid in order to push the dent out. The first plastic dolls appeared around 1920. The older examples are not colourfast. Because of their similarities, acrylic paints are ideal for touching up these dolls. Loose joints and seams can be glued with PVA adhesive.

Regardless of their condition, if the doll's original clothes have survived they must be retained. The clothing is of particular importance for doll collectors. Information about the different style periods can be found in a book about the history of

Unmarked wax doll on box in its original condition, circa 1900.

clothing. The restoration of the original doll's clothing is a very time consuming affair. The upper items of clothing in particular may have become very dirty over the years. The clothing must not be washed in a washing machine. The old textiles are far too delicate and need extreme care in their handling. At first any dirty marks need to be removed (for cleaning see under Textiles).

Washing of doll's clothes requires much thought. Firstly the colours have to be checked to see if they will run. If none of them run then the clothes can be hand washed by hand in hand hot water.

Some clothing may be too delicate to wash. They can be treated by carefully moving day old white bread over the surface or with fuller's earth. This method is certainly required for fabrics with non fast colours, brocades, velvet, moiré silk, and velours. White underclothes are often grey. These items can be bleached in a solution of two percent hydrogen peroxide in water but this needs to be done with care. The hydrogen peroxide will also affect the fabric and weaken it. It is better therefore to first try washing the underclothes to get them white. All the clothing must be rinsed thoroughly after washing and starch may be needed to get some items back into the correct shape and style.

There are many different approaches to fixing doll's hair. Doll's hair consists of strands of hair that is glued in place in a hole in the doll's head. Other dolls have a complete wig that is attached to the head. When dolls have been played with the hair becomes a mess and gradually also dirty and dull. Untangling of hair requires endless patience.

Little bits of hair have to be tackled at a time, starting at the end of the hair. Hair can be washed using a dry shampoo for pets or dry shampoo such as magnesium carbonate are equally effective.

Another method is to apply heated bran to the hair. This is worked through the

hair with the tips of the fingers and then brushed off after five minutes. All sorts of hair have been used for doll's hair.
When it has to be renewed then human hair is the best because it is the easiest to deal with. Wigmaker's hair is a good alternative because it is readily available. Doll makers closely followed the style of the times. The doll's hair should therefore match the style of the time it was made.

Up to 1870 dolls had fixed eyes, sometimes of glass, sometimes painted. After this dolls were fitted with sleeping eyes that moved and that are counterweighted. The eyes closed when the doll is laid down. The glass eyes are set in plaster and connected together by wires. A counterweight is at right angles to the connection that opens or closes the eyes. Dolls of biscuit or porcelain generally have an access to this mechanism in the head. This is usually covered with a piece of card that is covered by a wig. The eyes are dipped in molten wax. This serves as a lubricant and was intended to prevent scratches.

The eyelashes are usually also fixed with wax. These can usually be replaced quite easily with a pair of false eyelashes that can be cut to size.

The eyes need to be in the head in order to set the eyelashes in a natural position. They can be fixed using PVA adhesive.
Doll's bodies have been made of all manner of materials. Composition bodies can be glued with PVA adhesive. Arms and legs of stuffing filled fabric often have porcelain hands and feet sewn to them and certain leather bodies have this feature too.

It may be necessary to add new stuffing to a doll. Use the same material as the original. Moving elastic parts have usually perished. They can be replaced by sturdy round elastic available from specialist doll shops. Holes and breaks can be repaired with cellulose or epoxy resin based fillers and missing parts can be moulded in these materials. This also applies to missing hands and feet.

If old and new parts have to be joined together it is a good idea to reinforce the joint with a dowel. This requires adding filler within an existing part or boring a hole in it.

Edged arms

Although arms are predominantly made from iron and steel, other metals are used in their decoration. The most important task with arms is the removal of and protection against rust. Superbly decorated sheaths or scabbards also need to be considered. If a blade is allowed to rust inside a sheath it may be difficult to remove it. If penetrating oil is used to release a blade from a sheath then any leather parts must be protected against the oil. It may be necessary to leave penetrating oil to work for 24 hours.

Fix the sheath in a bench vice, protecting all metal parts with pieces of softwood. Tap the hilt with a rubber hammer. Sometimes the easiest way is to place a piece of wood against the hilt and to hit this.

When the weapon is cleaned it is worth checking whether the blade can be easily separated from its hilt. The handle, which is a continuation of the hilt, is attached to the blade by a nut or is riveted with a large bead or ring. When this is loosened the parts break down into easily cleaned pieces.

Cleaning of the blade requires special care when it is specially engraved. Use a very fine grade wire wool soaked in a mixture of paraffin and lubricating oil. A metal cleaner can also be used. During

Saudi state sabre with Damask blade. The sheath dates from 1920 but the blade is much older.

cleaning it is essential to continually monitor if any chemical is etching the metal. When the blade is badly rusted the rust needs to be removed without affecting the blade too greatly. It is important though that all traces of rust are removed. When one small area of corrosion remains it will spread itself. Polishing of steel is done with various types of waterproof sandpaper or emery paper.

Start with a coarser grade and finish with a finer one. A polishing disc with jeweller's rouge can also be used but this requires a certain amount of experience. Hilts and sheaths are made of all manner of materials.

For their restoration turn to the relevant sections in this book. In common with other antiques it is equally true of arms that it is better to restore than replace.

Firearms

If a firearm is in good condition it merely requires regular oiling. Twice per year is usually adequate. The correct type of gun oil must be used for this purpose. This can be bought from gun shops or gun smiths who sell hunting guns and firearms. The mechanism such as locks and other inaccessible parts should also be protected against rust. It is therefore best to avoid keeping firearms in a damp environment.

Unprotected steel and iron is quickly affected by rust. Plain steel is sometimes varnished to protect it. Because this affects the appearance of the firearm it is not advised.

Anyone taking hold of a firearm must first ensure that it is not loaded. With muzzle loaders the priming rod can be inserted into the barrel and the distance compared with the barrel length. Unloading a firearm needs to be done with extreme caution.

Balls can be removed with a cleaning rod equipped with a thread which can be screwed into the ball. Anyone who has no experience with firearms must play safe and leave the matter to an expert. Firearms must always be completely clean. First remove the lock. This can usually be unscrewed from the stock. Never force a screw or bolt (see also Screws).

The barrel, butt, and bracket can then usually be removed. These are usually held by bolts or pins. Make sure not to damage the wood when stripping the firearm down. Once the firearm is stripped down any rust or other corrosion can be removed. The traditional way is with gun oil and paraffin.
To be certain of no corrosion soak the parts for at least twelve hours in a bath of this mixture.

Goose gun, 18th century.

To prevent the metal being etched, a rust remover can also be used. Parts must be polished with the finest grade polishing paper. Start with a relatively coarse grain and finish with the finest. This gives the firearm a superb sheen.

All parts must be smeared with gun oil. Because fingerprints leave indelible marks no part should be touched with bare hands. The use of throw away surgical gloves is a handy solution. Anyone actually wanting to use the firearm must ensure that the barrel is completely clean with a cleaning rod. If irregularities or pitting can be seen in the barrel then it will need to be dealt with by an expert. Only gunsmiths are able to give steel parts their blue or brown finish.

Wooden parts of firearms are cleaned with turpentine and 000 gauge wire wool. This removes the worst possible dirt. Work always in the direction of the grain to prevent scratching the wood. Stubborn grime and old varnish can be removed with a varnish stripper. This must be neutralised after treatment with turpentine. Dents in the wood can be partially removed by covering with a damp cloth which will cause the wood to swell up. Protect the wood with either linseed oil or beeswax. Make sure that neither the oil or wax contain silicon.

This seals the surface of the firearm and is difficult to remove. Eventually it will harm the appearance of the firearm.

Gilt

IAll manner of objects have been gilded in the past. This varies from mirror frames to furniture. The traditional method of gilding was to apply gold leaf over a gesso ground. The finest method of gilding is with water.

Oil-based gilding was the most widely used in the Low Countries. The third method uses wax as the binding agent and is known as mordent gilding.

If gilding has not been maintained for a long time then it needs to be carefully cleaned with a little ammonia in water. This requires great care because the gilt layer is extremely thin and the gesso ground is easily affected by too much water.

Areas where the gold has disappeared or where the gesso ground has disappeared need to be restored. While experience and manual dexterity are not essential to the task of apply gold leaf these qualities do produce the best results. Fortunately there are also easier ways to restore gold leaf.

Where the gold leaf is worn there is often a patch of red or yellow under layer visible. This layer is intended to give the gold leaf a warm glow. Many collectors find these distressed areas exude a certain charm.

You may therefore decide to leave the worn places as they are but the missing gesso does have to be replaced first. This

Gilt Empire mantel clock. The classical figure is Hercules.

can be done with real gesso, synthetic gesso, or modern filler. After filling, the area will at least need to be rubbed down. There are gilt washes available in artist's material shops suitable for small areas of repair. These are available in various shades. Before applying gilding wax a yellow or red oxide layer needs to be applied. Instead of real iron or other oxide poster paint can be used. Wax is best applied with a finger.

Polishing with a soft brush makes the layer shine like gold. A new layer can be distressed if you wish to give the worn appearance.

One type of gold paint is much more attractive than another. It is worth finding out which type gives the best result. When spray paint is used then the areas that are not to be treated need to be well covered.
An advantage of spray cans is that it is easy to make a transition with spray from the old layer to the new.

All repairs can be coated with a coat of clear varnish. Applying oil based gilt yourself is a significantly more major task. It takes much longer but the results are much finer. The chalk base must first be sanded as smooth as possible. This is then given two or three coats of shellac mixed with ethanol.

Instead of shellac you may be able to find a supplier of a specialist undercoat paint by Lefranc & Bourgeois. When this is entirely dry the mixture from the same company is heated in a bain marie.

It is then applied sparingly. The mixture is then allowed to dry until it no longer sticks to the fingers. Now it is time to apply the gold leaf. For this purpose you need a gilding tool, a gilt cushion, and a gilding knife.

The gilding cushion is a plank with a piece of chamois leather stretched over it. Instead of a gilding knife a blunt knife will do provided it has no burrs. Because the gold leaf must be kept grease free it is placed on the gilding cushion. The gold leaf is lifted by carefully blowing on it.

The gilding tool is then placed over a small edge of the gold leaf which sticks to the tool. Each sheet must be placed upright and slightly overlapping the previous one. In difficult places to get at where the leaf has to be cut it can be helped into place with a brush. Continue until the entire surface has been covered. After a day the gilding can be cleaned with wads of cotton wool.

Glossary

ACANTHUS DECORATION
Widely used relief decoration in the form of this thistle like plant. The leaves of this plant are mainly found on furniture, specially on display pieces.

AJOURÉ
Silversmith's technique to create open-work or fret cut decoration. Otherwise generally used for open-work in other crafts.

A LA FAÇON DE VENISE
Venetian style glass not made in Venice.

A QUATRE COULEURS
Decoration of gold with different colours.

ARABESQUE
Islam forbids depiction of people or animals. Arabesque style uses stylised repeating geometric patterns and stylised plant stems. Arabesque is often used to fill in frames and small panels and is found horizontally in friezes. Neo-Classicism makes excessive use of Arabesque motifs.

ASTROLABE
Nautical instrument for determining elevation.

BALUSTRADE
Pear or vase-shaped column used in buildings and furniture for vertical support.

BANDED STYLE/BANDED WORK
Ornamentation of plaited-form banding first used in France in 1700 which then spread throughout Europe. Bandestil is the German variation.

BASALT WARE
Extremely hard, fine-grained, black stoneware by Wedgwood that can be decorated on a cutting wheel. By light sanding the surface it acquires a matt sheen.
The properties of Basalt ware allow for sharply defined detail in modelling.

BAS RELIEF
Slightly raised relief sculpture.

BEADED BORDER
Ornamental edge with tiny beads, used for silver and precious metals.

BERGÈRE
Sturdy easy chair. The area between the back rest and seat, and the seat are upholstered. The armrests also have partial upholstery.

BISCUIT
Normally used for unglazed porcelain. In a broader sense it is porcelain that is fired once, then decorated and glazed before being fired a second time.

BLEU DU ROI
A intensive royal blue underglaze used on porcelain discovered in 1749 by J. Heliot.

BLEU MOURANT
A matt, very pale blue used in porcelain.

BLEU PERSAN
Technique of the late seventeenth century originating in French *faience* from Nevers. Characteristic of this technique was floral decorations and birds painted in white and yellow on a ground of dark blue underglaze.

BOHEMIAN CRYSTAL (GLASS)
Also known as potash glass. A form of very clear and pure glass discovered in Bohemia with marked refractory properties with light.

BONE CHINA
Almost hard paste porcelain containing a large proportion of bone ash.

BROWNWARE
Imitation of the red Böttger stoneware produced in Bayreuth. It is a ceramic with a dark red glaze and red body which is decorated with banding and chinoiserie in gold and silver.

BROWN PORCELAIN
Imitation of the red Böttger stoneware produced in Ansbach. This is not porcelain but majolica with a dark brown glaze and red body that was decorated with reliefs in silver and gold paint.

BUFFET
Fairly low cabinet made from the sixteenth century with two doors and a rear panel. The top protrudes and is carried on columns or struts that rest on the top of the main part of the cabinet.

CAPITAL
The top of a column (that is often abundantly decorated).

CARTOUCHE
Rectangular or oval surface that may be framed by a curlicue moulding.
The central space is sometimes rounded and may carry an inscription or picture.

CARYATID
Column from Greek Ionic architecture in the form of women or muse.

CELADON
Earthenware with greasy grey-green glaze that was originally produced in China.

CHASING
Cutting or chiselling of a pattern in silverware (and other precious metals).

CHIMERA
Fire-breathing mythological monster with a lion's head, a goat's body, and a serpent's tail.

CHINE DE COMMANDE
Chinese porcelain of the eighteenth century made for western merchants who provided the Chinese with western-style decorations for them to copy.

CHINOISERIE
Object created or decorated in the Chinese manner.

COMMODE
Chest of drawers or cabinet on high legs.

CREAM WARE
See Queen's Ware.

CREDENCE
Two door cabinet with sliding leaves under a folding top.

DAMASK BLADE
Sword or dagger blade with metal continuo usly double folded during forging to produce a flexible blade from many thin layers of metal.

DAVIS QUADRANT
Nautical instrument for measuring elevation.

DECOR À LA GUIRLANDE
Decorative style originating in Moustiers with mythological scenes incorporated in a garland form on the rims of dishes and plates.

DRESSER
Wall cabinet with back and side panels reaching to the ground, often with open shelves for displaying/storing tableware.

EGG AND TONGUE MOULDING
Moulding in the form of carved 'eggs' interspersed with pointed forms. Found in moulding below pediments in furniture.

ENAMEL
Glass-like material that is applied as a thin protective layer to metal, glass, and stone objects.

ENCRUSTED
Precious metal beaten into another metal background.

ENGLISH CRYSTAL
Also known as flint glass. Glass developed by George Ravenscroft in the seventeenth century with a high level of lead added.

ENGRAVING
Technique used by works in precious metals and glass to decorate with a sharp stylus or (with glass) cutting wheel.

EN GRISAILLE
Grey painting of ceramics.

ETRURIA
Josiah Wedgwood's factory.

FAIENCE
Tin glazed decorated earthenware. The name comes from the Italian town of Faenza.

FILIGREE
Decorative technique for applying fine surface detail to (mainly) silver.

FRIEZE
A feature borrowed from architecture where a frieze was placed between a pediment and the architrave. In furniture this usually refers to the decorated top moulding of a cabinet or cupboard.

FRIT
Calcined mixture of silica and fluxes which can be melted to make glass; partially fused glass; a vitreous composition from which soft-paste porcelain or enamel is made.

GERMAN FLOWERS/DEUTSCH BLUMEN
A naturalistic representation of flowers in ceramic wares.

GLASHUT(TEN)
German name for glass works in singular (and plural) forms.

GRÈS
See Stoneware.

GROTESQUE
Classical ornamentation found for instance in the catacombs in Rome. Plants, animals, and humans are depicted between thin vine stems and banding.

HAUT RELIEF
Three dimensional sculpture on a wall or surface in which figures often rise out of the background.

HUMPEN
German sixteenth century beer glasses (singular is hump) that were initially cylindrical.

HUTTENGLAS
Glass that is decorated immediately during the blowing process at the glass works.

INTARSIA
A form of inlay using veneer, ivory, metal, bone, mother-of-pearl, and other materials that was much used during the Renaissance.

JACOB'S STAFF
Nautical instrument for measuring latitude.

JACK STONES/DIB STONES
Game played in many countries by children, sometimes with sheep vertebrae or other small bones.

JASPER WARE
A product of Wedgwood made by addition of barium sulphate. Jasper Ware is so hard that its exterior can be polished yet it is soft enough to be able to colour with metal oxide.

KAOLIN
Kaolin or china clay is the main raw material for hard paste porcelain. It is mainly derived from feldspar washed from granite rock.

LEAD CRYSTAL
A softer form of glass with additional lead added to the 25 percent used with other crystal. Se also English Crystal.

MAJOLICA
Opaque and lustrous tin glazed earthenware decorated with enamel paint.

MANUFACTURING
Large scale production introduced in Britain by the Industrial revolution where the entire production of e.g. porcelain was organised on a rational basis.

MARQUETRY
Inlay in furniture, usually with contrasting types of wood but also using other materials such as pewter, brass, and tortoiseshell in a geometric design.
Marquetry is a later refinement of Intarsia (q.v.) during Louis XIV.

MEANDER
Greek border design of broken rectangular forms.

METOPE
A square space between triglyphs in a Doric frieze. This can also be performed in relief.

MOSAIC DECORATION
A scale or floral motif used to decorate the edges of Gotzkowsky porcelain of Berlin (among others).

NETSUKE
Miniature carved sculpture figures in ivory on a cord that served to tie the purse. Worn around the waist. Highly sought after collector's item.

NIELLO
A black composition of sulphur with silver, lead, or copper, for filling engraved designs on silver or other metal; an example of such work.

0, 1, H0, 00 GUAGE ETC
Indication of the scale and track width of different scales of model railway.

OEIL DE PERDRIX
Favourite decorative style of Sèvres porcelain (partridge eye), consisting of a white ground with blue or green stipples and small golden dots.

PATINA
An coloured layer on bronze, brass, copper, or pewter that can result from weathering. Patina can also be applied with etching substances. Real patina is a sign of age.

PEDIMENT
The top part of a tall cabinet or cupboard or building.

PIETRA DURA
Florentine mosaic consisting of different coloured stones.

PILASTER
Architectural element forming an upright form projecting from the wall (or a piece of furniture).

QUEEN'S WARE
A technically better form of cream stoneware with tin glaze discovered by Josiah Wedgwood in 1759. Initially known as Cream Ware it later became known as Queen's Ware.

ROEMER
Specific type of German white wine glass that was first produced in the fifteenth century by applying prunts as decoration.

ROSE POMPADOUR
A plain pink porcelain body probably discovered by Heliot at Sèvres.

ROSETTE
Stylised flower form as seen from above (e.g. a rose) used as decoration in furniture to hide joints.

ROSSO ANTIQUO
Basalt Ware (see there) with a red colour.

SARCOPHAGUS
Stone coffin for a dead person displayed above ground and usually decorated with relief sculpture.

SEXTANT, OCTANT
Nautical instruments for measuring elevation.

SGRAFFITO
Scratched decoration used in ceramics.

SILVER PLATE
Also Sheffield Plate: copper sheet to which a layer of silver has been applied by rolling.

SOFA (TURKISH CANAPÉ)
A broad low upholstered form of seating with the side rests facing outwards; during Louis XV the side rests were upright.

STIPPLE
Technique or decorating glass in which hard or soft stippling is applied by hitting the glass with a stylus.

STONEWARE
Hard type of pottery also known as grès that is fired at 1,100–1,300°C (2,012–2,372°F).

STYLE RAYONNANT
Style used in Rouen for faience in which a basic motif is repeated in countless variations arranged in radial sequence.

TERRA SIGILLATA
Red earthenware of Roman times with a lustrous surface.

TOFT WARE
British earthenware of red clay of the seventeenth century made by the Toft family of Staffordshire.

TRIGLYPH
Architectural element: a block of vertical grooves alternating with metopes in a Doric frieze.

Bibliography

Paul Atterbury & Lars Tharp (ed.), *De geillustreerde antiekencyclopedie* (Zuid Boekproducties, Lisse, 1996)

Albrecht Bangert, *Porselein* (Moussault's Uitgeverij, Bussum)

Ernst von Bassermann-Jordan & Hans von Bertele, *Oude klokken* (Schuyt & Co., Haarlem 1978)

Carlernst J. Baecker & Botho G. Wagner, *Blechspielzeug: Eisenbahnen* (Verlag Eisenbahn, Villigen, 1982)

Emile Bayard, *Le Style Empire* (Garnier Frères, Paris)

Udo Becher, *Antieke modeltreinen* (Kluwer, Deventer/Antwerpen, 1979)

Dr. Anne Berendsen (ed.), *Groot tegelboek* (Elsevier, Amsterdam, 1975)

J.P. Blake, *Chippendale and his school,* (William Heinemann, London, 1912)

A.A. de Boer, *Uurwerken* (De Haan, Haarlem, 1980)

Huub van den Boom & Frans Mutsaers, *Het veilingwoordenboek* (Boekwerk, Groningen, 1990)

Claire Dauget & Dorothée Guilleme-Brulon, *Reconnâitre les origines des faïences* (Éditions Ch. Massin et Cie., Paris)

Lemile Decker & Christian Thevenin, La *Majolique de Sarreguemines* (Édition Association des amis du Musée de Sarreguemines 1990)

De grote encyclopedie van het antiek (Uitgeversmaatschappij Holland, Haarlem, 1970)

Marianne Fasse, *Von Flachs und Leinen in alter Zeit* (Güth Verlagsgesellschaft/ Heckman Verlag, Rheda-Wiedenbrück, 1989)

Tim Forrest, *Antieke meubelen* (Zuid Boekprodukties, Lisse, 1997)

Dr. H.E. van Gelder, *Glas en Keramiek* (Uitgeversmaatschappij W. De Haan, Utrecht, 1955)

Jan Pieter Glerum, *Antiek* (Tirion, Baarn, 1993)

Jan Pieter Glerum, *Zilver* (Tirion, Baarn, 1995)

Jan Pieter Glerum & Luca Melegati, *Glas* (Tirion, Baarn, 1997)

Jan Pieter Glerum & Luca Melegati, *Aardewerk en porselein* (Tirion, Baarn, 1997

E.H. Gombrich, *The story of art* (Phaidon, Oxford, 1982)

Hans Jürgen Hansen, *Europese volkskunst* (Gaade, Den Haag, date unknown)

Clarence P. Hornung, *Treasury of American design and antiques* (1950)

Emma Johnson & Lucinda Montefiore (ed.), *Techniques of the world's great masters of pottery and ceramics* (Phaidon, Oxford, 1984)

Chester Johnson, *Klokken en horloges,* (Elsevier, Amsterdam, 1965)

Keramika, uitgave Princessehof Nederlands Keramiek Museum, no. 4 1994

Jana Kybaloviïá, *La Faïence fine* (Librairie Gründ, Paris, 1991)

Sigmund A. Lavine, *Handmade in America: the heritage of the colonial craftsman* (l966)

Wolf Mankowitz, *Wedgwood* (Spring Books, London, 1966)

Agnes Melger, *Antieke poppen* (Zuid Boekprodukties, Lisse, 1996)

Hugo Morley-Fletcher, *Meissen porcelain in colour* (Ferndale Editions, London, 1971)

Anton van Oirschot, *Antiek in woord en beeld* (Uitgeverij Helmond, Helmond)

Tom Rowland, *Behoud en herstel van antiek* (Becht, Amsterdam, 1984)

C. Spierdijk, *Horloges en horlogemakers* (Becht, Amsterdam, 1973)

Hugh Tait, *Clocks and watches* (British Museum Publications, London 1983)

Christian Vaterlein & Botho G. Wagner, *Märklin Eisenbahnen* (Battenberg, Augsburg, 1996)

J.I. Woldring & K.A. van den Hoek (ed.), *Antiek* (Lekturama, Rotterdam 1982)

Index